E.G. West

E.G. West

Economic Liberalism and the Role of
Government in Education

JAMES TOOLEY

Bloomsbury Library of Educational Thought
Series Editor: Richard Bailey

B L O O M S B U R Y
LONDON · NEW DELHI · NEW YORK · SYDNEY

Bloomsbury Academic

An imprint of Bloomsbury Publishing Plc

50 Bedford Square	1385 Broadway
London	New York
WC1B 3DP	NY 10018
UK	USA

www.bloomsbury.com

First published 2008 by Continuum International Publishing Group
Paperback edition first published 2014 by Bloomsbury Academic

British Library Cataloguing-in-Publication Data
A catalogue record for this book is available from the British Library.

ISBN: PB: 978-1-4725-1878-1
ePUB: 978-1-4411-5262-6

Library of Congress Cataloguing-in-Publication Data
Tooley, James.
E. G. West/James Tooley.
p.   cm.
Includes bibliographical references.
ISBN-13: 978-0-8264-8413-0 (hardcover)
ISBN-10: 0-8264-8413-1 (hardcover)
1. West, E. G.   2. Educators–Great Britain–Biography.
3. Education–philosophy.   4. Education–History–19th century.   I. Title.
LA2375.G72W47   2008
370.92–dc22
[B]
2007030633

Typeset by Aptara Books Ltd.
Printed and bound in Great Britain

To Ann West

Contents

Series Editor's Preface

Education is sometimes presented as an essentially practical activity. It is, it seems, about teaching and learning, curriculum and what goes on in schools. It is about achieving certain ends, using certain methods, and these ends and methods are often prescribed for teachers, whose duty it is to deliver them with vigor and fidelity. With such a clear purpose, what is the value of theory?

Recent years have seen politicians and policy makers in different countries explicitly denying *any* value or need for educational theory. A clue to why this might be is offered by a remarkable comment by a British Secretary of State for Education in the 1990s: 'Having any ideas about how children learn, or develop, or feel, should be seen as subversive activity.' This pithy phrase captures the problem with theory: it subverts, challenges and undermines the very assumptions on which the practice of education is based.

Educational theorists, then, are troublemakers in the realm of ideas. They pose a threat to the status quo and lead us to question the commonsense presumptions of educational practices. But this is precisely what they should do, because the seemingly simple language of schools and schooling hides numerous contestable concepts that in their different usages reflect fundamental disagreements about the aims, values and activities of education.

Implicit within the *Bloomsbury Library of Educational Thought* is an assertion that theories and theorizing are vitally important for education. By gathering together the ideas of some of the most influential, important and interesting educational thinkers, from the ancient Greeks to contemporary scholars, the series has the ambitious task of providing an accessible yet authoritative resource for a generation of students and practitioners. Volumes within the series are written by acknowledged leaders in the field, who were selected both for their scholarship and for their ability to make often complex ideas accessible to a diverse audience.

It will always be possible to question the list of key thinkers who are represented in this series. Some may question the inclusion of certain thinkers; some may disagree with the exclusion of others. That is inevitably going to be the case. There is no suggestion that the list of thinkers represented within the *Bloomsbury Library of Educational Thought* is in any way definitive. What is incontestable is that these thinkers have fascinating ideas about education, and that, taken together, the Library can act as a powerful source of information and inspiration for those committed to the study of education.

Richard Bailey
Roehampton University, London

Foreword

James Tooley's *E.G. West: Economic Liberalism and the Role of Government in Education* is one of the most amazing books I have ever read. The book is, in effect, a much-improved, expanded fourth edition of E.G. West's *Education and the State*, with James Tooley as coauthor. Tooley provides an overview of West's perspective, examines the origin of West's ideas, gleans additional analysis from other West publications, critiques West, introduces new evidence, and gives it all exceptional modern relevance.

This book revisits the justifications of state intervention in schooling and contrasts them with the actual genesis of intervention, and its evolution over time. Tooley brilliantly makes the connection between disappointment with state-dominated schooling and the absence of market-determined prices to guide and energize decision making and innovation. He is among the very few ever to have produced those essential, not well known insights.

Of great significance is that the school policies in place now 'were explicitly *not* part of the original [intervention] plan, and even ran counter to it'. Tooley presents as a 'conundrum' an observation that should serve as an additional, powerful cautionary tale for all of us. Policy interventions evolve – typically grow – and the minimal state interventions suggested by West's analysis have much generally in common with the minimal nineteenth-century interventions that evolved into the extensively interventionist education policies of the present.

The book asks extremely important questions and provides an insightful, fair-minded examination of each. Topping the list: is there any intervention that avoids the slippery slope? Secondarily: are there any interventions that could incline the slope in the direction of reduced intervention? For either objective, can a well-managed, properly oriented think tank be decisive in determining which way the slope points? Tooley provides insightful discussion of how the United Kingdom's Institute of Economic Affairs (IEA) brought the policy-making process to the brink of significant liberalization of the school system, but ultimately failed to implement policy changes that would have unleashed the entrepreneurial initiative rhetorically favored by the government then in power. Tooley's analysis of unsuccessful efforts to leverage choice as a reform catalyst provides key lessons in the art of politics and program design.

Tooley's analysis of West's ideas about education and the state will 'be respected for the quality, consistency and rigor of his approach', to use a phrase applied to the IEA's work. Tooley explores several such interventions, including the 'voucherization' of current education funding as a stepping stone towards decreased public-sector provision of schooling, and market accountability as the sole basis of schooling and education. The latter approach amounts to accepting the slippery slope argument as a reason to tolerate possible market failures as the price of non-intervention – that is, keeping Leviathan from gradually replacing liberty with coercion in the provision and consumption of schooling.

Tooley's review of tuition voucher programs – real and possible – cautions reformers and opinion makers to pay attention to widely neglected critical factors. They should match ambition, expectations and rhetoric to the possibilities actually provided for, or severely undermine productive debate of the reform options.

Another tough, critical question: are the dissatisfactions with access to schooling according to family willingness to pay sufficient for us to accept the deficiencies and dangers of political control? Tooley outlines the more (total separation) and less ('Churchillian' universal vouchers) radical paths to reduced and improved intervention. For those inclined towards reduced intervention, which kind of voucher system to pursue is another quite critical issue addressed by Tooley.

West's original three editions dismantled the assumptions underlying state provision of compulsory schooling, and most other state interventions. Tooley's partnership with West in this book amounts to utter demolition and burial of the still popular ostensible justifications for significant government intervention in education. Since intellectual death does not necessarily lead to quick destruction of entrenched institutions, the intellectual corpse of government-run schooling would benefit from periodic exhumation and ceremonial reburial with new evidence piling on top of old.

With periodic rich reminders not to automatically equate education with formal schooling, Tooley helps the reader think outside the box. That process begins on page 1.

John Merrifield
Economics Professor
University of Texas, San Antonio

Acknowledgments

I should like to thank several people who have helped in the preparation of this book. First and foremost, Dr Pauline Dixon gave an extraordinary amount of her time in summarizing positions of key authors, elucidating tricky economic concepts, locating sources and ideas, for which I will always remain grateful. My PhD students James Stanfield and Liu Qiang both helped find further sources and catalogue references. I am grateful to Professor Charles Rowley for a particularly insightful interview, and for further pointers to ideas and references. Professor Gordon Tullock also very kindly gave of his time for an interview. Robert Enlow, of the Milton & Rose D. Friedman Foundation, gave valuable last-minute information about the Utah universal voucher scheme. I have had very useful conversations with Arthur Seldon, Lord (Ralph) Harris and John Blundell in the past couple of years which helped inform the ideas in the book. I am grateful to Anthony Haynes and Professor Richard Bailey for inviting me to write the book in the first place, and for sticking by me when it seemed the book might not be written in time. The book is dedicated to Ann West, Eddie West's widow, who has always been supportive of our work in the E.G. West Centre: she freely donated his archives to us, has always been at the end of the phone to answer queries and questions about his life and times, and has continually offered backing and encouragement to further our work.

James Tooley
President, The Education Fund, Orient Global;
Professor of Education Policy, Newcastle University

Introduction

What role should government have in education? This question has been of interest to philosophers since Plato and economists since Adam Smith; it was the question that motivated E.G. West's writing throughout his life.

E.G. West's first major work, *Education and the State*, published originally in 1965 by the Institute of Economic Affairs, has been highlighted as one of the two major works on the role of government in education in the twentieth century. Harold Noah, Professor Emeritus of Teachers College, Columbia, wrote that, chronologically, Milton Friedman's *Capitalism and Freedom*, 'which contained a forceful plea for the application of market principles to education', was followed 'by E.G. West's even more pointed *Education and the State* ... The two books set off a *seismic shift* in the basic principles of educational policy' (Noah, 2000, p. 220; emphasis added). The seismic shift was to challenge the accepted wisdom of 'a major (if not monopoly) role for the state in both the financing and provision of schooling'. Friedman and West made 'respectable, to an extent previously quite unthinkable, notions of a decreased role for the state and a larger role for the market ... in education'. Because of their influence, 'there has been an out-pouring of writings, pro and con, on the restructuring of education along more market-friendly lines' (p. 220).

Similarly, Professor Mark Blaug, then of the University of London Institute of Education and London School of Economics, in a critical commentary on *Education and the State*, argued that 'this is one of the most important books to have appeared on education in recent years ... It should be read, studied and debated, for it raises profound questions, not only about state provision of education but indeed about state provision of all the so-called "social services"' (Blaug, [1967] 1970, p. 23).

Usefully, West's seminal work, published early in his career (in 1965 he was 43, but a new university lecturer in economics), was republished with West's explicit support and encouragement in 1994 (when he was 72 and emeritus professor). The new third edition had some additional material and some small revisions (although West clearly left much of the initial argument untouched, even, as we shall see, where his later work may have suggested some revisions). Thus, as it is clear that West himself believed that this work had stood the test of time, in this book we shall follow the arguments of *Education and the State* in detail, supplementing them with insights from West's other work where these clarify or develop the themes raised.

Professor Mark Blaug's positive comments quoted above were followed by a 'Nevertheless . . .' Whatever its merits, he wrote, *Education and the State* is 'not an easy book to follow: it moves simultaneously on three or four levels, continuously jogging backwards and forwards, with the result that most topics are taken up several times in different places in the book' ([1967] 1970, p. 23). It *is* a difficult book to follow, for exactly the reasons Blaug gives. Here, we will separate West's arguments out into their four key elements – three of which are contained in *Education and the State*, while the fourth appears briefly in embryonic form. In Chapter 2, we shall look at West *qua* economist, exploring the classical economic arguments for state intervention in education. The two classical justifications are the 'protection of minors' principle and various arguments concerning externalities or neighborhood effects of education. West's discussion of these issues leads him to the need for evidence before arriving at any key conclusions about these justifications for state intervention in education. But in the absence of experiments or genuine contemporary alternative systems to state education which could provide such evidence, West points to *historical* evidence concerning what happened before the state got involved in education as the major source for discussion. We shall follow West's historical analysis in Chapter 3.

But West, *qua* economist, was also to be influenced – after he had written *Education and the State* – by the new theory of public choice, or the economics of bureaucracy. We shall follow his discussion of this, especially how he believes it illuminates some of the historical debates, in Chapter 4. Finally, West developed some embryonic policy proposals. In *Education and the State*, he outlined a thought experiment to explore justified levels of state intervention in education, linking this with discussion of school choice reforms, especially education vouchers. I shall outline this discussion in Chapter 5.

When West's *Education and the State* was first published in 1965, it provoked great controversy in the media. It was reviewed in many of the major newspapers and journals, and prompted a hugely polarized reception – so polarized, in fact, that it led to a libel case in the High Court, where the *New Statesman* had to make an apology, and pay full costs, for a particularly bad-tempered review of West's ideas. Partly as a result of the notoriety stemming from this court case, West himself received a bumpy reception in British academia. But notwithstanding any of this, West's ideas on the role of government in education have been hugely influential – inspiring in large part the education reforms of the Thatcher government in Britain, including the abortive attempt at introducing a voucher scheme, and influencing in important respects the understanding of the key proponent of school choice in the United States, Milton Friedman. Chapter 6 will explore the reception and influence of West's ideas.

Chapter 7 will then outline the relevance of West's ideas for today, in two respects. First, of obvious relevance are the continuing school choice ideas that have brought in aspects of market-oriented reforms in countries across the world with governments of varying political persuasions. I shall outline some of these reforms, called by some two 'ideal types' of privatization, and explore how West might have viewed them. But there is a third type of privatization that is also occurring, *de facto* rather than *de jure*. This would have been of great interest to West, for it potentially allows us to explore many of the questions raised by him, but in a contemporary, rather than historical, setting. This, the burgeoning growth of private schools for the poor in developing countries, completes the discussion of the relevance of West's ideas.

West was obviously not writing in a vacuum. Chapter 1 will set out his intellectual biography, setting his ideas firmly in the reemergence of the ideas of classical, or economic, liberalism in the mid-twentieth century, dubbed by the Fabians as the ideas of the 'New Right', associated with thinkers such as F.A. Hayek and Milton Friedman, and with two key institutions in particular, the Mont Pelerin Society and the

Institute of Economic Affairs. But the ideas influencing these people and institutions themselves went back to Adam Smith, who was to be a powerful influence on West's ideas and work.

Two points must be made at the outset. The first concerns West's underlying and explicit motivation for his work. West was writing with a sense of the widely acknowledged 'gathering crisis' in state schooling in England and Wales during the 1960s. State education, especially for the most disadvantaged parents and pupils, did not seem to be working well; West was interested in the reasons behind this. Throughout his writing, he reflects on these issues. For instance, he notes how a proposal for a 'charter for children' was put forward at the annual conference of the National Union of Teachers (NUT) in April 1968, in protest against poor heating and sanitation in state schools. A government survey of 1962 showed that about 500,000 children were in schools without hot water or central heating, and two million attended schools with outside lavatories (West, 1968a, pp. 11–12). In 1967, official figures showed that over 500,000 children were in classes of over 40 children – even though 40 children per class was supposed to be the absolute maximum.

Moreover, West points to a survey by the United Kingdom's National Foundation for Educational Research (NFER) in December 1966 which showed that 14 percent of a representative sample of children 'had not mastered the mechanics of reading by the age of 8. Over half of these children remained backward readers or semi-literate till the end of their schooldays. Generally it was felt that the poorest scholars had the poorest facilities' (1968a, p. 12). Another problem was teacher shortage, estimated then to be about 40,000, 'and which in 1967 was officially admitted to be aggravated by wastage from the teacher-training colleges' (p. 12). Indeed, West notes that some education authorities (notably Luton's) were so short-staffed 'that they were forced to cancel their programme for five-year olds for the whole year' (p. 12). This led to a feeling of powerlessness among parents, and a striking asymmetry of power between parents and the providers of schooling. The local education authorities could take parents to court if they were not sending their children to school; parents on the other hand were found to have no right of redress at all in the courts when the local authority canceled the whole school year. Genuine problems like this and a sense of unease about state education motivated West's inquiries.

Second, constraints of space and time mean that the focus of the book excludes West's writings on higher education. Although many considerations that apply are similar to those which inform West's ideas on non-higher education, we will not explore them further in this book. Nor will we explore West's general economic and public finance writings or his important and influential work on Adam Smith (see West, 1964a, 1969a, c, 1971c, 1975c, 1976e, f, 1977c, 1993d, 1996c, d, 1997b, 1999b). In fact, during his career, West became so immersed in the works of Adam Smith that he was teasingly called 'Eddie Smith' as he walked around the campus at Carleton University; *The Region* interviewed West as Adam Smith (West, 1994c). But in the broadest sense we can say that more or less everything that E.G. West wrote was communicating – sometimes translating into a modern context and adapting the ideas on the basis of empirical evidence – the views of Adam Smith. Nowhere is this truer than on West's ideas on the role of government in education.

Thus, the focus of this book is solely on the seminal contribution made by E.G. West to our understanding of the role of government in education in what has generally emerged as the years of *compulsory* schooling; whether or not such compulsion is justified was of course a major concern throughout West's work.

Part 1

Intellectual Biography

Chapter 1

From Adam Smith to the Mont Pelerin Society

Brief Biography

Edwin George West was born on 27 February 1922 in Goldthorpe, Yorkshire, where his father ran the local cinema. Later they moved to Exeter, where Eddie attended Hele's School. Leaving grammar school, he worked for the Ministry of Transport in Exeter until the age of 24, including a stint as a bus conductor, when he entered University College, Exeter (now Exeter University). He was awarded his BSc in Economics in 1948. Upon graduation, he worked as a schoolteacher for three years in Staffordshire, before taking up a position as a lecturer in economics at Guildford College of Technology in 1951. In 1956, he moved to the Oxford College of Technology as senior lecturer in economics. During this time, West enrolled for the degree of Master of Science as an external student at the University of London, graduating in 1959.

In 1962, at the age of 40, West was appointed lecturer in economics at what was about to become the new University of Newcastle upon Tyne (then still a constituent college of the University of Durham) by Professor Stanley Dennison, one of only a few senior free-market economists in Britain at that time. Dennison encouraged West to enroll for his PhD, for which he also studied as an external student at the University of London under the supervision of Professors Jack Wiseman and Lionel Robbins. His PhD was awarded in 1964 and became the foundation for his major work, *Education and the State*, first published in 1965. In that same year, West was invited by Milton Friedman, with whom he had been acquainted since 1962, to take up a one-year position as postdoctoral fellow at the University of

Chicago. West returned to England to take up a readership in economics at the University of Kent in 1966, a position he held until
1970, when he was appointed professor of economics at Carleton
University, Ottawa. He was made professor emeritus in 1993. During
his career, he held numerous visiting professorships, including particularly important years (1975–7) at the Virginia Polytechnic Institute
and State University in Blackburg, Virginia, where he became friends
with two other key influences, James Buchanan and Gordon Tullock.
West died on the morning of 6 October 2001 at his home in Ottawa,
Canada.

In this chapter, we explore the intellectual influences on E.G. West
that led to his groundbreaking work on the role of government in
education. We do this mainly through a chronology of the rise, fall
and subsequent reemergence of the ideas of classical (or economic)
liberalism. We identify two key institutional influences, together with
five key intellectuals who symbolize the pattern of influence on his
thought. The institutions are the Mont Pelerin Society and the Institute of Economic Affairs. The key intellectuals are F. A. Hayek, Milton
Friedman, James Buchanan and Gordon Tullock, together with the
founder of modern economics, Adam Smith. The institutions and
writers are intertwined. The Mont Pelerin Society was created by
Hayek, with Milton Friedman as a founding member and Buchanan
and Tullock as later leading members, together with West himself. The
Institute of Economic Affairs, created under Hayek's influence, was
itself also influenced by Friedman's, Tullock's and Buchanan's ideas,
and West became a leading player within it. And all were inspired by
the foundations laid by Adam Smith, and were part of the intellectual
movement that became known as the 'revival' of economic liberalism
in the mid-twentieth century.

The Decline and Reemergence of Economic Liberalism

The Central Tenets of Classical Liberalism

In the nineteenth century, the ideas of classical liberalism were in the
ascendancy. The belief in liberalism appeared justified because of the
remarkable progress, on economic, social and political fronts, during

that century. Policies based on classical liberal ideas were seen to have 'released the initiative and energy that produced the industrial revolution, world-wide trade, and economic growth on an unprecedented scale' (Hartwell, 1995, p. 7). Alongside economic progress based on the self-regulating free market, only minimally constrained by government, was coupled the expansion of the franchise and election of representative government.

What are the basic ideas of 'classical' or 'economic liberalism'? Its key commitment is to individual liberty set against the coercive powers of the state. Its intellectual roots lie primarily with Adam Smith (1723–90). Importantly, while Smith is often cited as the father of modern economics, his first two chairs at Glasgow University were as professor of logic (1751) followed by professor of moral philosophy (1752), during which period Smith was to write *The Theory of Moral Sentiments* ([1759] 1976). While Adam Smith's major contribution to economics was of course *The Wealth of Nations* (1776), West himself was to stress – something sometimes neglected by both free-market protagonists and their critics – how important it is to consider Smith's two major works as a coherent whole. West wrote that *The Theory of Moral Sentiments* was

> the work which revealed to the world the full stature of Smith's genius. If *The Wealth of Nations* had never been written this previous work would have earned him a prominent place in intellectual history. It is certainly unfortunate that the second book has overshadowed the first to the extent that it has.
>
> (West, 1976e, p. 95)

In particular, West notes how Adam Smith has been mischaracterized as 'the classical "apologist" of capitalism, the insensitive theorizer, the man who believed in the "survival of the fittest" in a world dominated by the cash-nexus and ruthless warlike competition' (ibid.). True, West concedes, much of Smith's economics in *The Wealth of Nations* 'is based on one predominant assumption about human behavior: that in his material pursuits man obeys the dictates of self-interest'. But it is important to observe that this was when Smith was focusing on economics only:

Where he confined himself to the role of the economist he remained fully conscious that he was concentrating only on one area of human behavior. There were many motives in life, some stronger than others, some more noble. In the ordinary business of getting a living, generalizations about human behavior required an assumption not about which motives were highest but which were strongest. Nobody knew more than Smith how exquisitely the higher motives were expressed elsewhere in life.

(pp. 97–8)

So, *The Wealth of Nations* deals with these strong motives, while *The Theory of Moral Sentiments* deals with the 'higher' ones. In total, Smith's theory of human behavior explores the various and disparate factors that prompt 'ordinary persons to be benevolent as well as self-interested, to be virtuous as well as mundane, to be humane as well as human' (p. 98).

But what of the major contributions in economics? In *The Wealth of Nations*, Smith explored how it was that some nations were able to become prosperous. It was an explicit reaction to 'the mercantilist, feudal and aristocratic societies of the *ancien régime*' (Cockett, 1994, p. 5). *The Wealth of Nations* set out a system 'in the grand scientific manner of Newton', based on one simple axiom: 'that of individual self-interest set in a world of what he called "natural liberty"' (West, 1999b, p. 8). Moreover, just as Newton used his axiom of gravity to explain the causes and effects of the movements of the planets, so Smith wanted to find a system of *economic* causes and effects. The key idea in book IV of *The Wealth of Nations* is now described as the Invisible Hand Theorem:

But it is only for the sake of profit that any man employs [his] capital . . . He will always, therefore, endeavour to employ it in the support of that industry of which the produce is likely to be of the greatest value, or to exchange for the greatest quantity either of money or of other goods . . . He is in this, as in many other cases, led by an invisible hand to promote an end which was no part of his intention. Nor is it always the worse for the society that it was no part of it. By pursuing his own interest he frequently promotes that of the society more effectually than when he really intends to promote it.

> (Smith, [1776] 1976, book IV, ch. II, p. 455)

Self-interest has virtuous consequences for society at large, argued Smith, in this famous paragraph:

> It is not from the benevolence of the butcher, the brewer, or the baker, that we expect our dinner, but from their regard to their own interest. We address ourselves, not to their humanity but to their self-love, and never talk to them of our own necessities but of their advantages. Nobody but a beggar chooses to depend chiefly upon the benevolence of his fellow-citizens.
>
> (Smith, [1776] 1976, book I, ch. II, pp. 26–7)

West outlined the issues in this way: 'How is it', he asked, that a city such as London

> can be regularly fed by converging food shipments from all corners of the earth, and without any governing plan to make sure that the Canadian farmer, the Scottish fisherman, and the South African orange grower actually deliver to the hungry city?

Yet somehow, London is fed, 'although none of its suppliers need to be motivated by any particular love and concern for Londoners' (1999b, p. 9). It is through the invisible hand and the axiom of self-interest that this happens. As Smith wrote in *The Wealth of Nations*, 'In civilised society [man] stands at all times in need of the cooperation and assistance of great multitudes, while his whole life is scarce sufficient to gain the friendship of a few persons' ([1776] 1976, book I, ch. II, p. 26). So, the invisible hand, says West, 'is what leads an individual to work for the good of other persons, practically all unknown to him, in an orderly economy and world market that has arisen without anyone having planned it that way' (1999b, p. 9).

One of the central questions for Adam Smith, says West, was as follows: 'If maximising a nation's wealth is agreed to be the main objective, how can it best be done?' (p. 12). The opening sentences of *The Wealth of Nations* pointed to features of activity that the mercantilists had completely missed, namely 'the importance of improving technology and productivity'; and for Smith, one of the key developments here was the division of labor. Smith's famous example for this was that of the manufacture of pins – where he described how 10 workers, if they were willing to come together out of their different workshops, could increase productivity by at least 240 times! For West this was the key:

> Dramatic and spontaneous productivity changes like this, Smith insisted, are what one should concentrate on, and to secure them government need confine itself simply to identifying and removing legal and other impediments to the effective working of the free market economy.
>
> (p. 13)

Importantly, if the development of the division of labor occurs voluntarily, then this benefits everyone, including the poorest: 'It is the great multiplication of the productions of *all* the different arts, in consequence of the division of labour, which occasions, in a well governed society, that universal opulence which extends itself to the lowest ranks of the people' (Smith, [1776] 1976, book I, ch. I, p. 22). Smith's emphasis was very different from that of the mercantilists whom he was challenging; they did not want the lot of the 'lowest ranks of the people' to be improved, fearing this would reduce their effort. Smith, however, 'was obviously interested in the well-being of everyone' (West, 1994b, p. 15).

It must be stressed, says West, that Smith's 'necessary condition for economic progress was "natural liberty", upheld and protected by respect for property rights and the rule of law' (ibid., p. 17). Here are Smith's words to this effect:

> All systems either of preference or of restraint, therefore, being thus completely taken away, the obvious and simple system of natural liberty establishes itself of its own accord. Every man, as long as he does not violate the laws of justice, is left perfectly free to pursue his own interest in his own way, and to bring both his industry and capital into competition with those of any other man, or order of men. The sovereign is completely discharged from a duty, in

the attempting to perform which he must always be exposed to innumerable delusions and for the proper performance of which no human wisdom or knowledge could ever be sufficient; the duty of superintending the industry of private people, and of directing it towards the employments most suitable to the interest of the society.

(Smith, [1776] 1976, book IV, ch. IX, para. IV.ix.51, p. 687)

In other words, under economic liberalism the foundations for the freedom of the individual rest on the 'twin institutions of private property and the free market' (Cockett, 1995, p. 5). The only guarantee for freedom and liberty comes from 'the wide dispersion of economic powers that could alone be brought about the working of the free-market economic system and the freedom of the individual to dispose of his or her private money and assets as he or she saw fit' (ibid., p. 5). Or as F.A. Hayek, one of the foremost modern exponents of classical liberalism, was to put it:

The central concept of liberalism is that under the enforcement of universal rules of just conduct, protecting a recognizable private domain of individuals, a spontaneous order of human activities of much greater complexity will form itself than could ever be produced by deliberate arrangement, and that in consequence the coercive activities of government should be limited to the enforcement of such rules.

(Hayet, 1967, pp. 162–3)

Such a free society can be distinguished from a 'collectivist' society, which 'establishes certain common goals or purposes that "society", governed and guided by the State, should strive for' (Cockett, 1994, p. 6).

The Rise of Collectivism

The preeminence of classical liberal ideas was to be challenged towards the end of the nineteenth century in Britain, gradually to be replaced by the spirit of the age which favored collectivism. The Fabian Society, founded in 1884 by Beatrice and Sidney Webb and

George Bernard Shaw, was a key influence here. The Fabians 'aggressively and successfully' promoted 'a coherent intellectual justification for the extension of the power of the State in pursuit of certain specific aims, such as the creation of a "national minimum" standard of living' (Cockett, 1994, p. 14). They influenced the Liberal Party and the nascent Labour Party in the early twentieth century. The demands of the First World War saw a huge increase in state control, characterized as 'the final buckling of the Victorian liberal State, giving way to an unprecedented degree of central control and central economic planning'; the coal industry was nationalized in 1917, and there was a 'proliferation of new Whitehall departments', including the Ministry of Foods (ibid., p. 16). Moreover, the success of the war effort seemed to vindicate the notion that collectivism was 'not only the route to a more just and equitable society, but that it was also a more efficient way of running a modern economy' (ibid.).

The collectivist measures begun during the war continued after it. The Housing Act of 1919 committed government for the first time 'to subsidizing local authority housing so that rents could be fixed at below the market price' (ibid.); the government intervened in all levels of the economy, including setting up the first state national monopoly, the Central Electricity Board, in 1926. By the time of the 'economic deluge of the 1930s', following the Wall Street crash of 1929, 'the ideological course towards collectivism was firmly set' (ibid., p. 17).

During the 1930s, classical liberal ideas were at their lowest ebb, replaced by 'contemporary enthusiasms for various forms of collectivism – planning, protectionism and Keynesianism' (ibid., p. 2). The impact of the destructive world war and the global depression led many to doubt the ability of capitalism to cope with modern problems. And fascism and communism appeared to demonstrate that 'alternative economic systems could work, and communism had a hypnotic attraction for idealists' (Hartwell, 1995, p. 17). But at what cost to liberty and the foundations of democracy? Such concerns led to the conscious revival of the ideas of economic liberalism, carried forward by key intellectuals and institutions, that was to make classical liberal ideas 'not only the governing orthodoxy in Britain – accepted by all the main political parties – but also the idea that helped precipitate the downfall of the Communist regimes in the Soviet Union and Eastern Europe in 1989–90 and elsewhere subsequently' (Cockett, 1994, p. 2).

From *The Road to Serfdom* to the Mont Pelerin Society

Why did the ideas of economic liberalism reemerge in the 1930s? Groups of intellectuals became deeply concerned by the potential of the collectivist movements building around Europe to undermine freedom and with it the basis for the good life. An early expression of this emerging countermovement was a colloquium organized in Paris in late August 1938 focused on Walter Lippmann's book *The Good Society*, hence called 'Le Colloque Walter Lippmann'. The opening chapter of *The Good Society* spelled out the warning in stark terms:

> Throughout the world, in the name of progress, men who call themselves Communists, Socialists, fascists, nationalists, progressives, and even liberals, are unanimous in holding that government with its instruments of coercion must, by commanding the people how they shall live, direct the course of civilization and fix the shape of things to come ... [So] [u]niversal is the dominion of this dogma over the minds of contemporary men that no one is taken seriously as a statesman or a theorist who does not come forward with proposals to magnify the power of public officials and to extend and to multiply their intervention in human affairs. Unless he is authoritarian and collectivist, he is a mossback, a reactionary, at best an amiable eccentric swimming hopelessly against the tide. It is a strong tide.
>
> (Lippmann (1937), quoted in Cockett, 1994, p. 10)

Present at the colloquium was one Friedrich A. Hayek, who was to become the foremost figure in the revival of economic liberalism. Hayek (1899–1992) was born in Vienna into a family of intellectuals. He had graduated from the University of Vienna with doctorates in law (1921) and political science (1923) and journeyed as a research student to the United States, where he remained for 14 months. Hayek was greatly influenced by the work of Ludwig von Mises (1881–1973), known as the father of Austrian economics, and, in particular, Mises' *Socialism*, published in 1922. Professor Lionel Robbins – perhaps the most prominent of the free-market economists in England at the time – invited Hayek to the London School of Economics in 1931 to deliver a series of lectures concerning the economic trade cycle. Hayek consequently moved to London that same year to take up a professorship at the London School of Economics, where he remained Tooke Professor of Economic Science and Statistics until 1950. Hayek became a British citizen in 1938. During his time in London, Hayek was an important figure debating economic policy with John Maynard Keynes, who perhaps above all was the key intellectual figure promoting the viability of government intervention to solve the social and economic problems of the 1930s. Hayek sought to show how Keynesian monetary theory and philosophy concerning the business cycle was misguided and destructive.

Hayek's career – and the whole revival of classical liberalism – was dramatically boosted by the 1944 publication of his *Road to Serfdom*. This was a polemical, political book, published by Routledge in England in 1944 and the University of Chicago Press in the United States in 1945. A condensed version was also published in April 1945 in the *Reader's Digest*. It was hugely influential succeeding, 'as Hayek had intended, in redefining the political debate in Britain' (Cockett, 1994, p. 97). In *The Road to Serfdom*, Hayek spelled out the dangers of socialism and how socialist planning led to totalitarianism:

> Our generation has forgotten that the system of private property is the most important guarantee of freedom. It is only because the control of the means of production is divided among many people acting independently that we as individuals can decide what to do with ourselves. When all the means of production are vested in a single hand, whether it be nominally that of 'society' as a whole or that of a dictator, whoever exercises this control has complete power over us. In the hands of private individuals, what is called economic power can be an instrument of coercion, but it is never control over the whole life of a person. But when economic power is centralized as an instrument of political power it creates a degree of dependence scarcely distinguishable from slavery.
>
> (Hayek, [1944] 1999, p. 3)

Hayek used his new-found fame and influence after the success of *The Road to Serfdom* to suggest building on 'Le Colloque Walter Lippmann' to create a new intellectual society, linking those who were against collectivism in both Europe and North America, building on the combined philosophies of Lord Acton and Alexis de Tocqueville. From 1 to 10 April 1947, a group of like-minded liberals met, at Hayek's invitation, at the Hotel du Parc on the slopes of Mont Pelerin above Lake Geneva, Switzerland. They came together sharing a 'feeling of crisis – that Western liberal civilization was in danger from illiberal doctrines and forces' (Hartwell, 1995, p. 27). There were 39 altogether, made up of economists, historians, philosophers, jurists, publicists, political scientists and literary critics. These included Milton and Rose Friedman, Ludwig von Mises, George Stigler and Franz Machlup. Professor Stanley Dennison, then of Cambridge University, who was to offer E.G. West his first university lectureship in economics at Newcastle, was also present, as were Professors Lionel Robbins, Arnold Plant, Karl Popper and John Jewkes, also attending from England. Four of those present at the inaugural meeting went on to win the Nobel Prize for economics, including Hayek in 1974 and Friedman in 1976. By 1997, the achievements of four further active Mont Pelerin Society members – James Buchanan, George Stigler, Ronald Coase and Gary Becker – had been similarly recognized.

The participants at the first meeting were concerned about a range of issues that they thought had the potential to undermine Western liberal civilization. These included the rapid growth of government and the way in which the state was increasingly intervening in economic life, leading to a decline in competitiveness. They were worried about the growth of industrial and labor monopolies, monetary instability, mass unemployment and the continued persistence of poverty. They were also concerned with developing theories of classical liberalism. They were clear that these theories did allow an important role for the state, particularly in defense, the maintenance of law and order, and the provision of some public works, but were also aware that the theories seemed inadequate to cope with the range of perceived social and economic problems that democratic governments were seeking to solve through state intervention. Hence, they saw a need to develop the theories and applications of classical liberalism to modern-day problems.

The commencing address to the meeting made clear its basis in the philosophy of Adam Smith: economic liberalism, it was explained, 'is the legitimate off-spring of the union between two first cousins: Adam Smith's penetrating and essentially sound scientific analysis of the economic world of his day, and Adam Smith's inborn love of freedom, constructive effort and wealth' (quoted in Cockett, 1994, p. 111).

The name of the society had still not been agreed by the last day of the meeting. Hayek favored 'the Acton-Tocqueville Society', while others favored using the names of Burke and Smith. The compromise was reached that they should simply settle on the place name of their first meeting. Hence, the Mont Pelerin Society was born. It was registered as a corporation on 6 November 1947 in Illinois, with Hayek as president.

Six central aims of the Mont Pelerin Society, drafted by Professor Robbins at the first meeting, were set out. These included the central issue of 'combating the misuse of history for the furtherance of creeds hostile to liberty' (quoted in Hartwell, 1995, pp. 42). Hayek's interest here led the 1951 Mont Pelerin Society meeting in Beauvallon, France, to focus solely on historical aspects; the papers of the meeting were published under the title *Capitalism and the Historians* (Hayek, [1954] 1963). In his introduction, Hayek argued how the history of capitalism in the industrial revolution in Britain and the United States had been distorted by enemies of capitalism such as Marx and Engels. Because of this perceived misrepresentation of the facts of history in order to strengthen the socialist cause, Hayek is at pains to suggest that history must be reexplored in order to overcome some of the myths of his time:

> There is, however, one supreme myth which more than any other has served to discredit the economic system to which we owe our present-day civilization and to the examination of which the present volume is devoted. It is the legend of the deterioration of the position of the working classes in consequence of the rise of 'capitalism' ... Who has not heard of the 'horrors of early

capitalism' and gained the impression that the advent of this system brought untold new suffering to large classes who before were
tolerably content and comfortable? We might justly hold in disre-
pute a system to which the blame attached that even for a time it
worsened the position of the poorest and most numerous class of
the population. The widespread emotional aversion to 'capitalism'
is closely connected with this belief that the undeniable growth of
wealth which the competitive order has produced was purchased at
the price of depressing the standard of life of the weakest elements
of society.

(Hayek, [1954] 1963, p. 10)

This concern of Hayek's may have been a critically important influence on E.G. West. As we shall see in Chapters 3 and 4, West was
to follow Hayek's injunction to explore the history of the industrial
revolution with regard to education in particular, leading to a radical
reappraisal of ideas concerning the justified role of government in
education.

E.G. West's first encounter with the Mont Pelerin Society was in
1962, when he was invited by Professor John Jewkes to attend the conference in Knokke, Belgium. (West was to become a member in 1964.)
The year 1962 was a portentous time to be introduced to the society
and the people within it: Milton Friedman had just published his now
classic work in defense of free markets, *Capitalism and Freedom*, which
included an important chapter on the role of government in education, and was present with his wife, Rose, at the Knokke meeting.
E.G. West was deeply honored to meet Friedman. In the acknowl-
edgments to his PhD thesis, he wrote, 'Finally I wish to express my
gratitude to Professor Milton Friedman of Chicago University for an
informal but most valuable conversation in September 1962' (West,
1963) – a conversation that took place at the Mont Pelerin Society meeting. It is clear that this discussion inspired him to continue
'thinking the unthinkable' in his work (letter from E.G. West to Milton
Friedman, *c.* 1965, E.G. West Archives); in one sense, from then on,
his PhD thesis and his subsequent *Education and the State* became
a virtual dialogue with Milton Friedman, building on the foundations of Friedman's ideas, challenging them in key places. (Note: the

E.G. West Archives are held at the E.G. West Centre, School of Educa-
tion, Communication and Language Sciences, Newcastle University.
They can be accessed by request to the author, who is Director of the
E.G. West Centre.)

Moreover, in 1962 the Mont Pelerin Society for the first time featured as one of its major sessions 'The Role of Government in Relation
to Education, Health Services and Support of Science'. The papers
here featured views that West was to find far too conservative: one
argued why education should, in fact 'be provided "free" by government' (Lees, 1962, p. III.43). The major argument given was that

> education is a pre-condition of rational choice: a minimum amount
> of literacy and knowledge is essential to the efficient functioning of
> markets and political processes . . . it is clear that education is part of
> the foundations of free activity, akin to defence and justice. Illiteracy
> and ignorance reduce the effectiveness of the whole political and
> economic system and not merely that of the individuals concerned.
> This, as I understand it, is the liberal (as in the sense of 'Old Whig',
> Hayekian) justification for compulsory education.
>
> (ibid.)

The paper also noted that 'some liberal economists', presumably
referring to Milton Friedman, 'would argue that nowadays the only
legitimate role for government in education is that of compulsion,
combined perhaps with subsidies' (ibid., p. III.44). However, the
author is not sure about this argument, pointing to the importance
of education as

> an equalising force in society, breaking down class barriers and
> other restrictions on mobility and reducing future inequalities of
> income . . . Many liberals, therefore, would support collective pro-
> vision, as well as compulsion, in education as a means of ensuring
> broad equality of consumption of education – something difficult to
> enforce in markets, with their potentialities for variety and differing
> standards.
>
> (ibid., p. III.43)

The discussion at the conference around these issues with Friedman and Hayek served to fire up West's enthusiasm. As Friedman's influence is so important, I shall temporarily abandon this chronological treatment of events to outline the basis of Friedman's ideas on the role of government in education, both linking them with Hayek's on the same subject and showing how these relate to the ideas of the founder of classical liberalism, Adam Smith.

Friedman and Classical Liberal Ideas on Education

Friedman, born in Brooklyn in 1912, had graduated from Rutgers University in 1932, majoring in mathematics and economics, from where he studied for his MA in economics at the University of Chicago (1933). He returned to University of Chicago as an associate professor in economic theory after obtaining his PhD from Columbia University in 1946. He died in late 2006, as this volume was being completed. He, like Hayek, was also a key player in debates with John Maynard Keynes on price theory, publishing in 1956 *Studies in the Quantity Theory of Money*, which challenged Keynes's theories. Friedman's monetarism came to the fore in 1963 when he published *Monetary History of the United States, 1867–1960*, coauthored with Anna Schwartz, which suggested that the Great Depression of the 1930s in the United States resulted from the disastrous monetary policies set up by the Federal Reserve System, rather than from any inherent defects of capitalism.

In 1962, Friedman published *Capitalism and Freedom*, his classic defense of capitalism and the economic liberal order. One of the important chapters in this book, Chapter 6, reprinted his earlier 1955 article 'The Role of Government in Education'. It has become known as the seminal statement in favor of educational vouchers (see, for instance, Enlow and Ealy, 2006), and was to be deeply influential on a whole generation of scholars, including E.G. West.

The key argument built on Friedman's economic treatment of cases where government intervention was required, the two relevant ones for education being where there are externalities, or neighborhood effects, and where the 'protection of minors' principle is invoked. In the cases of neighborhood effects, 'strictly voluntary exchange is impossible', as 'actions of individuals have effects on other individuals for which it is not feasible to charge or recompense them' (Friedman, 1962, p. 30). Importantly, Friedman noted that when governments intervene in order to overcome neighborhood effects, they introduce 'an additional set of neighborhood effects by failing to charge or to compensate individuals properly' (ibid., p. 32). So, government intervention has its own neighborhood effects, including the threat to individual freedom. Friedman argued that there were no hard and fast rules to determine when governments should intervene because of externalities; rather, each case should be decided on its own merits.

Furthermore, government intervention may be regarded as beneficial or desirable on paternalistic grounds – that is, in the case of mentally ill people or of children. Although the family is the best unit in which care can be given to children, parents are not free to do what they wish with other people, and this applies to their own children too.

How do these two principles apply to education? Together, both justify government intervention, Friedman argued. A major externality of education was the requirements of democracy: 'A stable and democratic society is impossible without a minimum degree of literacy and knowledge on the part of most citizens and without widespread acceptance of some common set of values' (ibid., p. 86). Because education contributes to both, and 'the gain from the education of a child accrues not only to the child or to his parents but to other members of the society' – that is, 'the education of my child contributes to other people's welfare by promoting a stable and democratic society' (ibid.) – this is a genuine 'externality' or 'neighborhood effect'. Thus, 'the action of one individual imposes significant costs on other individuals for which it is not feasible to make him compensate them or yields significant gains to them for which it is not feasible to make them compensate him' (ibid.).

This leads, for Friedman, to the justified state intervention of 'the imposition of a minimum required level of schooling and the financing of this schooling by the state' (ibid., p. 89). However, it certainly does not lead to the justification for the 'actual administration of educational institutions by the government, the "nationalization" as it were, of the bulk of the "education industry"' (ibid.).

Instead, Friedman proposes that government finance the compulsory elements of education by giving parents 'vouchers': 'Governments could require a minimum level of schooling financed by giving parents vouchers redeemable for a specified maximum sum per child per year if spent on "approved" educational services' (ibid.). Importantly, parents could supplement the sum available, and the educational services 'could be rendered by private enterprises operated for profit, or by non-profit institutions' (ibid.). For all educational institutions, government's role 'would be limited to insuring that the schools met certain minimum standards, such as the inclusion of a minimum common content in their programs, much as it now inspects restaurants to insure that they maintain minimum sanitary standards' (ibid.).

It is also relevant to note that these ideas on the role of government in education became the mainstay of those connected with the revival of classical liberal ideas through the Mont Pelerin Society. Hayek himself was to add nothing substantially to them. His treatment of education in his major three-volume work *Law, Legislation and Liberty* (Hayek, 1973) is cursory only, referring us back to his earlier work *The Constitution of Liberty*, first published in 1960, for a 'fuller treatment' (Heyek, 1973, III, p. 60). Here the discussion appears to be pure Milton Friedman: First, outlining the paternalistic role of the state with regard to children, Hayek notes that the significant fact is that 'they are not responsible individuals to whom the argument for freedom fully applies' (Hayek, 1960, p. 377). While responsibilities for their welfare should by and large be given to parents,

> this does not mean that parents should have unrestricted liberty to treat their children as they like. The other members of the community have a genuine stake in the welfare of the children. The case for requiring parents or guardians to provide for those under their care a certain minimum of education is clearly very strong.
>
> (ibid.)

The case for compulsory education 'up to a certain minimum standard', Hayek notes, following Friedman in the 'neighborhood effects' arguments, rests on two arguments: The first 'is the general argument that all of us will be exposed to [fewer] risks and will receive more benefits from our fellows if they share with us certain basic knowledge and beliefs' (ibid.). The second is that 'in a country with democratic institutions, there is the further important consideration that democracy is not likely to work, except on the smallest local scale, with a partly illiterate people' (ibid.). For both, partly what is required is an enforced 'certain common standards of values' (ibid.). However, again agreeing with Friedman, Hayek warns of the dangers of instituting these through public (state) education: 'The very magnitude of the power over men's minds that a highly centralized and government-dominated system of education places in the hands of the authorities ought to make one hesitate before accepting it too readily' (ibid., p. 379). Moreover,

> the more highly one rates the power that education can have over men's minds, the more convinced one should be of the danger of placing this power in the hands of any single authority ... And if, at present, one of the reasons why there should be the greatest variety of educational opportunities is that we really know so little about what educational techniques may achieve, the argument for variety would be even stronger if we knew more about the methods of producing certain types of results.
>
> (ibid., p. 380)

Finally, Hayek followed Milton Friedman's proposals for educational vouchers: 'it would now be entirely practicable to defray the costs of general education out of the public purse without maintaining government schools, by giving the parents vouchers covering the cost of education of each child' (ibid., p. 381); again, following Friedman, he points to the reason for public finance resting on the issue of compulsory schooling: 'It is probably a necessary consequence of the adoption of compulsory education that for those families to whom the cost would be a severe burden it should be defrayed out of public funds' (ibid., p. 378).

How did Friedman's ideas on the role of government in education (and hence Hayek's) relate back to the ideas of Adam Smith? Smith, too, believed that there was a role for government in education, although of a relatively minor kind; he was clearly not in favor of the kind of universal funding that Friedman and Hayek promoted. For clearly, Smith wrote, people of 'rank and fortune' are capable of gaining an education without any help from the 'public'. However, the 'common people's' education may require some 'attention of the public', namely the 'establishing in every parish or district a little school, where children may be taught for a reward so moderate that even a common labourer may afford it' (Smith, [1776] 1976, book V, ch. I, V.i.f.55, p. 785). Importantly, for Smith, although 'the master' should be partly reimbursed from the public purse, this should not cover even the majority of his pay, which should be made up by tuition fees from the pupils or their parents. Why? 'Because, if he was wholly, or even principally, paid by [the public], he would soon learn to neglect his business' (ibid.). In other words, the system favored by Smith was somewhat similar to that which had emerged in Scotland from 1696, where 'the establishment of such parish schools has taught almost the whole common people to read, and a very great proportion of them to write and account' (ibid.). Importantly, under this system there was some small provision for capital constructions while the teacher's salary came from a small fixed stipend, supplemented by pupil fees. (We shall further discuss the Scottish system at the end of Chapter 3.) By the time of Smith's writing, however, inflation had substantially reduced the real value of the stipend, so that, in effect, the more efficient teachers were dependent for their incomes largely on school fees. This was good as far as Smith was concerned: dependence on direct payments from customers meant a close correspondence between teachers' efforts and the desires of pupils and their parents, since a teacher's income would be closely related to the numbers of pupils enrolled.

Smith was able to contrast the Scottish situation with that in England, which had a conspicuously different system. In England, the Test Act of 1665 had excluded dissenters from schools and universities, and so placed serious restrictions upon the development of education in England. Catholics and Jews were excluded from universities, while grammar school teachers were governed by ecclesiastical licensing, meaning that many who would have been willing teachers were not allowed to practice, while those who became teachers were protected against competition. But another factor, apart from legislation, also led to reduced competition in the English schools: benefactors often bequeathed large 'endowments' on schools and colleges, which usually funded them in full. This had the unfortunate effect, observed by Adam Smith, that the greater the proportion of funding provided by the endowment, the more the school or college operated away from parental and pupil wishes. As Smith wrote, contrasting the English endowed institutions with the preferred Scottish method of fee-paying tuition,

> The endowments of schools and colleges have necessarily diminished more or less the necessity of application in the teachers. Their subsistence, so far as it arises from their salaries, is evidently derived from a fund altogether independent of their success and reputation in their particular professions.
>
> ([1776] 1976, book V, ch. I, p. 760)

Moreover, the endowed schools and colleges acted not only to corrupt the teachers but also to crowd out purely private provision: 'The endowments of schools and colleges have, in this manner, not only corrupted the diligence of public teachers, but have rendered it almost impossible to have any good private ones' (Smith, [1776] 1976, book V, ch. I, p. 780).

Smith also deliberately eschewed the notion of specially trained and selected teachers, both because he thought state training of teachers was undesirable and because he thought a system of licensing would undermine competition and erect barriers to entry to the profession. Those being taught should be allowed freely to choose their teachers, since 'they would soon find better teachers for themselves than any whom the state could provide for them' (Smith, [1776] 1976, book V, ch. I, p. 796). Smith gave historical evidence, including from classical Greece, in support of his objections to state-provided teachers, showing the superiority of freelance teachers. And in a letter to Dr Cullen, a colleague at Glasgow University, in 1778, Smith wrote, 'Monopolists seldom make good work, and a lecture which a certain number of students must attend, whether they profit by it or no, is certainly not very likely to be a good one' (Thomson, 1832).

Meanwhile, Smith's objections to the licensing of teachers were part of his rejection of the principles of occupational licensure in general. One of the major reasons here was the inefficiencies brought about by monopoly: In his letter to Dr Cullen, he continued on these themes:

> Had the Universities of Oxford and Cambridge been able to maintain themselves in the exclusive privilege of graduating all the doctors who could practise in England, the price of feeling a pulse might by this time have risen from two and three guineas, the price which it has now happily arrived at, to double or triple that sum; and English physicians might, and probably would, have been at the same time the most ignorant and quackish in the world.

In the next chapters, we shall see how E.G. West was to explore Friedman's ideas on the role of government in education in the light of Adam Smith's own prescriptions, leading to a much more radical version of how the state should be involved in education than that prescribed by Friedman and taken up by Hayek.

The Public Choice Theorists at the Mont Pelerin Society

Let us return to the influence of the Mont Pelerin Society on West. There were two other key players within it who were to have a key impact on West's thought, both of whom were to become personal friends when West was in the mid-1970s a visiting scholar at the Public Choice Center in Blacksburg, Virginia. These were James Buchanan and Gordon Tullock. Buchanan won the Nobel Prize for economics in 1986. West was introduced to James Buchanan's ideas around the same time as his first Mont Pelerin Society meeting in 1962, when his PhD supervisor, Jack Wiseman, suggested he should read Buchanan to relieve the tedium of much of what was being written in economics at the time: 'I found the material unexpected and stunning in its logic and implications', reported E.G. West (E.G. West Archives, undated). When West was a postdoctoral researcher at Chicago from 1965 to 1966, he also further encountered these ideas, and went back to the University of Kent to share them with Charles Rowley, who had independently been introduced to them while holidaying in the United States.

Buchanan, born in 1919, and Tullock, born in 1922, are considered to be the founders of public choice theory. They coauthored *The Calculus of Consent* (Buchanan and Tullock, 1962) which, along with Anthony Downs's book *An Economic Theory of Democracy* (1957), laid the foundations for this new theory. Traditional economic theory is built around individuals, the 'building blocks are living, choosing, economising persons' (Buchanan, 1978, p. 5). In public choice theory – the economic theory of politics – the tools and methods of economic theory are applied to 'the political or governmental sector, to politics, to the public economy' (Buchanan, 1999, p. 48). Public choice theory looks at the behavior of these individuals acting in their own self-interest in the governmental sector in the capacity of voters, leaders or members of political parties, bureaucrats, elected representatives, and candidates running for office. Public choice sees the actions of bureaucrats and politicians in the same way as those of *any* utility-maximizing individual, acting in their own self-interest to maximize their own benefit. These benefits could include wealth, political standing, reelection possibilities and 'empire' building. Actions are assumed to be undertaken aiming at this self-interest, rather than at serving the public interest. Just as entrepreneurs are driven by the desire to maximize profits, so the actions of those in politics may be driven by the maximizing of votes.

Bureaucrats acting in their own self-interest, as any other individual in society does, will wish to expand the size of the bureau of which they are a part. Expanding the size has benefits for the bureaucrat, such as an increased salary and more perquisites of office; the larger and more powerful the bureau, the greater the budget and the power of the bureaucrats within it (Buchanan, 1978). William Niskanen (1971) developed a model showing how bureaucracies could expand the size of their budgets to 'twice the size necessary to meet taxpayers' genuine demands for public goods and services' (referenced in Buchanan, 1978, p. 12). In doing so,

> taxpayers end up by being no better off than they would be without any public goods; all of their net benefits are 'squeezed out' by the bureaucrats. The implication is that each and every public good

or service, whether it be health services, education, transport, or defence, tends to be expanded well beyond any tolerable level of efficiency, as defined by the demands of the citizenry.

(Buchanan, 1978, p. 12)

Prior to public choice theory, the term 'market failure' was (and still is) used in order to describe the position where government action is required to correct the failures of the market. One such example might be a monopoly, or the need for government to provide public or merit goods. Public choice economists came up the with term 'government failure' to describe the position when government intervention does not achieve the corrective outcome it sets out to achieve.

Although West encountered these ideas relatively early on in his career, he was not to apply them fully to educational policy until after he had written *Education and the State*. We shall explore the influence of these ideas on West's subsequent intellectual development in Chapter 4, as well as noting some of their critics.

From the Mont Pelerin Society to the Institute of Economic Affairs

The Mont Pelerin Society was one vehicle for the revitalization of the ideas of classical liberalism, and an important source of influence on E.G. West. But the Mont Pelerin Society explicitly eschewed bringing the ideas of classical liberalism to a wider audience; in a sense, it remained in its early years as an environment to give 'reassurance, comfort and camaraderie to individual liberals at a time when they were few in number and geographically isolated' (quoted in Cockett, 1994, p. 118). But perhaps the revival of economic liberalism required more than this? Enter Antony Fisher, entrepreneur farmer, who was to be instrumental in founding the second institution that would be of paramount influence in spreading classical liberal ideas, and a second key influence on E.G. West. This was of course the Institute of Economic Affairs (IEA).

The Institute of Economic Affairs was created by Antony Fisher, whom Professor Milton Friedman has described as the 'single most important person in the development of Thatcherism' (interview with Richard Cockett, quoted in Cockett, 1994, p. 122). Fisher, born in June 1915, started dairy farming in 1947 after serving in the Second World War in 111 Hurricane Squadron. Fisher had read Hayek's *The Road to Serfdom* in 1945, which had articulated both his fears for the future and emerging ideas on the way forward. He became determined to meet its author and arranged a meeting in 1947 at the London School of Economics, as Hayek was preparing for the first meeting of the Mont Pelerin Society. Antony Fisher described the 'fateful meeting' as follows: 'My central question was what, if anything, could he advise me to do to help get discussion and policy on the right lines.' Hayek warned him against 'wasting time' with a political career, something by which Fisher was tempted at the time. Instead, Hayek explained that 'the decisive influence in the battle of ideas and policy was wielded by intellectuals', whom he characterized as the 'second-hand dealers in ideas'. Hayek pointed to how the Fabians had 'tilted the political debate in favor of growing government intervention'; what was needed was a parallel body to counter that influence. Hayek recommended that Fisher 'should join with others in forming a scholarly research organisation to supply intellectuals in universities, schools, journalism and broadcasting with authoritative studies of the economic theory of markets and its application to practical affairs' (Fisher, 1974, p. 103).

Hayek himself, looking back on the creation of the IEA, writing in December 1982, observed:

> One Institution I have watched from the beginning, and for the existence of which I am in some sense responsible, is the Institute of Economic Affairs in London ... What I insisted, and was strictly followed, was not to appeal to the large numbers but to the intellectuals – the journalists, teachers and so on ... The IEA has become the most powerful maker of opinion in England. Bookshops have a special rack of IEA papers. Even people on the Left feel compelled to keep informed of its publications.
>
> (quoted in Seldon, 2005, p. 84)

Following his meeting with Hayek, Fisher wrote his first book, *The Case for Freedom*, published in 1947, a 'comparatively simplistic but robust exposition of the free-market economy, laced with home-spun wisdom about politics and democracy' (Cockett, 1994,

p. 124). Fisher's cattle-farming business was all but wiped out in the foot and mouth epidemic of 1951, but his fortunes changed when he visited the United States in 1952 at the invitation of the Foundation for Economic Education in New York State – an early organization set up to popularize free-market ideas. On that visit, Fisher was both to see first hand the new method of broiler chicken farming in Ithaca – unknown in England at the time – and to observe the functioning of a free-market think tank. He returned to England inspired by both. 'Buxted Chickens' was founded in 1953, through which Fisher was to make his fortune. And two years later, on 9 November 1955, Fisher established the Institute of Economic Affairs (IEA). The IEA was formed as a non-political charity; as its trust deeds put it, 'a research and educational trust that specialises in the study of markets and pricing systems as technical devices for registering preferences and apportioning resources' (quoted in Cockett, 1994, p. 132). The IEA's first publication was *The Free Convertibility of Sterling* (Winder, 1955), which, through the influence of the *Newsweek* columnist and Fisher's fellow Mont Pelerin Society member Henry Hazlitt, received widespread publicity.

Fisher engaged Ralph Harris in 1956 to run the IEA. Harris had been taught by Professor Stanley Dennison at Cambridge (who was later to offer West his first university lectureship, at Newcastle). Arthur Seldon was recruited in 1957 as editorial director. Together, the 'duo of Harris and Seldon effectively ran the IEA from 1957 until the mid-1980s' (Cockett, 1994, p. 137). Both Harris and Seldon were of working-class origins and 'could thus attack Keynesianism and the Welfare State from the bottom up' (ibid., p. 138).

Arthur Seldon, looking back over 25 years of the IEA's work, set out the key principles that motivated the organization: the IEA

systematically mustered and presented in modern dress the truths of classical political economy: that government could not assemble the information required for the desired use of resources; that only individuals could derive the information from their local, voluntary, private lives; that they could reveal and apply the information only or most effectively by coming together as buyers and sellers in markets.

(Seldon, 2005, p. 4)

The IEA did accept, Seldon wrote, that

> some goods or services – the so-called 'public goods' – had to be supplied by government, national or local, and financed by taxes or rates, because they could not be refused to people who refused to pay and who would otherwise batten on those who did pay by taking 'free rides'.
>
> (ibid., p. 5)

But an important part of the work of the IEA was to discover *what were* these public goods that needed supplying: the IEA 'opened up questions that had lain dormant for decades'. It explored whether particular services should be supplied by government or whether they could better be supplied by markets. And '[i]f markets were not feasible, was that because choice for buyers or competition among suppliers was impracticable, or because government itself was putting legal or other obstacles in the way of individuals with goods or services to exchange?' (ibid.).

Seldon noted that there were two possibilities for provisions of goods and services: 'If markets were practicable', he wrote, then how could 'obstacles to them be removed?' If they were not practicable, then the question was: were there other methods 'of cooperation between buyers and suppliers' that *were* feasible? Seldon asked:

> Was it better to construct state monopolies – as in fuel or transport, education or medicine – and try to arrange they served buyers faithfully and efficiently? Or did such organisations have their own weaknesses of political and impersonal control, bureaucratic inflexibility, high taxation and restriction of choice between suppliers?
>
> (ibid.)

A key approach of the IEA was not to consider 'administrative practicability' or 'political possibility' (ibid., p. 6), but 'to apply economic analysis ruthlessly'. The IEA was there to 'think the unthinkable'. Administrative practicability 'could not be ascertained except by practical trial'. Political impossibility 'could be a pretext developed by politicians or bureaucrats who resisted reform that did not suit them however good the argument, and in any event because reasoned ideas could themselves make the "impossible" possible' (ibid.).

There were various 'fundamental economic truths' that were at the base of much of the writings of the IEA. One of these was that 'without the signalling device of price, man cannot spontaneously and voluntarily co-operate for prosperous co-existence' (ibid.) and another was that 'Competition is the environment – the *only* environment – in which commodities or services can be judged by *comparison* with alternatives ... And competition is the *only* effective method of defending the consumer by making every seller his ally against every other seller' (ibid.). For Seldon, the 'divorce of supply or demand from price' in a variety of services and goods, including 'electricity, gas, rail, road, education, medicine, housing, a host of local government services, not least in labour by incomes policies', had led to 'massive, de-stabilising, simultaneous wastes of surpluses and shortages' (ibid., p. 7).

In particular, early on the IEA saw the growing welfare state as showing key symptoms of the problems noted above: it has grown into

> an uncontrollable monster with an insatiable appetite for tax finance and incestuous administrators. It denies choice. It substitutes incorrigible differences in cultural power which determines access in the state for corrigible differences in purchasing power which determine access in the market. It demands increasing coercion as incomes rise, as in the suppression of private education and medicine. And it is largely unaccountable and therefore irresponsible because it is run by men spending other men's money.
>
> (ibid., pp. 7–8)

Those who justify the welfare state emphasize 'the external benefits of welfare', but these 'strangely overlook its external costs in tax disincentives, resistances to reform, diminished personal liberties, weakened family cohesion, and social conflict where political consensuses are enforced on minorities, groups or individuals' (ibid., p. 8).

One of Seldon's preoccupations very early on was education. He was pleased to recruit Professor Alan Peacock, founder of the Institute of Social and Economic Research at the University of York, and Professor Jack Wiseman, to write the first contribution on education, *Education for Democrats* (published in February 1964). In the preface to this volume, Seldon commented, 'Education is a service that too many social scientists, educationalists and politicians assume must be provided by government' (Seldon, 2005, p. 108). Recent government reports, he noted, 'all concluded with recommendations that would enlarge or entrench the role and intensify the control of the state' (ibid.). However, he observed that '[s]ince the mid-1950s, and earlier, economists in the USA [i.e. Milton Friedman] have considered the problems of establishing a private market in education' (ibid.). The IEA invited Peacock and Wiseman to consider a similar proposition for England, 'to reconsider the institutional framework and financial arrangements that seemed desirable to permit scope for a variety of private or state educational institutions from primary schools to universities that best met the requirements of a free society' (ibid.). One of the inspirations for the IEA's move was the result of its social surveys, which 'revealed a sizeable demand for a choice between state and private education' (ibid.). That is, the IEA had, from 1962 onwards, conducted field studies asking ordinary parents whether they would be prepared to pay for their children's education, and whether they would prefer to receive funding in terms of vouchers from government, to be used in schools of their choice, rather than the current system of free-at-the-point-of-delivery state-provided schooling. The results were analyzed in three reports: *Choice in Welfare*, 1963, 1965 and 1970: 'The conclusions of most of these works have challenged the conventional view held alike by academics, by politicians and by opinion-forming journalists on public preferences in welfare and on the possibilities of reform' (Seldon, 2005, p. 135). However, despite the results that showed parental preference for choice, 'academics concerned with education . . . persist in favouring a system of monopolistic, state-controlled, standardised, universal, comprehensive education' (ibid.). The IEA set out to challenge these premises.

At the time, however, it was touch and go whether Peacock and Wiseman's work would be the first published on education, or whether E.G. West's *Education and the State* would get in before theirs. Arthur Seldon had written to E.G. West (Seldon to E.G. West, 3 October 1963, E.G. West Archives), inviting him to 'write one of the first of a new series of paper-backs we are hoping to launch next year. The subject will, of course, be Education. The books are to be of, roughly, 60,000–70,000 words in length and will be aimed at the same range of readers who buy Pelicans and Penguins. The provisional name of our series (still on the secret list) is "Polar Bears"' – presumably a continuation of the Penguin theme. West accepted on 10 October. At the same time, there were considerable delays to the Peacock and Wiseman book (Seldon to E.G. West, 26 and 29 November, 1963, E.G. West Archives), so Arthur Seldon had it in mind that West's book could actually be the IEA's first on education: 'I need not tell you that I should not have minded at all if the Wiseman/Peacock alliance had let us down. I am sure we should have had a first-class Hobart Paper from you – as we may still have yet.' In the end, Wiseman and Peacock did deliver. As West was worried that his book might 'be too much of a duplication' of Wiseman/Peacock (E.G. West to Arthur Seldon, 18 October 1963, E.G. West Archives), he was given the manuscript to study before he had finished his own paper.

The basic argument of *Education for Democrats* that West would have read was a proposal for state-funded education, funded through vouchers, bursaries and some grants, and provided 'privately or by self-financing public institutions' (Peacock and Wiseman, 1964, p. 15). Public authorities 'would be responsible for setting examinations concerned with general standards, and with the general surveillance and accrediting of educational institutions' (ibid., p. 16). The reasons why there should be state funding of education were broadly those found in Milton Friedman's essay: 'education has a broader impact upon society', over and above its economic attributes, so these 'cannot be irrelevant to public policy. Education affects social behaviour, political attitudes, and so on, and these in turn have obvious implications for the evolution of a community' (ibid., p. 23). In particular, the IEA authors wrote, clearly influenced by, and referencing, Milton Friedman's 1955 paper, that 'education for citizenship' is of 'fundamental importance':

> A democratic society . . . depends for its continued and satisfactory life upon the existence of a sufficiently literate and informed electorate, which demands some minimum general level of education. At least, then, the community *qua* community has an interest in ensuring that children reach a minimum standard of literacy, whatever the views of parents.
>
> (ibid.)

In other words, there was a requirement for 'public (legal) compulsion, overriding parental wishes' (ibid., p. 27), to ensure 'universal education up to some minimum level' (ibid.). And universal compulsion implied, as it did for Friedman, universal state funding: education should be compulsory *for all*, the authors wrote. But since 'there is no operational way to distinguish the families upon whom financial assistance should be concentrated', and 'the enforcement of compulsion is likely to be much more difficult if parents also have to pay fees', and, finally, 'punishment for those who refuse to pay' would probably make the children suffer as much as the parents, these considerations suggested that education for all should be funded by the state (ibid., pp. 28–9).

Such was the background influence that West would have received from the IEA, which would inform his own development of the ideas on the role of government in education. Before we turn to the development of his ideas in response to this influence, to complete the picture, particularly for when we come to explore the reception and influence of West's ideas, it is worth noting how the IEA's general influence developed in the subsequent years. For its first 20 years, the IEA had 'endured . . . being ignored by government' (Cockett, 1994, p. 156). But this was to change in the mid-1970s. By then, the IEA had 'developed a coherent body of free-market ideas, applicable to all areas of the economy' (ibid.). This coherent set of ideas was labeled by the Fabian Society in 1968 as the philosophy of the 'New Right', a label that was to stick to the brand of economic liberalism purveyed by the IEA: In the Fabian's tract 387, *The New Right: A Critique*, by David

Collard, the author said 'the New Right must be respected for the quality, consistency and rigour of its approach' (quoted in Cockett, 1994, p. 157).

Importantly, West's work on education became part of that 'coherent body of free-market ideas'. As Arthur Seldon wrote, having 'persuaded a young economist' to write for the IEA about the role of government in education, that author 'blossomed into Professor E.G. West, the leading authority on the genesis of British education' (Seldon, 2005, pp. 273–4). West's work was to become part of the corpus critiquing the welfare state that became increasingly influential, as 'a stream of new, younger Conservative politicians were to beat a path for the IEA door' (Cockett, 1994, p. 167), particularly after their election defeat of 1964. Most notably these included Sir Keith Joseph (who was to become Secretary of State for Education under the first Thatcher government), who read avidly of the IEA's work, including on education, to develop 'his own philosophy of economic liberalism during the late 1960s' (ibid., p. 168), and Geoffrey Howe (later to be, among other roles, chancellor of the exchequer and foreign secretary under Thatcher), who was especially interested in the IEA's publication on health and welfare spending. In 1964, he wrote an article for the *Daily Telegraph* in which he asked, 'Is it not time for Conservatives to consider once again the politically difficult business of reducing the area over which the State collects and spends our money for us and increasing the area within which we are free to spend it for ourselves?' (quoted ibid., p. 169). Another important recruit to the IEA's ideas on education policy was Dr Rhodes Boyson (later to be a minister for education in the first Thatcher government), headmaster of Highbury Grove Comprehensive School in north London, who also came under the IEA's influence during the mid-1960s.

And finally, another rising star, introduced to the IEA in the early 1960s probably by Joseph and Howe, was one Margaret Thatcher herself, who was also particularly interested in the IEA's work on the welfare state. In 1969, she wrote, also in the *Daily Telegraph*, that whereas

[t]he left-wing believes that State ownership coupled with central government enables its government to plan the production of each product in relation to the other ... [t]he Conservative approach is

different. We dislike monopoly and seek to break it up, we believe
that competition is the best and the only test of efficiency, that
decisions should be made where the experience and knowledge
are to be found, and that the test of their correctness is the market-
place and that the consequences of wrong decisions should not be
borne by the taxpayer.

(quoted in Cockett, 1994, p. 172)

The IEA became an extremely influential part of Thatcher's intellectual development. It was Seldon and Harris who arranged for
Thatcher to meet with both Hayek and Friedman during her time
as leader of the Opposition. And on Thatcher's coming to power in
1979, one of her first nominees to go to the House of Lords was Ralph
Harris. Thatcher wrote to the IEA a few days after her election victory
in May 1979:

[A]bove all let me thank you for all that you have done for the cause
of free enterprise over the course of so many years. It was primarily
your foundation work which enabled us to rebuild the philosophy
upon which our Party succeeded in the past. The debt we owe to
you is immense and I am very grateful. With best wishes, Margaret.

(ibid., p. 173)

In Chapter 6, on the reception and influence of West's ideas, we
shall explore how these key figures took up West's ideas on education
during the early years of Margaret Thatcher's government.

Coda

It is sometimes argued that one's own personal biography reflects
one's ideas, particularly when it comes to sensitive areas of upbringing
such as schooling. Interestingly, in West's first published piece for
the IEA, an essay in the edited collection *Rebirth of Britain*, he wrote
(as did all the other contributors) a brief autobiographical note. It
provides some interesting reflections on how West perceived his own
educational circumstances, which may have influenced his own ideas,
and to this end is worth quoting in full:

I was born in 1922 in Goldthorpe and went to a co-educational grammar school after failing the then 'eleven plus' at the first attempt. My parents attribute this setback to the antics of local education officials who made me change my school to suit their 'zoning'. We moved to Exeter in 1936 where I attended a grammar school for boys, but by the time I had settled down in it my father thought I should get a nice quiet job somewhere. After working for a while in local government offices, I entered Exeter University in 1945 with a government grant. I emerged with a degree in economics and a teacher's diploma. Nervous as a student, I was terrified as a teacher. However, I survived my first post in a secondary school in the Black Country and moved to a technical college in Guildford to teach economics. In 1956 I went to teach at the Oxford College of Technology where a few staunch colleagues helped me launch a strenuous full-time London University degree course in 1958. Apart from this history, experience as a taxpayer has given me a vested interest in educational reform.

In 1962 I left Oxford and local authority education to become Lecturer at the University of Newcastle upon Tyne. Following articles on monopoly legislation, the history of economic thought, the economics of education and the problem of local unemployment, I am writing a book on the economics of education for the Institute of Economic Affairs.

(West, 1964d, p. 170)

That book was of course *Education and the State*. We shall turn now to explore its arguments that would contribute to the 'seismic shift' that challenged the ways in which people thought about the role of government in education.

Part 2

Critical Exposition of E.G. West's Work

Chapter 2

Economic Arguments for State Intervention in Education

West's Questions

West's overriding interest is in the role of government in education. It is important, in exploring his discussion on these issues, to disaggregate, as West does, the three ways in which governments can intervene in education, namely through funding, regulation and provision. Each of these three ways is independent of the others. For instance, governments can, for example, *provide* by supplying buildings and employing teachers, *fund* by supplying school places free of charge or heavily subsidized, and *regulate* through having compulsory attendance laws and national curricula and assessment systems. While we are used to all three aspects being together in state education now, it is important to note that each is logically independent of the others. In other areas of our lives, for instance, we are accustomed to the state *regulating* to ensure that all drivers on the road have passed their driving test, but there is no state *funding* of this, nor state *provision* of driving schools, both aspects of which are left to private initiative. Or we can have state *funding* of food for the poor, through welfare payments, but no state *provision* of food stores.

Given this context, throughout *Education and the State* and in West's other writings we can see questions being asked on two different levels. The first is: can we justify (using economic arguments) the *current system* of state 'education' as found, say, in England and Wales in the 1960s, when West was writing, which was not vastly different from the system today in 2007 – where governments regulate, fund *and* provide schools? The second level is the more abstract one: can we justify from first principles (using economic arguments) *any* of the three kinds of state intervention in education? For example, can we justify state intervention in *funding*, but not *provision*, of schools? Or can we find justification for *regulation* of aspects of the curriculum, say, but neither state *funding* nor *provision* of schooling? Both alternatives posed in these hypothetical questions were in fact, as West points out, some of the policy possibilities explored in the nineteenth century, to be ultimately rejected. Was the rejection for sound economic reasons or because of other considerations? Questions such as these are ones with which West is concerned throughout his writing.

Putting 'education' in scare quotes above when referring to the state schooling system was a deliberate move in keeping with West's analysis. Throughout his discussion, West is at pains to stress that he does not make the conflation between 'education' and 'schooling' that, he points out, is prevalent in the economic literature. (Here he may also have been influenced by Milton Friedman – for in his seminal essay 'The Role of Government in Education', Friedman reiterates that it is 'important to distinguish "schooling" and "education"' (1962, p. 86), although the two are often conflated: 'The proper subject of concern is education. The activities of government are mostly limited to schooling' (ibid., p. 86). For instance, when referring to the 'protection of minors' principle, West argues that schooling may be only one form of education (and therefore only one way of abating ignorance): 'There are additional sources of learning in real life: the parent, the family, ... friends, the church, books, television, radio, newspapers, correspondence courses, etc., "on the job training", and personal experience' (1994a, p. 7; see also pp. 11, 46, 55). This distinction has two implications. First, West's exploration is of whether state intervention in any parts of education in its broadest sense is justified, not just in schooling systems. Second, conversely, West asks whether and in what ways the broader definition of education impacts on given economic arguments for state intervention.

In *Education and the State*, West explores the standard two major economic arguments for state intervention in education: the 'protection of minors' principle and the argument from 'neighborhood effects'. We look at each in turn.

The 'Protection of Minors' Principle

The 'protection of minors' principle says that government is justified in intervening in education in order to protect children from 'the incompetent decisions of their parents' (Blaug, [1967], 1970, p. 26) because of the harm that such decisions could cause the children. West points out that this was a fundamental principle of the classical economists. Even 'the most ardent' proponents of *laissez-faire* were committed to a legal framework within which it should operate, and where, although disliking 'over-interfering government', they were prepared to make 'exceptions to their general principle of freedom of contract' in certain cases (West, 1994a, p. 3). Protection of children was one such case.

John Stuart Mill was adamant that in the case of education, 'the foundation of the *laissez faire* principle breaks down entirely', because the 'person most interested' – that is, the child – 'is not the best judge of the matter, nor a competent judge at all' (from *Principles of Political Economy*, quoted in West, 1994a, p. 4). His friend the classical economist Nassau Senior wrote that 'the main, almost sole, duty of Government is to give protection. Protection to all, to children as well as to adults' (from *Suggestions on Popular Education*, quoted in West, 1994a, p. 3). Such protection of children brought, for these classical economists, a 'strong presumption in favour of state intervention in education' (West, 1994a p. 4). Importantly, West notes that this view 'seems to have been readily accepted by liberal economists ever since', pointing to Milton Friedman's *Capitalism and Freedom* (1962, p. 86), the key source we noted in Chapter 1. It is an assumption of Friedman's, however, that West seeks to challenge.

There are three important questions that arise for West here. First, protection by whom? For he notes that even if we agree that 'the state should be responsible for seeing that children are protected', we still need to ask, '*whom* should it appoint to carry out this duty in practice?' (West, 1994a, p. 4; emphasis added). For, argues West, 'the state is not a disembodied entity' – that is, it has to work through some individual or individuals 'to whom it prescribes certain powers' (ibid., p. 5). Now, the usual candidates put forward for protecting children – say from hunger or the elements – are their parents. In the case of education, however, John Stuart Mill, in common with the other classical economists, was not satisfied that this was possible. Following the passage quoted above, Mill pointed out that 'In the case of children and young persons, it is common to say, that though they cannot judge for themselves, they have their parents or other relatives to judge for them' (quoted ibid., pp. 4–5). However, Mill argued against this, for 'this removes the question into a different category; making it no longer a question whether the government should interfere with individuals in the direction of their own conduct and interests, but whether it should leave *absolutely in their power* the conduct and interests of somebody else' (quoted ibid., p. 5; my emphasis added).

West points out the rather odd leap of Mill's logic here. For surely the usual argument that parents and relatives could judge on behalf of their children is *not* a claim for *absolute* power, as Mill suggests, but rather 'something in the nature of a *fiduciary* power to be removed in cases where abuse can be shown' (West, 1994a, p. 5). In that case, the power of Mill's argument is dissipated. West also points out the apparent logical inconsistency between Mill's argument here (and that of other classical economists) and their treatment of other of life's necessities. For, argues West, using the same logic as Mill has done above would surely show that the *laissez-faire* principle 'breaks down entirely' in the case of 'feeding, clothing, and sheltering children' too, because in each of these other cases 'there are the same impediments to responsible choice by dependent minors' (West, 1992a, p. 601). So why did Mill – and the other classical economists – treat education differently from these other areas? It is a question to which we shall return several times in this book.

The second question that arises for West is: Protection against what? What is the danger against which the classical economists are seeking protection? West suggests that they were seeking protection against 'ignorance'. But this term needs unpacking; 'we have to ask: ignorance of what?' (1994a, p. 7). Here West's discussion is not entirely satisfactory. He points out the many ways in which children – and adults – can learn things, as we noted above. Learning can take place, he argues, not just in schools but through parents, families, friends, churches, and so on. And he notes that J.S. Mill himself also seems to believe this:

> The business of life is an essential part of the practical education of a people; without which, book and school instruction, though most necessary and salutary, does not suffice to qualify them for conduct, and for the adaptation of means to ends. Instruction is only one of the desiderata of mental improvement; another, almost as indispensable, is a vigorous exercise of the active energies; labour, contrivance, judgment, self-control: and the natural stimulus to these is the difficulties of life.
>
> (Mill, 1909, p. 948, quoted in West, 1994a, pp. 7–8)

What this suggests for West is that the ways in which individuals will want to 'protect' both themselves and their children from 'ignorance' 'should therefore be open to constant comparative appraisal' (1994a, p. 8). So, for example, if a parent wishes to remove his or her child from school, this does not necessarily signify negligence but could mean that the parent acknowledges that the 'school has become less efficient than other means of education', and the parent may in fact 'be acting from motives of protection' by removing his or her child (ibid., p. 8). Indeed, West notes that J.S. Mill himself was kept away from school and taught at home by his father, 'lest the habit of work should be broken and a taste for idleness acquired' (Mill, 1873, p. 36, quoted in West, 1994a, p. 8).

But while all this may be interesting, West has not actually answered the question of what ignorance children might need to be protected against – and how one could judge the respective merit of, say, what James Mill was teaching his son and that of parents who withdraw their children from school to help with the harvest or housework. West does not explore this any further in the context of his discussion of the protection of minors principle. A couple of candidates – that of protection from ignorance about democracy and ignorance leading to social divisiveness – he explores in subsequent chapters, as these are noted as important 'neighborhood effects' of education. I shall defer discussion of these potential curriculum requirements.

Third, if we accept that children need protecting, through some kind of state intervention, and if we have some ideas on what kind of ignorance they need protecting from, then we need to look at the appropriate scope and form of protection. What level of state intervention, in terms of intervention in regulation, funding and provision, could be justified by the protection of minors principle? West switches his discussion here to consider whether or not our current state schooling system could possibly be justified, or whether some lesser forms of state intervention might be preferred.

In terms of what level of state intervention the protection of minors principle could justify, West explores two issues: first, whether it leads to the need for *universally prescribed* intervention; and second, whether it leads to the need for *schooling*. On the first, West points out the oddity that the protection of minors principle might seem 'to support pressure ... to educate a *minority* of neglected children', and yet it is put forward today to support '*universal* schooling whereby *every* child is provided for by the state' (1994a, p. 9). But this assumes that everyone needs protecting from ignorance, not just a minority – that is, that 'the *majority* of parents and relatives are either negligent or ignorant' (ibid., p. 9). But why is this assumed? West says that we need empirical evidence here. And in the absence of any suitable contemporary evidence, says West, the most opportune way of looking for evidence is likely to be to look at what was taking place *before* governments got involved in education – hence the need first arises for his important investigation of evidence from the nineteenth century, which we shall come to in the next chapter.

On the second issue, West asks why 'other forms of state intervention' could not perhaps 'achieve the intended result of state protection', and, crucially, whether other methods could be more efficient – that is, less costly 'than the present system of state schools'? (1994a, p. 10). West points out that even John Stuart Mill, while certainly invoking the protection of minors principle, did not see this as requiring compulsory *schooling*, whether public or private, but only 'compulsory *education*' (ibid.) – that is, bringing in a broader definition of education, as discussed above. For Mill had proposed compulsory examinations that could check the results of education, whatever its source, and the right to vote would be conditional on reaching the required standard. Under a Mill-type system today, West suggests, children might obtain their minimum necessary education through 'television, parental instruction, correspondence courses, evening classes, local libraries, etc.' (ibid., pp. 10–11).

To illuminate these issues, West draws parallels between feeding and learning, to question whether the current universal state schooling system might be the obvious way forward if protection of minors is the aim: 'Protection of a child against starvation or malnutrition is presumably just as important as protection against ignorance,' he notes, but this has not led to laws being passed for universal and compulsory eating, or for children's food to be provided free at local authority kitchens or shops. And it is hard to imagine, says West, people acquiescing in such a system where, for 'administrative reasons',

> parents were allocated those shops which happened to be nearest their homes; or that any complaint or special desire to change their pre-selected shops should be dealt with by special and quasi-judicial enquiry after a formal appointment with the local 'Child Food Officer' or, failing this, by pressure upon their respective representatives on the local 'Child Food Committee' or upon their local M.P.
>
> (1994a, p. 12)

But, says, West, 'strange as such hypothetical measures may appear when applied to the provision of food and clothing, they are typical of English state education as it has evolved by historical accident or administrative expediency' (1994a, p. 12). West has put forward this parallel argument apparently in order to challenge our conceptions, and to ask us to think outside of the box. He challenges us to ask why *market* mechanisms, which seem to be successfully used in these other areas of our lives, are eschewed when it comes to education.

In summary, West has pointed to the oddity, and apparent inconsistency, in the arguments of the classical liberals for the protection of minors in suggesting that *laissez-faire* breaks down concerning the provision of educational opportunities in a way that it does not for the provision of food, clothing or shelter, say. Yes, there is a risk in children being dependent on their parents in each of these cases for protection – against ignorance, hunger or the elements. But no, this does not lead us to the need for universal compulsory protection. It is sufficient that a parent's fiduciary responsibilities might be relieved if the parent is shown not to be carrying them out satisfactorily. Why is education different? This is an issue that we shall be exploring throughout the book, including in this chapter when we look at curriculum content suggested by the neighborhood effects of education, and in Chapter 4 when we explore West's discussion of public choice theory. Importantly, as West argues, we will certainly need further evidence to explain why the protection of minors principle should be seen as justifying *universal* state intervention, rather than just aimed at the minority of parents who are not protecting their children. We shall explore this in Chapter 3 when we look at West's discussion of the history of nineteenth-century education – where we find that the evidence, for West, does not support the need for universal intervention at all.

'Neighborhood Effects', or 'Externalities'

The second set of economic arguments concern what West calls 'neighborhood effects', commonly referred to in modern-day welfare economics literature as the 'externalities' of education. Some of these – notably the propositions that education reduces crime and is required to make democracy work – were put forward, at least implicitly, as neighborhood effects by the classical economists, while modern-day economists use a range of these arguments to provide justifications for state intervention in education today. Importantly, as we saw in Chapter 1, Milton Friedman used one of these neighborhood effects – education to make democracy work – as a crucial plank of his argument for state intervention in education, supporting his case for universal state-funded vouchers. In part, we can see that West's argument is an explicit challenge to Friedman on this issue.

West describes 'neighborhood effects', or 'externalities', as follows: Put simply, these exist when 'the costs (or benefits) of private transactions do not take into account spill-over costs (or benefits) to other individuals who do not participate in the transactions in question' (1970a, p. 68). For instance, whether I have myself or my children inoculated against dangerous diseases can have an impact more widely in the community on whether or not these diseases are communicated. If I do not get inoculated, this could cause widespread damage to the community. Hence, one approach where we see potential for individual action or inaction leading to such damage is 'to explore the possibility of government intervention' (West, 1994a, pp. 31–2).

West notes that one relatively uncontroversial instance is the 'establishment of a state system of law and order to curb and to make socially accountable individual acts of aggression' (ibid., p. 32); indeed, this is often seen as the 'basic *raison d'être* of the state in the first place' (ibid.). Another instance commonly cited in the economic literature to warrant state intervention is the case of factory chimneys, which, spewing smoke out over the neighborhood, lead to spillover effects such as an increase in illness (bronchitis, etc.) and higher laundry bills (to clean clothes made dirty by the smoke). But do such cases necessarily lead to justifications for state intervention? Not necessarily. West suggests that identifying a neighborhood effect 'is only a *necessary* but not a *sufficient* condition for intervention' (ibid., p. 33). One reason here is that '[t]he administrative costs of intervention alone may be so high as to exceed the net benefits which such action sought to secure, even if they could be measured' (ibid.). West asks to consider this in the context of the smoking chimneys. For neighborhood effects can be positive as well as negative, and there may be 'many instances' where the social costs produced, in the absence of government intervention, are both positive and negative. So, in the case of the smoking chimneys, it is true that the factory can cause pollution (a negative externality), but it can also reduce unemployment for the same neighborhood (a positive externality). Now, government could respond to the problem by levying a special pollution tax on the factory. But this might lead to an increase in the relative costs of production, which could lead to a decline in output or even the firm's removal elsewhere, to somewhere where the pollution tax was lower or non-existent. But then the government intervention might lead not only to a reduction in the negative neighborhood effect it set out to curb, namely smoke pollution, but also to an *increase* in another negative neighborhood effect, namely an increase in unemployment and/or reduction of the prosperity of the region or country. So, the easy assumption that finding a negative externality means that we have found an argument for state intervention cannot be made, West argues.

How does this discussion relate to education? Economists have argued that there *are* neighborhood effects – that is, '*social* benefits' – of education that are not confined to the person educated but 'spread to society as a whole' (West, 1994a, p. 34). Or, to put it the other way around, 'the private actions of an uneducated person may have unfortunate consequences for others in society' (ibid.). My decision whether or not to educate my child might impact on the 'lives of others in terms of a wide assortment of influences ranging from the securing of public order to economic growth and prosperity' (West, 1970a, p. 69). And it is this understanding that leads to the implication that, therefore, governments have to intervene in education.

In *Education and the State*, West considers a range of neighborhood effects of education that are or were commonly given in the economics literature, from the reduction of crime, the making possible of a suitable environment for democracy, an increase in equality of opportunity, an increase in social cohesion, and improved economic growth. After exploring each, West concludes that none is a substantial *theoretical* argument for state intervention in education. Crucially, each requires further *evidence* to explore whether it could be supported as an argument for state intervention, and some 'conceptual clarity' about what kind of 'education' is required to be intervened in.

Education and the Reduction of Crime

The idea that an educated citizenry is one that commits fewer crimes – that is, that education has a 'neighborhood effect' of reduced crime – was one of the main arguments used by the protagonists of state intervention in education in nineteenth-century England. For instance, the parliamentarian T.S. Macaulay asked, 'can it be denied that the education of the common people is the most effectual means of protecting persons and property?' (House of Commons, Hansard,

19 April 1847, quoted in West, 1994a, p. 35). The Utilitarian W.T. Thornton wrote that although state funding of schools might be expensive, the sums required would not exceed monies currently being spent on 'prisons, hulks, and convict ships'; and 'it is certainly better economy to spend money in training up people to conduct themselves properly, than in punishing them for their misdeeds' (Thornton, 1846, p. 379; quoted in West, 1994a, p. 35). Government intervention in education, although expensive, would be offset by the reduction in the need for prisons and other punishments associated with the crimes committed by uneducated people. Importantly, these observations were not confined to nineteenth-century debates: over 100 years later, and contemporaneous with when West was writing *Education and the State*, the Robbins Report on higher education (1963) argued that the social benefits to education included a 'less crime-prone population' (*Higher Education*, Cmnd 2154, appendix 4, part III, para. 54; quoted in West, 1994a, p. 36).

West's discussion of this possible 'neighborhood effect' starts with the system of the twentieth century – namely, *state provision, funding and regulation* of *schooling* – and asks what impact this system has had on crime reduction. He looks at a range of contemporary evidence, including a 1958 report financed by the Nuffield Foundation, the Newsome Report of 1963 and the Crowther Report of 1959, which seemed to show that increased schooling correlated *positively* with increased crime. Indeed, this appeared to be a long-standing finding: the Crowther Report noted the curious finding that when in 1947 the age of school leaving was raised from 14 to 15, 'there was an immediate change over in the delinquency record of the 13 year-olds (who until then had been the most troublesome age-group) and the 14 year-olds, who took their place in 1948 and have held it consistently ever since' (quoted in West, 1994a, p. 41). So, for West, the available evidence does not support the 'popular belief', as evidenced by the Robbins Report, that 'state education makes the public less crime prone' (ibid.). The relationship might appear to go in the opposite direction: that the system of state schooling 'involved *adverse* external effects and aggravated or even helped to cause the prevailing trend towards increased criminal behaviour' (ibid.).

However, importantly for West's approach, this explicitly leaves open whether the reduction of crime *is* a neighborhood effect of *education* understood more widely, rather, that is, than simply in terms of the current state schooling that has emerged in Britain, and other countries. 'What do we mean', he asks, 'when we say that *education* reduces crime?' (1994a, p. 44). Do we mean education considered in its broadest sense, or simply formal schooling? And if the latter, does this mean *state schooling*? West's examination of the neighborhood effect of reduced crime leaves open the possibility of some form of education, or some kind of schooling (e. g. 'non-state', p. 44), having the impact that was desired by the classical economists.

These themes were taken up, under West's influence, by one of his students. Interestingly, what John Lott found supports West's hypothesis that there may be some aspects of *education* that are important for reducing crime, but these are certainly not synonymous with the universal state schooling system. First, Lott (1987) showed that *functional illiteracy* correlates highly with crime rates, and was able to suggest why: A delinquent act is more likely to be carried out by those who have had a smaller investment made in their human capital: 'the lower the forgone human capital investment (and hence the forgone income from that investment), the lower the cost of crime' (ibid., p. 164). The opportunity cost of committing a crime (as opposed to carrying out paid employment – that is, the next best alternative) is small to those who are illiterate because there is little to lose from undertaking the criminal act.

Moreover, Lott was also able to show that the higher the proportion of children in public (state) schools, the higher the rates of juvenile delinquency – that is, that *state* schooling may exacerbate crime, rather than schooling per se. Lott used cross-sectional data for the state of California in 1970 and found that 'after accounting for other basic influences, an increase in the percentage of children in public schools out of all children in school is associated with an increase in juvenile delinquency' (1987, p. 169). His results also reject the hypothesis that 'increased government expenditures on education are associated with a decrease in the rate of juvenile delinquency' (ibid.). He does consider whether this effect is due to shifting children from non-religious public schools to religious private ones, but after 'dividing private school attendance between religious and non-religious schools', he shows that this hypothesis is not confirmed. Moreover, Lott also explored time series data for the United States from 1950 to 1978 and found that the higher the proportion of pupils in public (as opposed to private) schools, the higher the juvenile delinquency rate (ibid., p. 170). Lott notes:

> Given the vast resources devoted towards public provision of education based on the supposed link between crime and (public) education, it is surprising that work on the relative efficiencies of public and private schooling has not been extended to this area. We hope that these findings will question some long held presumptions.
>
> (ibid., p. 171)

In other words, there may be links between crime reduction and education, but it is clear that these links do *not* point towards the need for state intervention in education – at least, not of the kind with which we are familiar.

Education for Democracy

A second major 'neighborhood effect' put forward by economists concerns education for democracy. Importantly, one of the economists offering this perspective, as we saw in Chapter 1, was Milton Friedman (1962). West uses Friedman's discussion as a springboard to explore his own views. Friedman wrote, 'A stable and democratic society is impossible without a minimum degree of literacy and knowledge on the part of most citizens and without widespread acceptance of some common set of values. Education can contribute to both' (ibid., p. 86; quoted in West, 1994a, p. 45). The first aspect is covered under our rubric of 'education for democracy', while the second we shall consider separately under 'education for social cohesion'. Friedman was not alone in this view: Dr Burton Weisbrod, another American economist, saw an even 'more ambitious and wide-ranging' (ibid.) set of neighborhood effects of education, including both education for democracy and social cohesion. And in the first IEA pamphlet on education, again as noted in Chapter 1, Jack Wiseman and Alan Peacock also wrote of this particular neighborhood effect. We can also note that while John Stuart Mill rested 'his entire argument for state intervention in education' on the protection of minors principle (Blaug, [1967] 1970, p. 26), as discussed earlier, it was clear that he had in mind a compulsory curriculum that would reinforce education for democracy. Hence, his discussion of this has relevance for this section too.

West's argument concerning education for democracy has three dimensions. First, he says, we need some understanding of what education for democracy means. Here, West distinguishes *literacy* and *political literacy* (1994a, p. 53) as two aspects. For each of these areas, the usual further two levels of questioning arise for West: Does the need for it require state intervention in any parts of *education*, in its broadest sense? And, conversely, could the current state intervention, universal state schooling, be justified using these arguments?

On *literacy* itself, West agrees with economists such as Weisbrod, who had argued, 'Without widespread literacy the significance of books, newspapers and similar media for the transmission of information would dwindle; and it seems fair to say that the communication of information is of vital importance to the maintenance of . . . political democracy' (Weisbrod, 1962b, p. 119) However, although Weisbrod used this discussion to justify state intervention in education, for West it only raises questions about such a justification. First, West points out that the British government's role historically was one of 'saboteur' (1994a, p. 48) in the acquisition of popular literacy. For at the beginning of the nineteenth century in Britain, prior to any state intervention in education, 'it was a subject for government *complaint* that the ordinary people *had become literate*. For the government feared that too many people were developing the "wrong" uses of literacy by belonging to secret "corresponding societies" and by reading seditious pamphlets' (ibid.). Far from subsidizing literacy, notes West, 'early nineteenth-century English governments placed severe taxes on paper in order to discourage the exercise of the public's reading and writing abilities' (ibid.). However, while this may be of historical interest, West's discussion here is beside the point when it comes to examining whether or not the neighborhood effect of education for democracy justifies state intervention; at most, it can serve as a warning that government intervention in this respect is not necessarily benign.

Second, more substantially, West points out that if we assume that universal literacy is required for a functioning democratic society, this still leaves open the question of whether *government* needs to intervene to ensure it. Only if we can show that 'substantial numbers of people would not acquire a necessary minimum of education themselves without the help of government agencies' (1994a, p. 46) should we consider the need for government intervention. So, West argues, we need evidence about this – and so again we are pulled towards examination of the historical evidence of what was happening before governments got involved, to inform our judgment here. For West argues, crucially, 'If it *cannot* be shown that most people would fail to become literate by their own efforts', then the arguments of economists such as Weisbrod 'of all the possible beneficial external effects of literacy' become irrelevant (ibid., p. 52), or at best on a par with 'listing the beneficial "neighbourhood effects"' of our habit of, say, 'washing ourselves'. Such analysis would 'not point to any significant policy at all beyond possible marginal provision in exceptional instances' (ibid.). In other words, yes, washing ourselves has extremely beneficial neighborhood effects; the unwashed are a health hazard and aesthetically displeasing. But the vast majority of people will wash themselves (and their dependents) without any assistance from anyone else. Only in rare cases – such as irresponsible or mentally and physically unfit parents, or the very elderly without dependents – might we consider that there could potentially be policy implications, such as home help or the taking of children into care, etc. But for the majority, there would be no policy proposals arising.

West then moves on to look at 'political literacy', which includes 'the task of acquainting the ordinary electorate with the rules and spirit of their constitution' (ibid.). First, he adopts his usual method of first examining whether it might be met – and perhaps more effectively met – in ways other than through schooling. West argues that '[s]o long as a healthy opposition to an existing government is allowed, one can always rely to some extent at least on the organised pressure of minority parties and groups such as trade unions, trade associations, etc., to educate', in the sense of helping people understand the pros and cons of political policies (ibid.). Indeed, argues West, James Mill apparently concurred with something like this view, believing that political education could be promoted by widely dispersed groups airing their views in journals, books and newspapers. He had argued that 'a free press was all that was necessary for a healthy and stable democracy' (West, 1994a, p. 54). His son, John Stuart Mill, concurred; the existence of these routes to 'political literacy ... no doubt influenced J.S. Mill in his decision to confine his policy proposals to a system of compulsory *education* as distinct from compulsory schooling' (ibid., p. 55). West is optimistic that the 'enormous multiplication, improvement and cheapening of means of instructional media such as television, radio, paperback literature, weekly journals, correspondence courses, as well as newspapers' (ibid., p. 55), would strengthen the ways in which alternatives to schooling could help provide citizens' education for democracy. If he were writing today, he would no doubt similarly point to the power of the internet in this regard, too.

In sum, West's argument appears to be implying that, *at most*, the state intervention suggested by the need for the political literacy aspect of 'education for democracy' would be a compulsory core curriculum for citizenship – assessed as with Mill's proposals through an examination that did not necessarily require schooling whatsoever. But clearly West believes it likely that much of what is required could be picked up casually as it were, through various media in society. West does not spend time examining what the curriculum *content* of this curriculum might be, but clearly assumes that the prescriptions will be rather minimal. (Elsewhere, I have explored what others have argued would be the curriculum content of education for democracy and how that content might fit in with West's ideas on the topic; see Tooley, 1995, Chapter 3.) In any case, we will carry forward to a later chapter, when we explore West's policy ideas, the notion that this neighborhood effect may have some implications for the regulation of the curriculum.

Education for Equality of Opportunity

The third 'neighborhood effect' of education considered is 'equality of opportunity'. The American economist Weisbrod, suggests West, is perhaps the first economist to make explicit that this is a neighborhood effect of education:

Equality of opportunity seems to be a frequently expressed social goal. Education plays a prominent role in discussions of this goal, since the financial and other obstacles to education confronted by some people are important barriers to its achievement. If equality of opportunity is a social goal, then education pays social returns over and above the private returns to the recipients of the education.
(Weisbrod, 1962b, p. 119; quoted in West 1994a, p. 58)

The argument for state intervention on the grounds of ensuring equality of opportunity, West writes, 'reflects concern about the distributional implications of purely private provision'. For it is obvious that richer parents 'are likely to spend more than poorer parents to educate their children, just as they spend more on cars, homes, and clothes'. But it is 'widely accepted', he observes, that 'children's life chances should not depend on the wealth of their parents or the fortuitous circumstances of the community in which they live'. Hence, the 'prospect of upward mobility, of ensuring that one's children will be better off, has been a key-stone of political support for the public school system in the past' (West, 1997a, p. 84). However, argues West, this 'depends on the assumption that governments are best equipped to supply the appropriate institutions' (ibid.). But he offers several factors that are likely to inhibit government involvement from leading to equality of educational opportunity.

To begin with, just as he did in his discussion on literacy, West warns us to be skeptical about the potential for government action here. First, he points out that sometimes government intervention can be *explicitly* designed to promote *in*equality of opportunity, so we must not assume that governments always have benign intentions. In some countries – apartheid South Africa, for instance, and countries that had (or have) caste systems – there are *constitutional* barriers that are unlikely to be overcome by state-sponsored education: 'Certainly if the education programme is to be sponsored by a ruling class whose position depends upon the maintenance of these barriers', then 'we must be particularly sceptical of this as a "solution"' (West, 1994a, p. 59).

Second, he notes that government activity sometimes has the result of erecting barriers to equality of opportunity, perhaps inadvertently, while trying to correct other problems. (Here we can refer back to the general discussion of externalities earlier, where West suggested that government action to correct one negative externality – the smoking factory chimney – could have the impact of bringing about unintentionally another, perhaps worse, negative externality – increasing unemployment.) In this regard, West notes that it is commonly assumed that the main barrier to equality of opportunity will be economic (1994a, p. 59). But one aspect of this is often neglected in the literature on equality of opportunity, the problem of 'arrangements to erect obstacles against new entrants' (ibid.). These, West notes, can be sponsored by, among others, governments and labor unions. Such institutional restrictions, he says, 'may be more important than any lack of education for opportunity seekers' (ibid., p. 60). He gives the example of the monopoly labor union 'which forces a closed shop upon its employer and then rations the number of union cards available'; this 'creates a much more obvious barrier to workers or to school-leavers outside the union than does any deficiency in education' (ibid.). Another example is when 'a 16-year-old boy has no equality of opportunity at all with a boy of 15 years [the school-leaving age at the time of his writing was 15] to enter certain trades if the rules of apprenticeship decree that he is too old' (ibid.). A more modern example that fits with West's point here might be barriers to entry to professions that demand certain levels of higher education; a degree is an increasingly common requirement for a whole range of employment today. West's suggestion is that such barriers to entry – assuming that the degree is used as a 'sorting mechanism' rather than to point to the necessary requirements of the job – could lead to a negative externality of government intervention in education, *undermining* rather than promoting equality of opportunity. We shall continue this discussion when we look at education and economic growth.

Third, West points to the problem that once government is called upon to intervene to promote equality of opportunity, then this will inevitably lead to 'inequality of political power' (ibid., p. 71). Here he points to the problem that was made familiar a few years later by Albert Hirschman in his *Exit, Voice and Loyalty* (1970). Some people, argues West, will have greater ability to negotiate the political system (using 'voice', in Hirschman's terminology) than others – and it is likely to be those belonging to the more articulate middle classes who are able to do this. But the ability to take one's business elsewhere, as in the market (using 'exit'), might be more widely spread among the population, whatever their level of sophistication. For West, this means that 'inequality of opportunity will probably now stem from their misfortune, not this time in having parents who are poorer, but in having parents who are politically weak' (1994a, p. 72). West gives examples to illustrate this, from what he considered to be the reality of education provision in 1960s England. Here, he pointed out, it is 'a tricky business for any parent to try to get his child out of an inferior school and into a superior one even in his own district' (ibid., p. 71). Recent advice given by a government adviser reinforced his misgivings here: parents are counseled 'to be polite and courteous when dealing with state headmasters [*sic*] and to try to be particularly diplomatic when negotiating with the Education Officer' (quoted ibid., pp. 71–2). In order to change schools for their children, parents are advised 'to try to persuade the Education Officers to make an exception by a skilfully and reasonably argued case' (ibid., p. 72). But, West notes, 'English people do not usually have to be coaxed to be polite in their ordinary dealings with everyday suppliers of goods or services such as the grocer, the butcher or the newsagent anxious for their custom' (ibid.). Most significantly, this ability to argue 'skilfully and reasonably' may be 'distributed unequally among parents' (ibid.).

Fourth, West looks at the problem that geographical 'zoning' of state schools – where pupils are assigned schools on the basis of their neighborhoods by the local education authority – brings to the issue of inequality of opportunity. Zoning, he writes, 'can actually reduce mobility', rather than increase it, or even block it altogether, particularly if, as is usually the case, 'the quality of public education is better in middle-class zones than elsewhere'. In short, 'the public system can often narrow a child's options, forcing the child to attend an inferior school when a superior one may be physically within reach' (West, 1997a, p. 84). Within the state system, many pupils 'have substantial privilege over others by the chance "virtue" of their geographical loca-tion' (West, 1994a, p. 81). Again, we shall explore this issue further when we look at social cohesion below.

Finally, given these difficulties both with current state schooling and in theoretical considerations of the difficulties that *any* govern-ment intervention might face, West turns to consider whether equality of opportunity could arise *without* state intervention. West observes that most people usually offer the argument that there would be 'pronounced market imperfections' in this regard. But, he argues, evidence showing the inadequacies or imperfections of the market in leading to equality of educational opportunity is not enough: 'What has also to be shown is that the shortcomings of the state system will not be even worse' (ibid., p. 74), hence his listing of some of these shortcomings, as enumerated above. West concludes: 'to treat the "social goal" of equality of opportunity as a neighbourhood effect which can inevitably be fostered by state education is unwarranted and unproven since it overlooks the probability that such a cure makes things worse than before' (ibid., p. 83).

Ultimately, again, West says that we need some evidence of how the private sector in education might work – and the extent to which it can serve the poor, and so help overcome inequality of opportunity. We shall turn to his discussion of the historical evidence in the next chapter to help illuminate these issues. The evidence suggests for West that the poor were doing pretty well, educationally speaking, before the intervention of the state, and that its impact on reducing inequality should be treated with some skepticism.

'Common Values' and Social Cohesion

The fourth neighborhood effect of education discussed by West is the communication of common values and its impact on social cohesion. In *Education and the State*, West notes that the British economist Pro-fessor Jack Wiseman (who had advised West on his PhD thesis) argued that '[s]ociety as a group benefits from the existence of some mini-mum standards of education among its citizens, in the understanding of common values and acceptance of community obligation' (from a lecture by Wiseman, quoted in West, 1994a, p. 46). He also notes that

Milton Friedman supports this claim of the importance of 'a common set of values' for 'a stable and democratic society' as a justification for state intervention in education. So again, in his discussion here, West is explicitly challenging the beliefs of his intellectual mentors.

The need for social cohesion is given as one of the major arguments for state intervention in education. For Professor Mark Blaug ([1967] 1983, p. 43), the argument for social cohesion is indeed the *only* valid justification for state provision of education (although other justifications might suggest the need for state funding). Professor Henry Levin argues:

> Beyond the fulfilment of private needs, schools must provide students with a common set of values and knowledge to create citizens who can function democratically . . . They must contribute to equality of social, economic and political opportunities among persons drawn from different racial and social class origins . . . To a large extent these requirements suggest that all students be exposed to a common educational experience that cannot be left to the vagaries of individual or family choice.
>
> (1991a, p. 139)

In other words, one of the major reasons for state intervention in education is that 'public schools have an absolute advantage or a unique ability to produce the "common values" or to pursue the "social purposes" of education' (West, 1991a, p. 164). Professor Michael Krashinsky makes precisely the same claim: 'In the current system, the public school serves as a melting pot, bringing students from different backgrounds together and providing equal opportunity' (1986a, p. 142).

The key elements, then, are that through common state schools, social segregation can be overcome, and so social cohesion ensured. West is dismissive of these kinds of claims. The problem is that the provision of state schooling has led to 'zoning', and this will inevitably undermine the possibility of social cohesion. West notes that 'the official practice of assigning students to the government school nearest their home' is a universal phenomenon associated with public schooling. He points to a survey by John Lott that found such 'exclusive territories' for public education 'prevailing in all the countries in his survey', including the United States, the United Kingdom, France, New Zealand, Sweden, Canada, Italy, South Korea and Russia (West, 1990a, p. 371). (We can also note that in those countries, such as New Zealand and England and Wales, where reforms were introduced in the 1980s to try to undermine zoning of schools in order to enhance parental choice, the effectiveness of these reforms has been explicitly reduced, and zoning reintroduced either *de facto* or *de jure*; see Merrifield, 2005.) West does explore some theoretical reasons as to why this might be the case, including public choice theory explanations, to be discussed in Chapter 5. But it certainly is an empirical fact that reinforces his suggestion that state schooling has the potential to increase, rather than decrease, social segregation and hence undermine social cohesion.

West points to the evidence from societies when he was writing in the 1960s. In the United States, he says, the public school 'exacerbates rather than ameliorates class distinction'. He notes that in Chicago and Boston, numerous schools are wholly or 90 percent African American. 'Although they pay taxes, most Negroes are excluded from these better schools because, since they cannot afford high property prices, they do not have the necessary residential qualifications' (1994a, pp. 68–9). West suggests that similar problems are being found in Britain too, especially where housing is subsidized through government:

> Neighbourhood schools serving exclusively whole council house estates are quite typical. The families in these estates, of course, are much less mobile, since the privilege of a council house subsidy cannot be transferred to areas of private accommodation which enjoy better school facilities and the opportunity to mix.
>
> (ibid., p. 69)

The trend towards comprehensive schools 'seems to be emphasising' social stratification, West argued, rather than reinforcing social cohesion.

Is there any evidence that has accumulated since West was writing that can inform the debate on the relative merits of public and private schooling with regard to social segregation? Certainly the debate still rages about whether public education can help promote social cohesion, or whether school choice reforms will better facilitate this. A recent argument against school choice reform made what West would have found a very interesting concession, however: Belfield and Levin (2002) argue that some parents would be against vouchers and private schools because they undermine the value of their homes:

> Some parents would face big asset losses: voucher programs would break the link between house prices and school quality, so parents who paid high prices to live near good schools would be clearly opposed. These parents would suffer big losses in the value of their most important asset, their home.
>
> (Belfield and Levin, 2002, p. 5)

Certainly this argument would reinforce West's point about the problems of zoning of state schools increasing social segregation. But what of other evidence? First, the evidence on reforms to overcome segregation arising from zoning of schools shows that these reforms have not been particularly promising. 'Busing' is one way, where children are moved, by bus, from one district to another in order to facilitate integration. But this has been unpopular with parents, 'who have to get their children up before dawn and wait until evening for their return' (Forster, 2006, p. 10). Efforts to increase public school choice through the provision of 'magnet' schools and open enrollment policies have also apparently failed to reduce segregation, although they have other reported benefits (Ravitch, 1985; Pride and Woodard, 1985).

Some of the evidence on segregation in public and private schools appears to be methodologically flawed, first, because of the way segregation is measured and defined. One issue is the problem of segregation within the administrative unit itself; '[m]uch of the segregation in the public school system occurs because school districts and municipal boundaries themselves are segregated' (Forster, 2006, p. 11). Thus, if a school is 98 percent white, it will be deemed perfectly integrated if the school district it is located within is also 98 percent white. The same perfect score would be achieved even if the immediately neighboring school district were 98 percent minority.

A second problem when looking at comparisons is that elementary and secondary schools differ in the amount of segregation within them: for elementary schools are generally more segregated than secondary schools, drawing as they do from a smaller geographic area. In addition, it is also the case that there are more private than public elementary schools, so comparing *all* private and public schools will give a 'false impression of greater segregation in private schools' (Forster, 2006, p. 11). An example is the study by Yun and Reardon (2005), which finds that private schools are more segregated than public ones. But the authors themselves point to the possibility that, as they have not compared grades to like grades, their results are compromised. Comparing students in kindergarten or pre-kindergarten is also misleading and will be likely to skew the result of any analysis that includes such data. This is because white parents are more likely to send their children to kindergarten and are also more likely to pay for this at a private school. An example here is the study by Ritter et al. (2002), which again shows that private schools are more segregated than public, but includes data on kindergartens that may have skewed the result.

Two studies that look at classroom-level (as opposed to school-level) data that do not seem to fall foul of these methodological problems are those of Greene (1998) and Greene and Mellow (2000). Greene (1998) took a nationally representative sample of twelfth-grade classes in both private and public schools. Fifty-four percent of public school students learned in classrooms that were racially homogeneous – more than 90 percent white or 90 percent minority. In the private schools, 41 percent of classes were homogeneous in this way. In the second study, visits were made to a random sample of schools during lunchtime in Austin and San Antonio, Texas. Data were gathered concerning the pupils' seating arrangements. Greene and Mellow (2000) observed how often students sat in racially mixed groups during their lunchtime. They found that 64 percent of private pupils and 50 percent of public pupils sat in a group where there was at least one other person from a different race. After city, seating restrictions, school size and grade had been controlled for, the predicted difference widened, with 79 percent of private pupils and 43 percent of public pupils sitting in mixed groups.

Five other studies look at data at the school level, comparing segregation in schools receiving vouchers and public schools (Greene, 1999; Fuller and Mitchell, 1999, 2000; Fuller and Greiveldinger, 2002; Greene and Winters, 2005). In each of these studies, it was found that public school students were more likely to be in racially homogeneous schools (that is, with more than 90 percent white or 90 percent minority students) than voucher students.

The evidence available would seem to lend weight to West's notions that private education systems may have greater racial integration than public ones, and hence that the requirement for social cohesion is *not* one that can justify state intervention in the provision of education. Of course, the evidence currently available is limited, and further evidence is required to explore these issues in more depth. Nevertheless, the picture does not seem to be as clear-cut as critics of West appear to argue. West's skepticism about the potential for state intervention in education to overcome social segregation and reinforce social cohesion seems to be reasonably well supported by the evidence.

Education and Economic Growth

The final 'neighborhood effect' of education that West examines concerns education and economic growth. Education, this argument goes, 'is an investment which increases the real income of all', regardless of whether or not they have used it or paid for it themselves (West, 1994a, p. 107). But what implications does this have for government intervention in education?

West's exploration here has two main parts. First, on the level of seeking justifications for the current system of formal state schooling (in schools, colleges and universities) that has emerged in Britain and the United States, West points to some problems with identifying economic growth as being caused by this government intervention. Second, he asks what the supposed 'market imperfections' are that would exist without government intervention in formal schooling, and that such government intervention is supposed to fix.

Here, West reiterates the need for a definition of education. Far too many economists – West quotes those writing for the Robbins Report on higher education reform as examples – simply combine the premise that 'knowledge is a major source of economic growth' with the proposition that 'education is the major channel for knowledge growth and dissemination' and arrive at the outcome that, therefore, 'society will benefit by more public expenditure on education' (West, 1994a, p. 110), meaning public expenditure on schools and colleges. But this misses the important point, again, that education is broader than schooling, and much that is economically relevant may be obtained outside of formal schooling. In this regard, West points to the research of the American economist Professor George J. Stigler, which found that of the education that led to an increase in earning power for the individual, 'as much as *two-thirds* of it was acquired not in colleges or schools but by experience and instruction within the factory or office' (ibid., p. 111). Data such as these should make us cautious, says West, in making too much of a link between formal education and economic growth, and hence in making too easy a link between the need for government intervention for this neighborhood effect of education.

What about the argument that many occupations requiring high formal educational qualifications for entry confer higher incomes than others? Does this not reinforce the importance of formal schooling for the economy, and hence suggest a role for government? Reflecting his earlier discussion under 'equality of opportunity', West argues that these higher incomes may be paid *not* because being able to do the job requires a greater amount of education, but because strong monopoly power exists in the sector that allows incomes to be raised (ibid., p. 115). The power of professional groups in securing high wages for their members, through creating barriers to entry into the profession, distorts the market. West cites Milton Friedman's argument that 'the relatively high earnings enjoyed by American doctors can be partly attributed to the American Medical Association's success in limiting new entrants to the profession' (ibid.). For West, this suggests the need for 'breaking down such artificial barriers', not the need for more (government-funded) education: 'In so far as stiffer and stiffer examinations are used as a means of keeping down the annual rates of entry, the associated increases in education cannot claim credit for economic growth' (ibid.). Indeed, the opposite is true: 'such increases are evidence of obstacles to growth and a relative waste of resources' (ibid.).

West is disparaging of the way the professional associations raise the virtue of improved 'social returns' to society (and the individual) from higher levels of education. This is 'seriously misleading', he writes. If professional restrictions, combined with political lobbying, have led to the need for further 'educational' requirements, then this does not lead to society being better off at all. 'Society' could have obtained the services of the person now with the higher qualifications 'at lower cost had it concentrated its attention on weakening the monopoly power of the professional group' (ibid., p. 116).

Overall West is doubtful that we can find genuine neighborhood effects of formal schooling, as opposed to neighborhood effects of education more broadly understood. In a critique of West's argument, however, Professor Mark Blaug suggests that West has missed at least one genuine neighborhood effect of formal education that requires government intervention – that is, 'a convenient mechanism for discovering and cultivating potential talent'. Blaug argues that this function has 'somehow to be performed in any viable economy', and it is an external benefit of education: 'consider the costs that would be imposed on business firms if they had to assess the ability of every job applicant without any prior indication of native ability in the form of an educational paper qualification.' And, most importantly, it is, says Blaug, a genuine external benefit, in the sense that it will not be

registered, or at least not fully registered, in the earnings of people or the prices of goods and services. Hence, if educational decisions were left entirely in private hands, there would be social under-investment in education because no one would be motivated to bear the cost of discovering potential talent.

(Blaug, [1967] 1970, pp. 29–30)

West's response to this, I suggest, would be first to question why Blaug is assuming that state intervention will be efficient in this regard – for it is precisely the opposite accusation that West has leveled against professional associations: In collaboration with governments, they can impose entry restrictions through formal qualifications that lead to inefficiencies. Moreover, the suggestion that government intervention in setting qualifications leads to inefficiencies was also the argument of Ronald Dore's seminal work *The Diploma Disease*. Dore's analysis suggests that it is precisely when *governments* get involved in the educational process that credentialism – where the requirements of employment become removed from the diplomas required to gain such employment – becomes pathological: 'It is not a bad generalisation that the almightiness of the certificate varies in direct proportion to the predominance of the state in the development process' (Dore, 1976, p. 74).

Moreover, West could also ask: Why wouldn't the cost of this benefit be registered in the earnings or prices? Where is Blaug's evidence for this? The problem of course is that there is little evidence of how a fully private system would operate. However, in a fully private system, school fees, for instance, could easily include the full price of the examination. And if no entrepreneur in a fully private system had created a system of school-leaving examinations, for whatever reason, then businesses could easily conduct some form of testing themselves, or contract this out to other bodies, and then deduct this from the first wages of those they employed.

Blaug's unsuccessful counterexample leads us to the second strand of West's argument: why is the alternative of no government intervention in formal education not considered as a way of promoting the neighborhood effect of economic growth? West sets out the market alternative for education: 'One way would be to leave it to individuals after returning to them the taxes which are normally used for state education expenditure and to assist them with both information and a suitable market for educational loans' (West, 1994a, p. 118). There may be the problem, says West, of 'intelligent but poor candidates' not being able to find the money 'to invest themselves', but we must not jump to the conclusion that this requires government finance and planning of education, rather than assistance in the capital loan markets: 'A more appropriate solution would be to make individuals bear their own costs of educational investment but to make capital available on terms equivalent to those for physical capital; in other words to institute a loan system' (ibid., p. 125).

West also offers the theoretical suggestion that

[i]f the demand for any service has increased and its price likewise, the prospect of a high income differential spread over a future lifetime will be an incentive to more young people to invest in the appropriate training and more will offer themselves until the increased supply sufficiently dampens their price advantage.

(ibid.)

There may be a time lag, which would make this process less than perfect, but the same would be true of government planning of educational places: West points to examples such as the shortage of medical doctors in 1965 being attributable to a 1957 committee's decision to cut the intake of medical students (ibid., p. 121). The key question to be addressed, then, is which is worse, government failure or market failure? West suggests that he knows of no evidence that challenges the argument that leaving educational provision outside of the state would not lead to 'at least the same quantity' of education being bought privately (ibid., p. 124). But of course his critics could argue that there is no evidence that shows the converse: that left to its own devices, the private market *would* supply enough education, that there would not be 'market failure' here. For West, the reason why there is no evidence is the same one that has been encountered throughout this chapter: governments have intervened to create near-monopolies in education in the developed nations where data are available, and so nowhere can we see what a true market in education might be like. For West, this points in one direction: the need for historical evidence of what happened before the state got involved in education.

The upshot of these arguments is that West is skeptical that the neighborhood effect of economic growth is a justification for government intervention in education. However, he does concede that further 'empirical research' is required to see whether the argument for government intervention can be strengthened (1994a, p. 280). So, what has more recent empirical research added to the discussion here? It would seem that it lends support to West's skepticism that government intervention in education is 'an investment which increases the real income of all taxpayers regardless of the degree to which the "free" education service is used by any of them for his own direct purposes' (ibid., p. 87) – in other words, that there is a genuine externality that requires government intervention.

This is certainly the position with which William Easterly would seem to concur, in his examination of the evidence from developing countries. He notes that from 1960 onwards,

> there was a remarkable expansion of [state] schooling. Fueled by the emphasis of the World Bank and other donors on basic education, primary enrollment had reached 100 percent in half of the world's countries by 1990. In 1960, only 28 percent of the world's nations had had 100 percent enrollment. The median primary enrollment increased from 80 percent in 1960 to 99 percent in 1990. Behind these figures lie educational miracles like Nepal, going from 10 percent primary enrollment in 1960 to 80 percent in 1990.
>
> (Easterly, 2001, p. 73)

Similarly, for secondary education the median rate of secondary enrollment increased 'from 13 percent of secondary school age children in 1960 to 45 percent in 1990', and in college-level enrollment the median enrollment rate has increased more than sevenfold, from 1 percent to 7.5 percent.

Yet what has been the economic growth spurred by this 'educational explosion'? Easterly says it has been 'little or none' (2001, p. 73). He points to data over the 1960–87 period comparing East Asia and sub-Saharan Africa, for instance, and shows the absence of any correlation between economic growth and government educational investment. African countries that invested heavily and had rapid growth in schooling, such as Angola, Mozambique, Ghana, Zambia, Madagascar, Sudan and Senegal, were all 'growth disasters'. On the other hand, Japan, which had 'modest growth in human capital', was nonetheless a growth miracle. And while it is true that other

East Asian 'growth miracles', such as Singapore, Korea, China and Indonesia, did experience 'rapid growth in human capital', this was at best equal to, and usually less than, the level in the African 'growth disasters': 'To take one comparison, Zambia had slightly faster expansion in human capital than Korea, but Zambia's growth rate was seven percentage points lower' (ibid., p. 74).

Moreover, it was not just the African cases that skewed the data. The evidence also shows that while Eastern Europe and the former Soviet Union compared very favorably with Western Europe and the United States in terms of levels of schooling attained by the population, 'their GDP per worker was only a fraction of Western European and North American levels' (ibid.). The data showed unequivocally that 'the decline in growth [globally] happened at the same time as the massive educational expansion in the poor countries' (ibid.).

Easterly also points to some of the reasons why educational expansion in developing countries in particular may have no impact on economic growth, reasons again that would reinforce West's skepticism about *state* intervention in education (but which would be less likely to apply to an expansion of *private* educational opportunities). Easterly argues that 'the state largely drove the educational expansion by providing free public schooling and requiring that children attend school'. But

Administrative targets for universal primary education do not in themselves create the incentives for investing in the future that matter for growth. The quality of education will be different in an economy with incentives to invest in the future versus an economy where there are none. In an economy with incentives to invest in the future, students will apply themselves to their studies, parents will monitor the quality of education, and teachers will face pressure to teach. In a stagnant economy without incentives to invest in the future, students will goof off in the classroom or sometimes not show up at all, parents will often pull their children away to work on the farm, and teachers will while the time away as overqualified babysitters.

(Easterly, 2001, p. 82)

Easterly concludes:

> [T]he growth response to the dramatic educational expansion of
> the last four decades has been distinctly disappointing. The failure
> of government-sponsored educational growth is once again due to
> our motto: people respond to incentives. If the incentives to invest
> in the future are not there, expanding education is worth little.
> Having the government force you to go to school does not change
> your incentives to invest in the future. Creating people with high
> skill in countries where the only profitable activity is lobbying the
> government for favors is not a formula for success. Creating skills
> where there exists no technology to use them is not going to foster
> economic growth.
>
> (ibid., p. 73)

Alison Wolf arrives at a similar conclusion with regard to developing
countries: can we argue that education causes prosperity, 'that spending on schools and universities spills over into general well-being?'
(2002, p. 38). The answer, she says, is clearly 'no'. South Korea is often
held up as the model to show how expansion of education leads to
growth. From the 1960s to the 1998 crash, it took primary education
from 'near-universal to universal', and secondary education from 'a
quarter to the whole cohort'; it also rapidly grew its university system. Alongside all of this educational expansion, its economy grew
at a rate of 7 percent per year in terms of income per capita. So
was it the educational investment that caused this economic growth?
Wolf is skeptical, for she compares South Korea with Egypt, which
experienced comparable dramatic educational growth yet stagnated
economically: 'So you grow economically and also expand your education system enormously; or, like Egypt, you fail dismally to achieve
economic success, alongside huge educational expansion' (ibid.,
p. 39).

Indeed, a range of World Bank studies show that across developing
countries 'there exists a negative relationship between [state] education levels and growth' (ibid.). She admits, 'This finding seems
profoundly anti-intuitive' (ibid.). Perhaps West would not have found
it so.

So much for the picture in developing countries. But Wolf arrives at a skeptical conclusion concerning the relationship between education and economic growth with regard to Western countries, too. For studies show a mixed picture: 'among the most successful economies, there is in fact no clear link between growth and spending on education, let alone between growth and central-government involvement in education planning' (ibid., p. 41). Hong Kong had nothing like the central direction of education in Singapore and Korea, but comparable growth rates (ibid., p. 42). Switzerland laid claim to being the richest developed country in the world in 1980 and 1993, yet its proportion of young people in higher education is far below the average for developed countries: about one-third of the average for OECD members, with some OECD countries registering enrollment rates five or six times higher (ibid.).

Moreover, evidence from the Third Trends in International Mathematics and Science Study (TIMSS) in the late 1990s showed that the 'correlation between maths scores and GNP per capita is so weak as to be insignificant' (ibid.). And, perhaps most significantly of all, the United States did very poorly in these international tests, accused of being caught in a 'low-skills equilibrium'. Yet not only did it manage 'record-breaking growth in both output and employment', but also it was 'the main source of innovation and product development' in the last 20 or 30 years of the twentieth century (ibid., p. 43).

The possibility that Wolf suggests is that the causation goes the other way around: 'growth causes education, rather than education causing growth' (ibid.). Children in Hong Kong, if Wolf is correct,

> may be pouring into higher education, and outperforming the English at maths, *after* the meteoric growth rate of their economy, and indeed because of it. They are doing so in order to compete for jobs in an economy which, as the number of professional jobs grows, increasingly uses credentials for hiring. And their prosperous parents can now afford long schooling, and indeed encourage it, pushing them to compete academically and so get into the best classes, the best schools, the best universities.
>
> (ibid.)

In short, Wolf argues that there is no evidence either way for the argument that there are spillover or neighborhood effects from highly educated people who 'don't just produce more themselves but create an environment in which *everyone* is more productive' (ibid., p. 53). There is little in the more recent evidence, in other words, that would have assuaged West's skepticism about the role of government in promoting the externality of economic growth through education.

In each of these economic arguments, we have come across West's skepticism about the role of government in education. Each of the arguments has pointed to the need for further evidence to substantiate the claims made either way. West, *qua* economist, is not able to make a convincing argument against state intervention in education, although he is able to raise doubts about its efficacy, and questions about the possibilities of the alternative. However, through West's search for historical evidence, his skepticism about the role of the state in education was to find an empirical anchor.

Chapter 3

Historical Excursions

The History of Nineteenth-Century Education in England and Wales

It is commonly assumed that in nineteenth-century England, before state intervention in education, provision for the working classes was totally inadequate in terms of both quantity and quality of provision. In a recent BBC Radio 4 program, *The Long View* (14 March 2006), for instance, education historian Professor Roy Carr of the University of London's Institute of Education took this line, stating that state intervention in 1870 was absolutely necessary to provide education for the masses, and pointing to the gross inadequacies of the reportedly few private schools that were available at the time.

This stance is the one that many of us will have acquired from history texts. For instance, in *British History in the Nineteenth Century*, G.M. Trevelyan notes that on the eve of the 1870 Act that laid the foundations for state education in England and Wales, '[o]nly about half the children in the country were educated at all, and most of these very indifferently. England, for all her wealth, lagged far behind . . . several foreign countries' (1922, p. 354). Sir Arthur Bryant's *English Saga* has a similar perspective: 'The great mass of the nation was illiterate. In 1869 only one British child in two was receiving any education at all.' And on the *quality* of Victorian education before state intervention, many of us have gained our impressions of doubtful quality from reading Charles Dickens's *Nicholas Nickleby*, and of the horrific behavior of headmaster Wackford Squeers of the private boarding school Dotheboys Hall. Indeed, it is not just the popular imagination that uses these sources. The historian S.J. Curtis (1965, p. 234) points to Dotheboys Hall to illustrate the 'terrible conditions' of the private schools of Victorian England.

West was to turn this received wisdom completely on its head. Perhaps inspired by Hayek's stressing of the need for a new historical perspective (see Chapter 1), West went back to investigate original sources and parliamentary debates, and suggested that the accepted view is entirely misguided. In fact, he was to observe, before state intervention in education there was an extensive system of private education, educating the vast majority of the working class. In this chapter, I outline West's basic findings on the history of education in nineteenth-century England and Wales, followed by discussion of Scotland. In the following chapter, we shall explore more deeply into the history of education in England, New York State and New South Wales, Australia, to explore West's understanding of how and why these systems of state education may have emerged.

West is concerned with evidence of both the *quantity* and the *quality* of education before the state got involved in England and Wales. He looks at schooling, but, bearing in mind his oft-repeated assertion that education is broader than schooling, he looks at literacy levels too – and literacy levels have emerged in the previous chapter as important in their own right, as well as in the discussion of the neighborhood effect of 'education for democracy', and in John Stuart Mill's paternalistic approach to the need for state intervention.

Throughout this discussion, we must bear in mind that the first state intervention in England in education was in 1833 in the form of modest subsidies for a small number of schools; the exact level and extent of these will be discussed in due course. State intervention on any larger level did not take place until Forster's Education Act of 1870, and even this was on a much more constrained level than is commonly believed, as we shall see.

Literacy in Victorian England

Literacy is defined as 'the ability to read and write' (West, 1994a, p. 158). Did bringing literacy to the working classes require government intervention, or were there mechanisms outside of the state that allowed them to achieve it? West's examination of the evidence suggests that high levels of literacy were achieved in the main without *any* state intervention. Indeed, as we noted in the discussion of education for democracy above, West notes that, far from encouraging the literacy of the masses, for the first 33 years of the nineteenth century it appears that one of the British state's aims was 'one of deliberate hindrance' of working-class literacy (ibid.). The government was clearly concerned about the ability of the 'lower orders' to read materials that could be damaging and critical of government (ibid.). Included in this seditious material were Tom Paine's *The Rights of Man* and William Cobbett's *Address to the Journeymen and Labourers*. The government used both legal and fiscal actions against newspaper circulation in order to control the reading habits of the masses, including advertising duties, stamp taxes and excise taxes (which were not removed, respectively, until 1853, 1855 and 1861).

Crucially, West points out that this suppression came about *because it was accepted that* 'reading ability was widespread' – that is, widespread *before* any positive state intervention (ibid., p. 159). Tom Paine's *The Rights of Man*, for instance, is claimed to have sold one and a half million copies, while William Cobbett's *Address to the Journeymen and Labourers* is reported to have sold 200,000 copies in only two months. Reading of the Bible and religious tracts was even more widespread. Concerning widespread literacy, a report from 1838, for instance, showed that 87 percent of *pauper* children aged 9 to 16 years housed in the workhouses of Norfolk and Suffolk could read to some extent (*The Report of the Poor Law Commissioners*, 1841; cited in West, 1994a, p. 161). An investigation into levels of literacy in mining communities in 1840 showed that of 843 miners in Northumberland and Durham, 79 percent could read, while 52 percent could read *and* write (*Minutes of the Committee of Council on Education*, 1840–1, appendix III, p. 138, cited in West 1994a, p. 161). But most of these miners would have left school by the time of the, in any case minimal, state intervention of 1833. For 'shoploom' weavers in Gloucestershire, an inspector's report of 1839 showed that only 8 percent could neither read nor write, while a special survey of over-21s in Hull (also in 1839) found that 92 percent could read, and indeed that 97 percent had attended day or evening school ('Report on the State of Education in the Borough of Kingston upon Hull', *Journal of the Statistical Society of London*, July 1841; cited in West, 1994a, pp. 162–3). Again, hardly any of these people could have benefited from state-subsidized schools, as by 1833 they would have been at least 15 years old, and hence not in school.

Importantly, the rate of growth of literacy appeared to be increasing during the nineteenth century, with younger people becoming more accomplished than their parents. For instance, an 1865 return on the educational requirements of men in the Navy and Marines revealed that around 99 percent of the boys could read, compared with 89 percent of the seamen, 80 percent of the marines and 94 percent of the petty officers. Research from the historian R.K. Webb (1950, 1963) estimated that around 1840, 'at least two-thirds of the working classes were literate', a proportion that increased to around 90 percent by the middle of the 1860s (cited in West, 1994a, p. 164).

How much was this increase in literacy due to government intervention, through the small state subsidies to education from 1833? We shall explore this in more detail below, when we look at schooling per se. But for now we can note that even as late as 1869, around two-thirds of school expenditure came from non-government sources, especially parents; this was directly through fees, but also indirectly through 'so-called religious "charity"' (West, 1994a, p. 163). For much of this 'charity' came out of the church subscriptions or tithes of ordinary working people, partly out of their Christian duty but no doubt also partly out of the expectation that the funds would benefit the schooling of their children.

Moreover, even the third of the cost of schooling from state subsidies would have come through taxation, and, West notes, the tax system at the time was highly 'regressive, falling heavily ... on food and tobacco' (ibid., p. 165). Crucially for West, and a point that we will also take up below, had these taxes not been levied, the working people would have had more disposable income, and 'it is not easy to demonstrate that had the state not raised the money through taxation to subsidise the schools the total expenditure on them would have been lower' (ibid.).

Perhaps it could be argued that these statistics on literacy are optimistic, because they too generously interpreted what was meant by reading and writing? West suggests that the 'remarkable consistency between all the various surveys in different parts of the country ... by different types of investigators' suggests that the statistics should not be so easily dismissed. But also 'there is evidence that the education inspectors who made some of the tests were so demanding that their figures were, if anything, underestimates' (1994a, p. 163). Most of the inspectors, it has been argued by R.K. Webb, for instance, were reformers, 'and an unconscious bias led them naturally to dwell on unsavoury aspects' (1950, p. 337). In other words, the reformers wanted to show why the current situation needed state intervention and hence were keen to show how bad it was. This point we shall also investigate further in the next chapter.

Another indicator of literacy used by some historians is the signing of marriage registers – although of course this could be objected to as showing only the ability to perform a one-off 'gimmick designed to win social prestige' (West, 1994a, p. 167). Nevertheless, such data have been used by some commentators to show the *beneficial* impact of government intervention in 1870, so it is at least useful to see how these arguments shape up. West points to Professor David Glass's (1962) argument to this effect. Glass showed that 'a third of the men marrying in 1840 in England and Wales, and half of the women, signed the registers by a mark', and even in 1870 the figures were still 20 percent and 27 percent respectively. Glass uses these figures to suggest that the achievement of presumably near-universal literacy since then shows the beneficial impact of the 1870 intervention. However, West suggests this is far too hasty. For looking at the figures for 1870 is surely wrong, as the 20 percent of men who could not sign the marriage register in 1870 would, on average, have left school 17 years before, given that the average age of marriage at this time, according to the Registrar-General Report (*Census of England and Wales*, vol. 4), was about 28 years, and a typical school leaving age might be about 11 years. So, the 1870 marriage registers would reflect the schooling situation (assuming people learn to read and write only in school, as seems to be Glass's assumption) in the early 1850s.

A better indication of the impact of schooling immediately prior to the 1870 Act is available in the 1891 Census, which showed only 6.4 percent of men (and 7.3 percent of women) unable to sign the marriage register. These men would have left school around 1874 on average (using the same assumptions as above), and therefore would have barely benefited, if at all, from the 1870 board school provisions, since the building program for board schools 'had scarcely got under way at this time' (West, 1994a, p. 167). In other words, if we are to accept the marriage signature as a useful indicator of literacy (writing), then we could conclude that around 93 percent of school leavers were already literate by the time the 1870 board schools began to operate. In any case, contrary to Glass's suggestion, the 1870 provisions did *not* introduce a state education system as we would understand it now. We shall explore this further later; for now, we note that the 1870 Act, 'contrary to popular belief, did not establish universal compulsion, nor abolish fee-paying' (ibid.). Universal compulsion came in 1880, and elementary school fees were not entirely abolished until 1918.

West then turns from literacy to look at the *quantity of schooling* available before the state got involved. But before doing so, he reminds us that literacy and other education may have come from sources other than schools – again stressing that education is broader than schooling:

> [T]he twentieth-century reader must be reminded of those private agencies which are no longer familiar: the Mechanics Institute, the Literary and Philosophic Societies, the Sunday schools. Moreover, systematic tuition in the home, often given by the parents themselves, was also quite common.
>
> (ibid., p. 170)

But there were also schools. So what is the evidence on these?

The Quantity of Schooling in Nineteenth-Century England and Wales

In the early nineteenth century, there were many anecdotal observations about the role of private schools in meeting the needs of the poor. James Mill, father of John Stuart Mill, writing in 1813, noted:

> From observation and inquiry . . . we can ourselves speak decidedly as to the rapid progress which the love of education is making among the lower orders in England. Even around London, in a

circle of fifty miles radius, which is far from the most instructed and virtuous part of the kingdom, there is hardly a village that has not something of a school; and not many children of either sex who are not taught more or less, reading and writing.

(James Mill, *Edinburgh Review*, October 1813,
quoted in West, 1994a, p. 170)

This 'love of education' was being demonstrated by the working classes a full 57 years before the 1870 Act, and 20 years before any subsidies at all were provided by the state. How were such schools funded? Mill added, 'We have met with families in which, for weeks together, not an article of sustenance but potatoes had been used; yet for every child the hard-earned sum was provided to send them to school' (West, 1994a, p. 171).

In 1816, the third report of the Select Parliamentary Committee of inquiry into the 'Education of the Lower Orders' noted

unquestionable evidence that the anxiety of the poor for education continues not only unabated but daily increasing; that it extends to every part of the country, and is to be found equally prevalent in those smaller towns and country districts, where no means of gratifying it are provided by the charitable efforts of the richer classes.

(ibid.)

Henry Brougham's Select Committee of 1820 provided the first official and comprehensives statistics on schooling. It established that in 1818, between 1 in 14 and 1 in 15 of the population was being schooled, claiming that this was a big improvement on earlier on, reflecting the zealous expansion of groups such as the National Society and the British and Foreign School Society, 'but also the increasing willingness of parents to send their children' to school and 'to pay the fees which were nearly always asked' (West, 1994a, p. 171). In 1828, Brougham followed up with a smaller (5 percent) sample, using the same sources as before (the parochial clergy), and was astonished to find a doubling of the number of children in schools. However, other accounts of gross educational deficiencies, particularly in towns of the Northwest, which were being flooded by immigration from

Ireland, captured the popular imagination more – but clearly they were not 'representative of the whole country', argues West, as were Brougham's figures (ibid., p. 172).

In part because of the conclusions of these other, more anecdotal surveys, the principle of state subsidies to schools was first accepted in 1833. The first annual grant was only £20,000, and was given to the two large voluntary organizations, the National Society and the British and Foreign School Society.

Parliament authorized a further survey of schooling across the whole country in 1833 under a parliamentary motion put forward by Lord Kerry, hence known as the Kerry Report. These figures did not become available until 1835, however. This survey seemed to support Brougham's own private estimate of 'the rate of growth'. The 1833 figures showed 1,294,000 children in school, an increase from the 1818 figure of 478,000 (West, 1994a, p. 172). These children attended schools 'without any imposition of the Government or public authorities' (ibid., quoting a speech by Henry Brougham in the House of Lords, 21 May 1835).

In *Education and the State*, West notes that some have disputed these figures, but 'as far as I know they have never supported their complaint with specific reasons or alternative evidence' (ibid.). However, in a paper that appeared after the first edition of *Education and the State* (West, 1970a) West shows that he was now aware of the source of these disputes and was keen to address them – so it is odd that in the revised editions of *Education and the State* (1970c, 1994a) he did not do so. In fact, the 'complaint' came from the Manchester Statistical Society. But, crucially, the complaint was not what many seem to have assumed: West cites S.J. Curtis's *History of Education in Great Britain* (1965), noting that the Kerry figures were 'untrustworthy' (p. 232), along with a similar observation made by Frank Smith in *A History of English Elementary Education* (1931, p. 151), both suggesting that the figures should be *revised downwards*. However, in fact the complaint of the Manchester Statistical Society was that the figures were significant *under*estimates! In Manchester, for instance, it was complained that the Kerry Report had underestimated by a total of 8,646 scholars, mostly day scholars, an error of 27 percent of the total scholars (day, evening and Sunday scholars), and at least one-third and possibly as much as one-half of the day scholar total (West, 1970a, p. 79). Nor was Manchester unique in this regard. In the borough of Salford, the underestimate of day scholars was also 50 percent (ibid., p. 83), while in Hulme it was about one-third, and in Birmingham again there was about a 50 percent deficiency in the 1833 returns (ibid., p. 83, citing reports of the Manchester and Birmingham Statistical Societies). So how should we revise the Kerry figures? The 1851 Census report on education suggested, without any explanation, that for the whole country the figures underestimated by about 10 percent, but this included all scholars, including those in day and Sunday schools. But the local statistical societies had found the greatest underestimate to be for day schools, so West (1970a, p. 84) suggests revising the figures upwards by 20 percent or more. With a 20 percent upward adjustment, the figure for children in day schools in 1833 would have been nearly 1.6 million.

West commented about these findings, 'It seems reasonable, therefore to infer that when the government made its debut in education in 1833 mainly in the role of a subsidiser it was as if it jumped into the saddle of a horse that was already galloping' (1994a, p. 173). For West, the key question was, continuing the metaphor, 'would the new rider improve its speed and if so, could this be done without injury?' (ibid.).

Brougham was so impressed by this growth in schooling that he spoke of the 'irresistible conclusion' that, given

> such a number of schools and such means of education furnished *by the parents themselves from their own earnings*, and by the contributions of well-disposed individuals in aid of those whose earnings were insufficient, it behoves us to take the greatest care how we interfere with a system which prospers so well of itself.
>
> (Henry Brougham's speech to the House of Lords, as above, quoted in West, 1994a, p. 173)

That is, Brougham saw the schools provided by philanthropy and by parental fees, and worried about what might replace them if government intervened. We need, he argued, to think well and long and anxiously, and with all circumspection and all foresight, before we thrust our hands into a machinery which is now in such a steady, constant, and rapid movement; for if we do in the least degree incautiously, we may occasion ourselves no little mischief, and may stop that movement which it is our wish to accelerate.

(quoted ibid.)

Brougham's fear, says West, was that if working-class parents were made to pay new rates and taxes for funding subsidies for state education – and the taxation system, as we have noted, being heavily 'regressive', hit working-class people hardest (with 60 percent of taxation falling on food and tobacco around this time) – they would simply be unable to afford to pay for schooling. And so private schools would disappear: 'There would be ultimately be no net increase in the growth of schooling but simply a change in the pattern of the existing provision' (ibid.).

Brougham implied that parental fees were an important contribution to total schooling costs at the time. Was he correct? How was this system of education funded? We have seen that there were some small government subsidies from 1833, and there are also contributions from charity and religious groups. A key part of West's argument, supporting Brougham's contention, is that during the early part of the nineteenth century the '*biggest* part of the cost of day schooling . . . was covered neither by the church nor by philanthropy, but from direct payments (fees) from working families' (West, 1970, p. 84; emphasis added). He gives three sources of evidence for this, from the Bristol Statistical Society (BSS), the Manchester Statistical Society (MSS) and the Kerry Report. In Bristol, for instance, the 1841 report showed that 'a very big majority of its schools and scholars received no support whatsoever except from the parents' (ibid.). In these 446 schools, where parents paid full fees, their contribution was, according to the BSS, £32,000 annually. In those 42 schools where parents paid 'part' fees, with the rest of costs coming from subscriptions, parents paid £2,500. Only in 24 schools was education free and endowed (ibid.). (It is useful to note that at this time, the government's annual education subsidy to the *whole* of

England and Wales was only £30,000 – that is, less than was contributed by the parents of Bristol alone.) In Manchester, the MSS reported that 79 percent of parents paid full fees, while 10 percent of parents paid part fees (ibid.). The Kerry Report showed that 73 percent of day scholars paid fees, and in 58 percent of total cases, parental fees covered the entire cost. Thus, it is clear that parental contributions were making up the largest proportion of the costs of schooling.

The numbers of scholars continued to rise, until by 1851 there were 2,144,378 children in day schools out of a total population (children and adults) of about 18 million – that is, 1 in 8.36. Of these, over 85 percent were in purely private schools – that is, 'schools which derive their income solely from [fee] payments or which are maintained with a view to pecuniary advantage' (1851 Census, pp. 134–5, quoted in West, 1994a, p. 175). It is also important to note that the remaining 15 percent were in so-called public schools, but this meant schools 'supported *in any degree*' by government subsidies – which were usually rather minimal at this stage (West, 1994a, p. 175).

Finally, there was the 'mammoth report' of the Newcastle Commission on Popular Education, set up in 1858 and reporting in 1861. One of its members was the economist Nassau Senior, who supported state intervention in education on the same grounds as John Stuart Mill: the protection of minors principle. West spends some time elaborating its method of enquiry, to illustrate the depth and compass of its survey, and the advanced statistical techniques employed. It was the first enquiry 'to be directed entirely and purposefully to a survey of schooling' (ibid., p. 176). Its statistical methods included a combination 'of an assessment of aggregated statistics' cross-checked by 'intensive sample examinations from selected areas'. The former, covering the whole of England and Wales, collated data 'obtained through religious societies connected with education and through public departments' (ibid.). The smaller samples were made up of reports from ten 'specimen areas' by assistant commissioners 'who in many cases, either personally or by their clerks, assisted in filling up the forms issued from the office of the Commission' (quoted from the Education Commission, *Report of the Commissioners appointed to enquire into the State of Popular Education in England*, vol. 1, 1861,

p. 553; quoted in West, 1994a, p. 176). The specimen districts made up about one-eighth of the whole population. In these, the assistant commissioners were looking for the 'non-inspected' schools – that is, non-subsidized schools, which would not appear in other official statistics – and comparing their proportions with those of the inspected, subsidized schools. The commissioners then assumed that these proportions were true of the country as a whole, and so adjusted the figures found in the general survey upwards to accommodate these additional schools.

The Newcastle Commission estimated that for England and Wales as a whole, in 1858 there were 2,535,462 scholars in day schools – 'a figure', says West, 'which seems quite compatible with the 1851 census which showed that the two million mark had already been topped' (ibid., p. 177). In other words, the figures are consistent, strengthening for West the notion that they are more or less reliable. The key question then was: how many children were *not* in school? For this was the key figure that would lead to any conclusions about the need for state intervention, and the extent to which it was required.

The commissioners suggested from their evidence that the average length of school attendance 'did not exceed six years'. Hence, they assumed that one-half of the total number of children aged between 3 and 15 years (i.e. a 12-year interval) would be at school. Half of the official figure (from the registrar-general) of the appropriate age group was 2,655,767. Therefore, the commissioners reported that the shortfall of those not in school was only 120,305 children, or about 4.5 percent of the relevant age group. Indeed, many of these children, the commissioners suggested, were 'children who had bodily and mental infirmities', and West adds that some, too, may have been children educated at home.

Moreover, the more detailed investigation in the specimen districts actually showed an average attendance of 5.7 years. If the commissioners had used this more precise figure rather than the six years they used, then there would be no children unaccounted for: if we use 5.7/12 rather than 6/12 in our calculation, we get a figure of 2,522,979 children who should have been at school, or 12,483 fewer than were actually found! But, of course, we do not know the correct distribution of the population across the age group, so these figures are only approximations. But the key point is, in summary, that the commission found that more or less all children 'were having some schooling' (West, 1994a, p. 177).

Moreover, the Newcastle Commission very significantly also reported that the proportion of scholars to the population *as a whole* was now 1:7.7, compared with the ratio of 1:8.36 found by the 1851 Census. On this basis, the commissioners concluded:

> The proportion of children receiving instruction to the whole population is, in our opinion, nearly as high as can be reasonably expected. In Prussia, where it is compulsory, it is 1 in 6.27 ... in Holland it is 1 in 8.11; in France it is 1 in 9.0. The presence of this proportion of the population in school implies ... that almost every one receives some amount of school education at some period or other'
>
> (Education Commission, *Report of the Commissioners appointed to enquire into the State of Popular Education in England,* vol. 1, 1861, p. 293, quoted in West, 1994a, p. 180)

What government policy did all of this suggest? The commissioners, because they had found an 'extensive' network of what we would now call private schools, believed that the government should avoid any form of state schooling, either local or general. It recommended a system of improved direct grants to the private schools and a better inspection procedure, but nothing more. Generally, the theme was one of 'control and encouragement' for the private framework that already existed, not the creation of new types of schools (West, 1994a, p. 179).

In other words, the picture revealed by West, using contemporaneous sources, is nothing like the 'lagging far behind' other countries portrayed by Trevelyan, or the suggestion of mass illiteracy offered by Sir Arthur Bryant, as in the quotations above. If the Newcastle Commission data are correct, where did the historians get their figures from? They surely did not just pluck them out of thin air?

It seems that they are likely to have got their figures from the architect of the 1870 Education Act himself. For when W.E. Forster introduced his Education Bill of 1870 into Parliament, oddly he made hardly any reference to the Newcastle Commission's findings. Instead, he relied on evidence from a small-scale survey conducted by two inspectors, J.G. Fitch and D.R. Fearon, in 1869 over a period of a few months in four industrial towns, Liverpool, Manchester, Leeds and Birmingham – in contrast to the Newcastle Commission, which had taken three years to produce its findings, using five commissioners and ten assistant commissioners (West, 1994a, p. 180). In Liverpool, for example, Forster argued that out of an estimated 80,000 children of school age, '20,000 of them attend no school whatever, while at least another 20,000 attend schools where they get an education not worth having' (quoted ibid., p. 181). In other words, here we have at least 25 percent and, if the quality judgment is believed, up to 50 percent of the relevant population not in schooling at all, or in schooling of any suitable quality – hence the figures used by the historians Trevelyan and Bryant (although we note that even then they have exaggerated them, and ignored the caveats concerning quality).

We shall look further at the discussion of poor quality in the schools later. But, concerning the quantity of schooling, at first glance this seems a major discrepancy. And, as we have noted, later historians have tended to side with Forster's figures, rather than those of the Newcastle Commission, with the suggestion that the Newcastle Commission might have been trying to paint 'so favourable a picture as to relieve the government from too embarrassing a growth of educational expenditure in the future' (ibid.). Historians have pointed to both the composition of the Newcastle Commission and its terms of reference, which may have led to this kind of prejudice in its findings. The commission was directed to 'Inquire into the Present State of Popular Education in England, and to Consider and Report what Measures, if any, are required for the Extension of *Sound and Cheap Elementary Instruction* to all classes of the People' (ibid.; West's emphasis). In other words, say such critics, 'having spent "alarming sums" on the Crimea War, the 1858 government was looking with apprehension at its expenditure programmes and not least the increasing cost of the annual education grant' (ibid.). Hence, the authorities were keen to present facts which would show that education was not an area that required much growth in expenditure. Moreover, it may be that the commissioners were concerned only that the masses had the most elementary of schooling, and therefore content with what they found, whereas more objective observers might have decided that the state of education was unsatisfactory. West agrees that 'such suspicions are not easy to handle' (ibid.). But he points out we can also impute parallel biases in Forster's inspectors and departmental advisers, given their own potential desire to *increase* their power and influence. If one is to 'deconstruct' one set of statistics, then one should, in fairness, also deconstruct the other side too. Perhaps the opposite conclusion could then be levied at Forster's inspectors: that they wanted to paint 'so bad a picture' in order to ensure that their own department was entrusted with the expansion of the education system? We shall be exploring this issue in the next chapter in more detail (and also looking at a more positive interpretation of Forster's argument). However, we do not need to engage with the discussion at this level, for there is a more obvious discrepancy that can resolve the dispute rather easily.

For the Newcastle Commission had assumed a typical child was in school for about six years. But Forster in calculating his figures had assumed that the school-age population was for *eight years* – that is, between the ages of 5 and 13 (and we can observe that the school-leaving age was not even raised to 12 until 1899). This alone, clearly, will cause the major discrepancy between the two sets of figures. For instead of Forster's estimated 80,000 children of school age, we are likely to find a reduced figure of (assuming the proportions of children in each year group are proportional to the whole) 60,000 (i.e. six-eighths of 80,000) who were *actually* of school age. But this was exactly the figure that Forster's survey *did* find in school!

So, the source of the popular misapprehension about the quantity of schooling in England and Wales is easily found – and just as easily dismissed. Now in *Education and the State*, West does not give any references for this observation, which led at least one critical reader, Professor Mark Blaug, to assume that this was West's *own* 'ingenious argument to explain the discrepancy between Forster and Newcastle' (Blaug, [1967] 1970, p. 25). However, in later work (West, 1992a – published before *Education and the State* was revised in 1994), West points out that it was Lord Robert Montagu, a participant in the parliamentary debate in 1870, who first noticed the discrepancy. There, Lord Montagu argued:

> The right hon. gentleman alluded to the case of Liverpool, where he said there were 80,000 children between the ages of five and thirteen. Of these he said that 20,000 were in no school; and 20,000 went to inferior schools. The [Newcastle] Commissioners thought that for the children of the working class, six years schooling would be sufficient. Now, as there are eight years between five and thirteen, if every one were to attend school for six years, three-fourths of the number ought to be at school in each year; and according to the showing of the right hon. gentleman, there were three-fourths of the number at school.
>
> (quoted from Education Bill, first reading, 17 February 1870, Hansard, vol. 99, in West, 1992a, pp. 607–8)

Whatever the source of this explanation, it is clear that it *does* explain the discrepancy between Forster and the Newcastle Commission; both in effect give the same figures. And it suggests that historians of education like those I have quoted are entirely incorrect in pointing to the educational deficiencies in England and Wales, at least without further caveats and discussion pointing out that this is only one interpretation of the data. I shall have more to say on the kind of figures put forward by Forster in the next chapter, where we shall find that West argues there are numerous instances taking place of similar 'erroneous calculations'.

So much for the impetus that led to Forster's Act, and the subsequent 1870 intervention. It would seem that at least as far as the *quantity* of schooling is concerned, proponents of the need for state intervention were not on strong grounds. A very substantial piece of evidence in support of this statement is that Forster introduced his 1870 Bill *explicitly* as a measure to cater for those children who were not being provided by existing voluntary measures. It was not designed to cater universally for all children, but only to fill in the gaps in the current private system. Moreover, under the Act the country was divided into school districts, a survey of the educational needs of each district conducted, and voluntary sources given six months to rectify the deficiencies (Reid, [1888] 1970, pp. 479, 506). Clearly, Forster was aware that voluntary private provision was a very valuable resource in educational provision, and simply needed to be supplemented by his new board schools as required, not replaced.

The Quantity of Schooling and the Economic Arguments for State Intervention

I shall have more to say about the impact of the 1870 Act and the 'crowding out' of the private sector in a later section. However, as far as the *quantity* of schooling is concerned, we are in a position to make some links between the historical evidence and West's discussion of the economic justifications for state intervention in education, namely the neighborhood effects of education and the protection of minors principle. What West's analysis suggests is that in order to promote universal literacy and schooling more generally, the kind of state education with which we are familiar – namely, state-provided, state-funded and regulated schooling – is *not* required. The small level of public subsidies that had been provided since 1833 had led to a more or less sufficient number of school places. It is also arguable, says West, that even if these subsidies had not been provided, the disposable income of the poor would have been higher, and hence the amount of funding that they might have been prepared to spend on schooling could also have been higher – but clearly this is a counterfactual that we cannot further explore. If critics might claim that the length of time in school needed to be increased, then there is no obvious reason why this also could not have been accomplished through further subsidies, perhaps including subsidies to parents to offset the opportunity costs of young people not working to support the family. What this discussion suggests is that, at most, what is *justified* by the economic arguments for state intervention in education, taken in parallel with the historical findings explored here, as far as quantity of school places is concerned, is some targeted funding, not provision of schooling. This is an important conclusion that West takes with him to his policy proposals.

Crucially, this conclusion also applies if one is looking at whether government intervention was required to produce a more optimal

Table 3.1   Percentage of Net National Income
Spent on Day Schooling, 1833–1965

	1833	1920	1965
Children of all ages	1.0%	0.70%	2.00%
Children < 11 years	0.8%	0.58%	0.86%

Source: West (1970a) p. 87.

total expenditure on education. An argument is often put forward concerning nineteenth-century 'underinvestment' in education. West gives estimates using the 1833 Kerry Report of the percentage of net national income spent on day schooling, and compares his findings with official data for 1920 and 1965. The estimates are that the percentage of national income spent on the schooling of children under the age of 11 was *superior* in 1833 to that in 1920, and *roughly comparable* with what was spent in 1965 (Table 3.1).

This evidence, West argues, suggests that there may not have been underinvestment in education at all in the early nineteenth century, given that the percentage of net national income spent on schooling was of superior or comparable levels to those found later. All this, of course, was before there were *any* public subsidies for education.

Critiques of West's Approach to Quantity of Schooling

West's conclusions on the quantity of schooling in the nineteenth century have been subject to criticisms from a variety of sources. Some of the criticisms concern the general use of nineteenth-century statistics to arrive at firm conclusions. For instance, Professor Kiesling suggests, 'Surely *no competent student* of this period would deny that the quality of the educational data makes it impossible to provide support for *any* thesis about English education which is as strong as West's' (1983, p. 425). The evidence is 'simply not good enough to support broad generalizations of the kind West has tried to make' (ibid.). Kiesling accuses West of using nineteenth-century data to show that private education produced an 'optimal' outcome. West's defense is to suggest the opposite was his method: he was challenging those who were suggesting that *state* intervention was needed to produce the optimal outcome. In other words, he argues, 'Usually my position has been that of a reappraiser of data that other historians have deemed useful. Implicitly, I suppose, I have been accepting whatever degree of confidence in the sources *they* were assuming' (ibid.).

Others have addressed concerns at particular sources used by West. J.S. Hurt suggested that West showed 'a remarkable faith in the accuracy of the educational statistics that were collected in the first half of the nineteenth century' (Hurt, 1971, p. 624), in particular condemning the use of the Kerry Report statistics of 1833. But we have already seen that West himself was clear about the very same kind of problems with the Kerry Report data. Hurt also points to the problem that Kerry's survey on the state of education in England and Wales

> was conducted at a time of bitter rivalry between the main parties interested in education. The two leading religious societies, the Anglican National Society and the nonconformist British and Foreign School Society, had only one interest in common. They were both resolutely opposed to the principle of state control. In every other respect, they were at loggerheads. Hence they fought out with each other, and with the state, a battle of statistics.
>
> (ibid.)

Hurt claims that *they* claimed they each had 1.5 million in schools by 1839. But it was also claimed by others that there were 3,024,000 children in school between the age of 3 and 12 by this time, so 'the two societies had apparently cornered the market' (ibid.). Unfortunately, Hurt is completely wrong in his use of evidence here. He has cited a parliamentary answer by Mr Henry Dunn, Secretary of the British and Foreign School Society. But if the original source is checked, we find that Dunn was claiming one and a half million in *Sunday* schools, not day schools (see Kiesling, 1983, p. 421, fn. 21).

Hurt also suggests that West's use of the Newcastle Commission data is misguided: he writes, 'the accuracy of the figures cited by the Newcastle Commissioners, even after their lengthy and careful investigation, is open to legitimate doubt' (Hurt, 1971, p. 631). The specific problem that he points to is that schools receiving subsidies may have exaggerated their numbers in order to increase the grant, which was based 'mainly on attendance' (ibid.). As evidence for potential inaccuracies he points to the 1851 Census figures. These showed that 'the state-aided voluntary schools claimed an average attendance of 250,214'; however, the inspectors 'on their long-heralded visits – the day of the year when one would have expected every child on the books to be in attendance' found only 236,656. For Hurt, this means that '[c]learly school managers and teachers alike conspired to inflate the numbers of their pupils' (ibid., p. 632). Three points can be made here. First, the difference in what was found was tiny – only 5.4 percent of the reported total school population. So, if this is exaggeration, it is pretty minor. (In a school reporting 100 pupils, say, there would actually be only 95 pupils. Exaggerated, true, but hardly earth-shatteringly so.)

Second, Hurt is assuming that the inspectors' visits would have overridden everything else. But it is not clear why this would have been the case. If the visit coincided with important harvest-time activities, for instance, or with other significant events in the child's life – a death in the family, a funeral, a child's or relative's illness, etc., which might be randomly distributed across the school year – or with a period when the parents could not afford the school fees – again, randomly distributed – then there would be no reason to expect the child to drop everything and go to school simply because the inspector was coming. In other words, it is possible that the discrepancy between the figures actually showed something like the normal level of absenteeism in the schools – and, moreover, that this was rather low. It is also possible that particular children may have been actively *discouraged* from attending on the day of the inspector's visit if they were badly behaved or not so good at learning, in order to ensure that the inspector gained the most favorable impression of the school.

Third, Hurt is pointing to a discrepancy in the *small minority* of publicly supported schools – where attendance was in any case reported to be lower than in the majority fully fee-paying schools. 'These schools accounted for only about one-eighth of the total school population reported in the census' (West, 1971a, p. 640). West had used the figures on attendance to arrive at an estimate of the percentage of national income spent on education used above. As the census found that reported attendance in the non-subsidized sector (the seven-eighths) was 91 percent, while that in the public sector was 79 percent, West's use of 80 percent overall attendance is very conservative, 'more than sufficient to take account of Hurt's adjustments' (ibid.).

The Quality of Schooling Before and After 1870

John Stuart Mill, writing in 1834, observed that 'As far, therefore, as *quantity* of teaching is concerned, the education of our people is, or will speedily be, amply provided for' (quoted in Garforth, 1980, p. 114). This seems to concur with West's conclusion outlined earlier: that the quantity of schooling and the degree of literacy of the population *were* perfectly adequate, with only minimal state assistance. However, those who argue that the government needed to intervene in education in England and Wales do have another possible avenue of approach. This would be to question the *quality* of schooling offered at the time. This was certainly John Stuart Mill's problem with the private alternative in education in the nineteenth century; he followed the quotation given above with the comment: 'It is the *quality* which so grievously demands the amending hand of government. And this is the demand which is principally in danger of being obstructed by popular apathy and ignorance' (quoted ibid.).

What evidence can we adduce about the quality of the private schools that were provided in the nineteenth century? West has two major points to make about this evidence. First, he warns that much of the subjective material written about school quality may be clouded by value judgments held by individuals and not based upon measurable evidence (West 1994a, p. 199). Second, West also cautions that some of the, especially later, criticisms of the inferior education quality in private schools may well have been assessing the *impact* of unfair competition from the board schools post-1870, or earlier government subsidies from 1833. We shall look at both of these points in turn.

As a way into the first part of this discussion, let us use the argument of a staunch critic of West, W.B. Stephens (1987). Stephens explicitly takes West to task on several points concerning the quality of private education in the nineteenth century. He believes that it was government intervention from 1833 that led to improvements in education, improvements that could not have occurred without the state. For example, Stephens notes:

> With the advent of government funding and inspection, followed by the introduction into public schools of pupil teachers, increasing numbers of trained teachers, better buildings and equipment, more generous provision of books and so on, the benefit of a sound curriculum and teaching methods, and the pressure for regular attendance, standards in inspected public schools, particularly from the 1850s, *must certainly have outstripped* those of schools reliant on local funding and school pence and under less external pressure.
>
> (Stephens 1987, p. 25; emphasis added)

That is, the intervention of government had the effect of improving the quality ('standards') of schooling, and the improvement would not otherwise have occurred. Is this true? First, West would argue that it is not true that these 'improvements' could have come about only through state intervention. Some of them were simply the result of more funds (buildings, equipment, books), and more funds could have come from other sources besides the state – from voluntary contributions, charities, or simply the improved wealth over time of the people buying schooling, enabling them to afford higher school fees. Moreover, Stephens cannot mean that 'the pressure for regular attendance' was state induced, because schooling did not become compulsory for some years after the period he is surveying. So, this must have been something that happened irrespective of state involvement. We can also note that the type of state intervention he is referring to is pretty minimal. These 'public schools' he is describing are simply publicly inspected schools, with some small government subsidy. They are not what we would term 'publicly provided' today. So, even if Stephens is correct, and these were of much higher quality than the non-inspected schools, then this would be an argument only for inspection and very small subsidy – intervention more in line with what we shall refer to in a subsequent chapter as West's 'market model', and not an argument for state provision or funding in general.

Moreover, how can we be so sure that the 'improvements' Stephens is describing *did* lead to higher standards? It is a common assumption today that better buildings, more resources, trained teachers, etc. do lead to higher quality. But as far as the situation in the nineteenth century is concerned, there may be other factors that undermine Stephens's conclusions. Concerning perhaps the most significant criticism of the private schooling of the nineteenth century, lack of trained teachers, it is important to note that the accusations of the poor standard of unqualified teachers were often made by state inspectors who had received some formal training themselves and therefore felt animosity towards 'amateurs' without training (West, 1994a, p. 207). Often the private school teachers carried out other professions or had begun their career doing something very different from teaching. These private school teachers were regarded by the professional teacher in the nineteenth century as 'a collection of uncolleged, and therefore untrained, individuals with no redeeming qualities of possible benefit to the schools' (ibid., p. 209). But were the 'professionals' correct in thus dismissing the private school teachers? West suggests that the problem of the private school teachers, who had 'picked up' their knowledge 'promiscuously', as they were accused of doing, may not have been a problem at all. He quotes from the Newcastle Commission Report:

Of the private school masters in Devonport, one had been a blacksmith and afterwards an exciseman, another was a journeyman tanner, a third a clerk in a solicitor's office, a fourth (who was very successful in preparing lads for the competitive examination in the dockyards) keeps an evening school and works as a dockyard labourer, a fifth was a seaman, and others had been engaged in other callings.

> (The Royal Commission on Popular Education, vol. 1, 1861, p. 93, quoted in West, 1994a, pp. 208–9)

But, West suggests, 'the average small schoolboy would today no doubt display wonder at the prospect of having such a colourful variety of experienced adults to teach him' (ibid., p. 209).

In any case, West explores what the standard of Stephens's preferred trained teacher must have been at the time. He points out that the teacher training colleges at the time overwhelmingly favored rote learning, which was the preferred method of teaching picked out by the inspectors, too. It seems 'at least arguable', says West,

> that the communication of adults from varied occupations might, on average, have been more useful and inspiring to children in school rooms than parroting of English Literature before young school teachers who, in their own lives, had had little time to do anything else.
>
> (ibid., p. 210)

But couldn't some of the teachers and/or proprietors in the private schools have been below par? West agrees that, given the 'extremely buoyant demand for schooling', it is certainly possible that some 'charlatans' could have made their appearance in schools. 'What is more difficult to believe is that many such persons could have typically established themselves on any *permanent* basis' (ibid., p. 208). He points to the evidence of one of the assistant commissioners to the Newcastle Commission, Mr Coode (evidence that is also relevant when we consider the problem perceived in the private system of low attendance), who noted:

> It is a subject of wonder how people so destitute of education as labouring parents commonly are, can be such just judges as they also commonly are of the effective qualifications of a teacher. Good school buildings and the apparatus of education are found for years to be practically useless and deserted, when, if a master chance to be appointed who understands his work, a few weeks suffice to make the fact known, and his school is soon filled, and perhaps found inadequate to the demand of the neighbourhood, and a separate girls' school or infants' school is soon found to be necessary.
>
> (quoted from the Royal Commission on Popular Education, 1861, p. 175, in West, 1994a, p. 205)

Mr Coode's evidence, West suggests, 'is testimony to the shrewdness of parents in detecting and effectively rejecting the "quacks". In other words, that some teachers were incompetent does not seem to have been one of those secrets known only to the learned!' (1994a, p. 208).

Doubts must also be cast on Stephens's suggestion that government inspection also led to a higher quality of education: the inspectors' early official concept of educational efficiency meant 'a schooling which scored high marks in divinity and morality' (West, 1994a, p. 104). Indeed, some schools were deemed worthless precisely because of failure in moral and religious training. The Manchester Statistical Society, for instance, was critical of the private schools, where 'Religious instruction is seldom attended to beyond the rehearsal of "a catechism", and moral education, real cultivation of the mind and improvement of character, are totally neglected' (*Report of a Committee of the Manchester Statistical Society on the State of Education in the Borough of Manchester in 1834*, 2nd edition, 1837, p. 10, quoted in West, 1994a, p. 90). But it is likely that many parents felt that these aspects of education were being largely catered for in the family and in the Sunday schools: 'on week-days families were demanding education in more "practical" matters' (ibid., p. 91), such as reading, writing and arithmetic. Moreover, it must be noted that inspectors making these criticisms are known to have had particular biases. For example, the school inspector H.S. Tremenheere noted in the early 1850s that the people's education enabled them to read 'seditious literature without having the moral or intellectual strength to discern its falseness' (quoted in Stephens, 1987, p. 133). This was literature that was 'exaggerating the principle of equality before God and the law', encouraging workers to be antagonistic towards their employers (ibid.). With prejudices like these, it may well be that the inspectors' reports were not as valuable as Stephens elsewhere suggests, nor as likely to lead to improved quality of educational experiences. Moreover, the Victorian inspectors were 'often regarded with fear' by teachers as well as pupils, so we cannot be sure that their observations of the performance of pupils of unqualified teachers 'were made under the best of conditions', something admitted to by Sir James Kay Shuttleworth, the first secretary of the Committee of Council on Education, when he wrote, 'All inspectors are not perfect either in manner, utterance, choice of words for poor children, method of examining them; nor in the skill, kindness and patience required to bring out the true state of the child's knowledge' (quoted from a letter to Lord Granville, 4 November 1861, in West, 1994a, p. 207).

Moreover, we can also make some comments on the findings of the school inspectors who provided evidence for Forster when he introduced his 1870 Bill. We noted above that Inspectors J.G. Fitch and D.R. Fearon reported that in Liverpool, for instance, of the 60,000 children in school, 20,000 were getting an education that was 'not worth having'. How did they arrive at this figure? The number of children considered to be taught effectively was those who passed to the satisfaction of the inspectors. However, to qualify even *to be examined* by the inspectors, a child 'must have attended *that same* school for at least 200 times in the course of the year' (West, 1992a, p. 608). For this reason, many were simply ruled out of the inspections, and hence discarded as receiving an ineffective education, part of the reported 20,000 children getting an education 'not worth having'. But West suggests that some of these children might have left before the day of the inspection, or were ill on the day of the inspection, and others could have moved between schools, so had not been in the particular school inspected for 200 days although they had been in school and might well have passed had they been examined. So, the figure of 20,000 may have been an exaggeration; we simply do not know.

To return to Stephens's criticisms, he also deplores the poor-quality premises in which private schooling was carried out without state intervention. But, of course, as West points out, it is difficult to judge what was meant by 'poor' or 'inferior' quality as regards the school buildings at the time. West states that as well as poor school buildings there would have been poor houses, shops, hospitals and offices. Probably the state of the private schools reflected life at the time (1994a, p. 206). Tastes also change: 'It is interesting that when people protest about children still being taught inside Victorian "monstrosities" they are usually referring to the Board Schools which ... were feverishly erected after 1870' (ibid.). Schooling in the new board schools may have had no positive impact at all on children, *pace* Stephens; indeed, it may well have meant schooling in large, cold, regimented, factory-like surroundings, rather than the cozy school-room of the private school, and may in fact have been detrimental to education.

Finally, we move to two criticisms aired by Stephens – and other historians – that point to the inadequacies of the private system and the need for government intervention, this time concerning compulsory attendance. These were the problems of low and irregular school attendance, and the low school-leaving age. First, we can observe that Stephens at least grudgingly notes:

> Since schooling generally was not free and did not begin to become compulsory until the 1870s, the rising school attendance figures over the two generations before that must reflect a growing demand from working-class parents for formal schooling, however minimal.
> (1987, pp. 48–9)

The 'however minimal' seems rather ungenerous: in fact, while the real growth in income over the period 1801–71 was just over 1 per cent, the average annual growth rate of school pupils was over 2 per cent (West, 1994b, p. 13). However, Stephens thinks that not too much must be read into this growth rate: he notes that 'despite what has been said of the growth of working-class demand, all the evidence suggests that *only some form of compulsion* combined with state assistance could bring what was generally considered as adequate schooling' to the poorest children (Stephens 1987, p. 52; emphasis added).

If compulsion was required, then this must have been because of negative parental or child attitudes towards schooling. In fact, when Stephens's evidence is surveyed, it is not clear how he is able to arrive at this conclusion regarding the necessity of compulsion. First, he himself is able to offer many positive findings regarding parental attitudes to schooling. He notes that there were not only economic benefits to schooling but also political and social ones. There were desires to be respectable in the eyes of 'local clergy and others' (ibid., p. 49), as well as the attractions of 'reading for pleasure and the ability to communicate with relations living at a distance'. Moreover, 'as schooling became the norm the completely unschooled became increasingly untypical, a situation which must have brought its own pressure to conform' (ibid., p. 50):

> From 1840 schooling appears increasingly desirable socially and also functionally advantageous in an increasing number of jobs . . .
>
> Moreover, the vast expansion from the 1830s of didactic evangelical and utilitarian publications, of political and commercial literature, and of newspapers, radical and otherwise, attest to a working-class society in which the ability to read must have added to the economic advantages political and social ones.
>
> (ibid., p. 51)

This trend in schooling norms would have a considerable bearing on the thesis that compulsion would be necessary to ensure an adequate education for all. If there were social and political, as well as economic, advantages in sending children to school, and if there were norms that made this more favorable, then it is likely the rate of schooling would have continued to increase. However, let us ignore this (substantial) part of Stephens's evidence – which would provide strong support to West's argument – and concentrate instead on seeing whether Stephens's remaining criticisms substantially undermine West's position.

What are the negative attitudes of parents that Stephens says would need state compulsion to overcome? And what were the reasons for these attitudes? Reviewing his evidence seems to show *four* main reasons given. *Three* of these concern economic factors that may have influenced parental choice about sending children to school. The first is the actual fees for schooling; the second the *opportunity costs* of sending children to school – that is, the benefits forgone of children's income and assistance around the house that could have been had if the children had not gone to school. This is likely to have been quite a considerable deterrent to many poor parents. Stephens notes, 'Certainly not all families were able to view the loss of children's earnings with equanimity' (ibid., p. 52). Moreover, he notes the remarks of the Reverend J.P. Norris (one of Her Majesty's Inspectors in the 1850s), who suggests that school fees were far less important than another factor: parents 'cannot afford *to give up the value of their child's time* . . .

the school fee is a mere trifle' (quoted in Stephens, 1987, p. 128). These first two factors would be influenced by poverty; and Stephens points out that '[p]overty was, indeed, the main reason given' by working-class parents for not sending children to school (ibid., p. 25).

Sometimes, in any case, parents sent their children to school, but attendance was 'erratic'. This is certainly what the school inspectors noted during the mid-nineteenth century, particularly around harvest time. But West points out that in farming communities, the opportunity cost of sending a child to school during certain busy times of the year may be too high. The benefit from keeping the child away from school in increased income and productivity outweighs the education benefit gained by the child's going to school. Therefore, this periodic absence must be considered not parental neglect but rational assessment (West, 1994a, p. 201). It is significant, says West, that when education was made compulsory, 'special holidays were frequently granted at harvest times' (ibid.). And school holidays today can often be traced back to these origins.

Third, another economic factor would relate to the economic benefits that were considered to be obtained from schooling. It may well be that many parents could see no economic benefit to be derived from schooling for their children, and so were not prepared to make the necessary sacrifices for no economic return. Stephens notes that for some parents, their relative prosperity did not depend on schooling, and they did not see why it would for their children either. It was important for some children to learn manual dexterity early on, and 'in the iron and coal districts there were many prosperous employers who had risen from the lowest occupations in the pit, the furnace or the forge, and even the nailers' shop without ever acquiring the rudiments of reading or writing' (Stephens, 1987, p. 123). A common saying, he notes, was 'The father went down the pit and he made a fortune, his son went to school and lost it' (ibid.). This attitude was reinforced by some employers: 'even employers active in promoting schooling admitted that their most skilful and best paid workmen were not necessarily those who were literate' (ibid., p. 124). Moreover, when parents preferred to send their children to vocational schools, again this could have been for sound economic factors:

The lace and plait schools, so disliked by contemporary educationalists and philanthropists, could be regarded less as evidence of
parental exploitation than indicative of parental responsibility in
securing for their children the practical education of the appren-
tice in crafts where skills had necessarily to be mastered at an early
age.

(ibid., p. 175)

Each of these three reasons depends upon economic factors.
To undermine West's position that compulsion was not required
in order to bring out more or less universal schooling, our interest is whether or not these factors would have continued to be of
importance towards the end of the nineteenth and into the twentieth century. Clearly, if the wealth of the nation had continued to
increase, the importance of the first two of these factors would be
likely to have rapidly diminished. The third factor is clearly influenced by the demands of employment, and Stephens observes that as
industrialization increased, the demands of employers for a schooled,
skilled workforce likewise increased. A survey in the 1840s found that
employers in Nottinghamshire, Derbyshire, Leicestershire and Birmingham unanimously agreed that education led to workers who were
'more trustworthy, more respectful – more accessible to reason in
disputes over wages or changes in routine, better conducted in their
social duties, and more refined in their tastes and use of language'
(Stephens, 1987, p. 136, quoting Parliamentary Papers of 1843). So,
again there seem to be very strong pressures from industry for educated workers, pressures that would have found their way down to
parents and children. Similar views were expressed in other parts of
the country and at later times. There were also technical advantages
in having a better-educated workforce in the metal, pottery and tex-
tile trades, although not in the coal and iron industries (ibid., p. 137).
An uneducated workforce led to 'the loss of immense sums of money'
(ibid.).

The fourth factor noted by Stephens as influencing parental attitudes towards education is of a different type. He observes that the
middle classes tended to overlook the three economic factors, instead
criticizing the working classes for parental greed and laziness. Some

parents, it was reported, did live off their children's wages, but these were a small minority of reported cases (ibid., p. 126). There were also savage indictments of working-class drunkenness, with parents spending money on drink rather than the education of their children. Now clearly, in these cases, it would seem that compulsion would have been necessary in order to ensure that these children received an adequate education. But let us repeat: Stephens's evidence suggests – in support of West's discussion – that these are likely to have been a very small minority of cases; moreover, given the discussion above about the process of modernization, it is plausible that such attitudes would not have lasted very long as society became more industrialized.

The Declining Quality of Private Schools *Caused* by the 1870 Intervention

We now return to West's second approach to evidence of low quality, where he warns that some of the later criticisms of inferior education quality in private schools may well have been assessing the *impact* of unfair competition, especially from the board schools post-1870. For the school boards were allowed to point to gaps that were caused by the provision of 'inefficient' – that is, low-quality – private schools, and so the need for new board schools. But often they did this, contemporary observers reported, because of 'extravagant notions about what efficiency really required in terms of buildings, playgrounds, etc.' (West, 1994a, p. 190). West quotes Inspector Matthew Arnold's report on the London School Board in 1878:

> It cannot be right, it is extravagant and absurd, that the London boy's education should be so managed as to cost three times as much as that of the Paris one … Both in London and elsewhere, school boards are apt to conceive what is requisite in these respects rather as benevolent, intelligent, and scientific educationists in Utopia, than as practical school-managers. I am quite sure that their conception of what is required in the way of accommodations, studies, salaries, administration, is pitched too high.
>
> (quoted in West, 1994a, p. 190)

The competition between the new board schools and the existing private schools became intense. It was not fair competition, however. Board schools were financed through rate aid and could therefore afford to drop their fees below those of the private schools. They could also offer staff higher wages and better working conditions. At the same time, parents were now paying rates to support the board schools, while poor parents not liable to rate payment had the price of their accommodation increased in order to cover these rates. With less disposable income, parents may have been inclined to choose the lower fees of the board schools; West quotes the report of Inspector Fitch for the Lambeth district in 1878:

> During the few months in which I have had charge of the district several national and British schools have been closed, and there is no prospect of any school of either class. All the new schools … are those of the School Board for London. Nor can this occasion any surprise. In the densely-peopled districts of Walworth, Kennington, and North Camberwell there are few or no rich residents; the inhabitants are chiefly shopkeepers and others who form precisely the class most keenly sensible of the pressure of the rates, and most likely to regard the existence of the education rate as a reason for withholding all subscriptions from Church or other voluntary schools. The clergy of these parishes assure me of the increasing difficulty of obtaining local aid; and complain, not unnaturally, that as soon as they get a skilled and successful teacher he is tempted to leave them by the higher pay and more assured position offered by the Board.
>
> (West, 1994a, p. 191)

West notes the 'bitter complaints' of some private schools that were apparently being forced out of business by the new board schools. He gives one extraordinary account, a letter of 24 April 1876 from the rector of St Paul's, Hulme, to the Manchester School Board about the unfair competition of the board schools. The school board wanted to put the rector's schools, the St Paul's Church of England schools, under the board because they were now 'not flourishing' – that is, their quality was perceived to have declined, and was now below tolerable levels. However, writes the rector, this was principally the result of the nearby Zion Chapel Schools becoming board schools, and the unfair competition that resulted. There, fees had been set at 3d per week, whereas in his and other schools, fees were from 3d to 6d per week. The board schools also supplied 'free of charge Books, Copy Books, Slates, etc. . . . which is not done in any of the denominational schools in the neighbourhood' (quoted ibid., p. 197). The case, the rector said, was 'simply one of under-selling', having such low fees in schools 'in the *same street*'.

Moreover, the rector complained:

> Let it not be imagined that I am opposed to giving a cheap and good education to the people. If their circumstances require it, I would gladly aid to the utmost of my power in providing for the education of their children at the lowest possible charges. But I submit that their circumstances do not require it. They are well able to pay, as they have done heretofore, 6d and 8d per week. In the adjoining parish of St Michael's, where the circumstances of the parishioners are not near as good as in my parish, the parents are paying up to 8d per week for their children [with even higher fees elsewhere]. Under these circumstances I would ask whether it is right to pay out of the public rates for the education of children where parents are well able to pay for themselves? And is it right to members of Christian Churches, which have made great sacrifices of time and money to erect schools in connection with their places of worship, to set up rival schools which, as ratepayers, they are compelled to support, in addition to their having to support their own denominational schools?'
>
> (quoted ibid., pp. 197–8)

In short, he does not want his school taken over. He sees the board schools as a 'menace' (quoted ibid., p. 198).

However, some historians have suggested that the 'competition' of board schools 'performed a necessary task of stimulating existing schools into greater efficiency' (ibid., p. 192). But for competition to stimulate efficiency, *all* schools would need to be able to go out of business if inefficient. But the new board schools were protected from this fate by being able to increase their funding through public revenues (that is, not through raising fees). The 1870 Act stated that '[a]ny sum required to meet any deficiency in the school fund, whether for satisfying past or future liabilities, shall be paid by the rating authority out of the local rate' (Education Act 1870, section 54, quoted in West, 1994a, p. 193). Bankruptcy was not an option for the board schools, propped up by taxation, irrespective of efficiency or cost.

Thus, it should come as no surprise, says West, that the board schools were able to drive out the private ones, and could do this by pointing to the declining 'efficiency' – that is, quality – of the private schools on offer. He gives us an analogy to help explain this:

> Assume that a government of today declared its opinion that there were marginal gaps in the provision of retail shops. Suppose that it set up its own shops and subsidised one or two 'gap-filling' private groups. Imagine that these shops, on the strength of revenues from rates and taxes [that is, rather than profits, as with chains of super-markets today], then started selling the goods at half their normal price and also proceeded to provide the highest wages and best conditions for their employees. Very soon other shops far and wide would be forced into cutting their prices to prevent the transfer of their customers to state shops. Their buildings would then fall into disrepair and they would lose the best shop assistants to the state shops.
>
> (ibid., p. 200)

The crucial point, then, is that any historian of the future, 'looking at the forlorn state of twentieth-century private shops', would *not* 'be justified in concluding that, with such bad quality service, the state was fully justified in subsequently entering the whole field of retailing as soon as was possible in order to make "proper retail provision" for the people' (ibid.).

The Quality of Schooling and the Economic Arguments for State Intervention

West is skeptical about criticisms of low-quality private education in England and Wales, and the ways in which they are used to support state intervention. He suggests that the accusation of low-quality teaching may simply have reflected the prejudices of the rote-trained 'state' teachers and inspectors. Accusations of low-quality buildings may have been based on 'extravagant' notions of what was possible, and in any case may have replaced cozy comfort with austerity. And criticisms of parental indifference and complacency – leading to the need for state intervention for compulsory attendance – may have ignored the economic realities, and the likelihood that as parents increased in wealth, they would have forgone the opportunity costs of sending their children to school.

We can link these considerations again of educational quality back to West's discussion of the economic arguments for state intervention in education. It does not seem that the arguments here have added much to the justified level of state intervention of the earlier section. Without the state, it is certainly possible that the quality of educational provision might have been adequate, particularly as the wealth of the people increased. At most, the discussion here reinforces the notion that the maximum justified level of state intervention in education, in order to satisfy the economic principles explored in the previous chapter, would be some regulation of the curriculum – to ensure education for democracy and social cohesion – together with some small subsidies for those too poor to access schooling. The discussion of educational quality in the nineteenth century does not undermine these central propositions. Certainly, the level of state intervention in education that we take for granted today would not be justified by this discussion.

However, there is one common criticism from historians which suggests that West has missed an important point of comparison here. Whatever might be said about the success of the English system without state intervention, once this is put into a *relative* context the superiority of state intervention in education soon becomes apparent. For instance, the educational historian Professor Andy Green states that West 'has attempted to rehabilitate the reputation of English educational *laissez-faire*, arguing that reformers ... exaggerated English deficiencies. However, comparative data, which West largely ignores, vindicates the deficiency verdict, *at least in terms of the relative position of English education*' (Green, 1990, p. 11; emphasis added). That is, Green suggests that the main argument against the English system is that it was failing to achieve the same levels of enrollment and literacy as the heavily interventionist European states. However, when he actually gets around to reviewing this evidence, it transpires that even according to him, England's relative position in the mid-nineteenth century was *better than France's* as regards the percentage of the population receiving schooling (ibid., p. 15), and with regard to adult literacy (ibid., p. 25). Green does not dispute that there was a widespread 'national network' of schools in Victorian England and Wales without the state (ibid., p. 8), nor does he dispute that this was more effective than the centralized French state educational system. It does not seem that his challenge to West is as substantial as he suggests. Other historians concur: Stephens notes that in the period 1850–90, 'the proportion of literate persons in England' was higher than in France, although lower than in Germany (Stephens, 1987, p. 16).

However, one of the key points for comparison often given is England's neighbor, Scotland, which is reported to have had a much more advanced system of education than did England, and this superior system is said to have been *the result of state intervention*. Thus, Kiesling castigates West: 'The Scottish educational system, with well-paid schoolmasters in parish schools funded by taxes on large landowners was quite different from the situation in England and Wales' (Kiesling, 1983, p. 425). G.M. Trevelyan, in *British History in the Nineteenth Century* (1922), argued that education in England 'lagged far behind [that in] Scotland' (p. 355). Does Scotland offer a counter to West on the benefits or otherwise of state intervention in education? The Scottish evidence is also interesting to examine because, as we saw in Chapter 1, the Scottish system was the model that Adam Smith endorsed as being the best way forward for state intervention in education. What is the evidence of how it fared?

It is true that the Scottish state became involved much earlier than that in England in legislating about education. The earliest and most important legislation was the Act of Settling of Schools of 1696, which set out that a school should be established in every parish, and that teachers' salaries were to be met by local taxes. Education was neither compulsory nor free, as the taxes raised were certainly not enough to cover the full costs of schooling. Instead, public funding was largely for the capital costs of buildings, and some small stipends for

Table 3.2 Schools in Scotland, from the 1818 Digest

	Pupils	Schools
Parochial schools	54,161 (34%)	942
Private (unendowed, unaided) schools	106,627 (66%)	2,222
Total	160,788	3,164

Source: West ([1975a] 2001a, p. 87).

teachers. The main part of teachers' salaries was made up by school fees, which were charged to the vast majority of parents. However, the very poorest of families were given free tuition, subsidized by the Kirk. Nothing much further had been added from 1696 until 1803, when some further legislation increased teacher salaries and introduced new regulations.

How did this system fare during the early nineteenth century? Some useful evidence is found in the 'Digest of the Parochial Returns made to the Select Committee, appointed to enquire into the Education of the Poor' in 1818, the '1818 Digest'. The figures given in Table 3.2 exclude Sunday schools, dame schools, and schools for the wealthy. These figures show that by 1818 the population 'explosion' of the late eighteenth century was far too great to be catered for by the system of parochial schools. Instead, the majority of schoolchildren were being catered for by a boom in 'non-legislated' private schools. The earlier legislation had typically provided one school in each parish. But it was reported by the 1760s that class sizes were reaching 50 or 60 children. One response was to reduce the number of years of schooling. But population growth in the new industrial regions continued to explode. In the absence of any publicly provided schools, the private schools took up the strain.

The authorities were suspicious of these private schools, partly because they feared they took children away from the public schools and partly because they were concerned about teacher incompetence or lack of doctrinal orthodoxy. But although they reserved the right to close down any schools they did not approve of, this did not curb the massive growth of the private sector. Indeed, several of these private 'adventure' schools, as they were dubbed, had as alumni Scots of great distinction, such as Robert Burns, educated at 'John Murdoch's adventure school in Alloway, opened in 1765' (West, 2001a, p. 86).

One authority who was unhappy about this private school explosion was Dr Thomas Chalmers, who wrote his *Considerations on the System of Parochial Schools in Scotland, and on the Advantage of establishing them in Large Towns* in 1819, and whose report was to receive favorable attention in the United States (see Chapter 4). He noted the 'deficient quality' of the growing private schools in the rapidly growing new industrial cities. He wrote:

> These stations, too, whither children repair for their education, are continually shifting; and the teachers often being unconnected by any ties of residence or local vicinity with the parents, there is positively, in spite of the sacredness of their mutual trust, as little of the feeling of any moral relationship between them, as there is between an ordinary shopkeeper and his customers.
>
> (quoted in West, [1975] 2001a, pp. 86–7)

But, of course, *celebration* of the relationship between 'the ordinary shopkeeper and his customers' had a long vintage in Scotland, with Adam Smith proclaiming its virtues in *The Wealth of Nations*, published in 1776. He also there referred to his faith in the parochial schools, particularly the payment of fees within them, 'for the very reason that it insured some respect by the supplier for the consumer' (quoted ibid., p. 87).

One important question is: how well did the parochial (i.e. publicly supported) schools serve the rural poor? In 1822, a society at Inverness was opened to educate the 'poor in the Highlands'. Its report, *Moral Statistics of the Highlands and Islands of Scotland: compiled from Returns received by the Inverness Society for the Education of the Poor in the Highlands*, was published in 1826. It found that one-third of the population was more than 2 miles, and many thousands more than 5 miles, from the nearest public school. Half the population was unable to read, while in the remotest parts, the Hebrides and western parts of Inverness and Ross, 70 percent could not read. The population of the Highlands at the time was 416,000, of whom 52,000 were school-aged. Of these, only 8,550 (16 percent) scholars were in school. The parochial schools legislation had not been particularly successful, the report concluded.

In the rural Lowlands, however, the picture was more optimistic, although not because of the publicly supported system. The *Statistical Account* of the 1790s showed that there was one school in every Lowland parish. However, given the average population of 250 school-aged children, the system was considerably supplemented by private and charity schools. Moreover, the private ('adventure') schools outnumbered the parochial schools, as Table 3.2 shows, and, as almost every child could read and write, evidently they were serving the poor, with fees paid for by parents.

> Considering that 'almost everyone' could read and write in the rural Lowlands, and since on the average there were two adventure school pupils for every parochial pupil in Scotland, the private (adventure) schools must have been remarkably efficient. What is even more arresting is that they contained the children of the working class and that these families were paying fees that typically covered the full cost of the schooling.
>
> (West, [1975] 2001a, p. 90)

Just as in England and Wales, these 'adventure' schools were usually described (and criticized) as 'containing less well-qualified teachers and having lower educational standards than the parish schools' (ibid.). But West again is wary of taking these criticisms at face value, just as he was for England and Wales. 'Better qualified' meant having the ability to teach Latin and other classical languages, and greater competence in teaching religious doctrine. But parents – even those in the parochial schools – were protesting that too much time was being spent on these (the '4th R') rather than the 3Rs, which were seen to have much more commercial relevance. Indeed, parents from Adam Smith's old school in Kirkcaldy were to rebel against the extended syllabus, complaining that children were being short-changed 'by not having been teached writing' (quoted in Fay, 1956, p. 51). The school was thus forced to revise its syllabus to deflect this rebellion, offering an à la carte menu of 'fees per quarter', including: English by itself (1s 6d); English writing and vulgar arithmetic with one hour's writing daily (2s 0d); Latin by itself (3s 0d); Latin with writing and arithmetic (3s 6d); decimal arithmetic, mensuration, trigonometry and algebra (3s 0d), and church music (gratis). As West noted, such a menu 'reveals native shrewdness and discrimination among the Scottish clientele' (ibid., p. 88). Moreover, he reminds us that Robert Lowe was to remark, *approvingly*, 'In Scotland they sell education like a grocer sells figs' (quoted ibid.).

What of comparisons with England – often made to England's detriment? Even in legislative terms, the comparisons made are misplaced. The parochial system was neither free nor compulsory. Compulsion did not come until 1872 in Scotland. In England it was in 1881. Free schooling was established in 1891 in both countries. And in terms of the total population receiving schooling? In 1818, it was estimated to be 1 in 12 in Scotland, while in England it was 1 in 14. One similarity is clear: 'the majority of Scottish schools, as in England, were unendowed and unsubsidized private establishments at which fees were being paid by large sections of the poor' (ibid., p. 98). For West, the principal 'achievement' of the much-favored Scottish system 'was to supply educational subsidies to the benefit of about one-third of the total school population' – that is, the minority who were in the parochial schools. 'Even this favoured section still had to contribute a significant part of the educational costs through school fees' (ibid., pp. 96–7).

Chapter 4

Why Did State Education Emerge?

West's quest has been to explore whether or not the kind of state intervention in education with which we are familiar today, with universal compulsion, funding and provision of schooling, can be justified. I outlined his exploration of the economic justifications for state intervention in education in Chapter 2, showing how West found them lacking in substance, or at least in need of much further empirical support before they could justify the kind of state intervention in education that we take for granted today. At most they justified some rather minimal state intervention in education, not the wholesale intervention to which we are accustomed. West then went on to look at the history of education in the nineteenth century, the history of education 'without the state', to see whether there could be further empirical justifications for state intervention. We explored his evidence in Chapter 3, suggesting that it did not appear to strengthen the justifications for state intervention in education that actually occurred in the nineteenth century. Perhaps some regulations may have been justified (particularly taking into account some curriculum requirements for education for democracy and social cohesion), but again, nothing like the kind of state intervention in education that actually occurred seems to be justified by this historical excursion. Even evidence from Scotland – supposed to offer an alternative, celebrated route to state intervention – shows that it appears to have offered nothing of the sort: for it appeared to be the private schools, rather than the (public) parochial schools, that were catering for the educational needs of the growing population.

A key question that emerges from West's historical discussion, however, is not addressed in *Education and the State*: why did the state system that we see today in England and Wales, say, emerge from the relatively inauspicious beginnings put forward by Forster in 1870? For *W.E. Forster himself* only proposed *rather minor interventions* in education in order to fulfill the goal of universal provision. True, he did introduce a new kind of school, the board school, and a new set of institutions, the school boards, to manage these, and in West's view these were an unnecessary intrusion. But the school boards had rather limited powers in the beginning – basically to make sure that there were no pockets of educational inadequacy, either by encouraging voluntary provision to fill in the gaps, or, if all else failed, by introducing board schools to do the job. There was no compulsory schooling or education, other regulations were not extensive, and parental fees still made up a large proportion of the education budget in the board schools as well the largest proportion in private provision. So what, as West would put it, *went wrong*? Why did the universal system of state schooling emerge out of these small beginnings? Clearly, an answer to this question has profound implications for the kinds of policy proposals that West might put forward – as we shall see in the next chapter.

There are some hints of answers to these questions in *Education and the State*, but nothing more. For instance, there are West's observations of the way those in educational organizations can act apparently in *self-interest* to preserve or extend their reach. In a section entitled 'Education inbreeding', for instance, he notes the interaction of the 'organised teaching profession' with politicians, leading to recommendations for huge expansion of the public sector. He also offers some simple explanations as to why this might be the case: When 'a government requires advice on education,' he writes, 'it resorts first and foremost to "those in education"' (West, 1994a, p. 112), which of course it takes to mean those in the formal public sector – which misses out all of those involved in education in the broad sense in which West prefers to use the term, as well as those in the private sector too. But these groups are too 'untidy' and 'heterogeneous', and 'do not lend themselves so conveniently to such direct political representation' (ibid., p. 113). The government wants counsel on whether the expansion of higher education is required, asks advice from those in the formal state education sector, and, not surprisingly, is told of the need for a massive increase in public expenditure, 'without too much attention to ... the external opportunity-costs of alternative types of education forgone' (ibid.).

West does not take this kind of analysis much further in *Education and the State*. But, as was noted in Chapter 1, West was introduced to the new theory of public choice, or the economics of bureaucracy, and his reading of this was to influence his later work. This theory was to play a large role in clarifying West's thought on why and how the expansion of state intervention occurred, out of Forster's relatively minor reforms in England and Wales in the late nineteenth century. In this chapter, we explore four of West's applications of this theory, looking at the growth of state education in New York, England and Wales and New South Wales, Australia.

Public Choice Theory and Its Relevance for West

As was noted in Chapter 1, the distinguishing approach of public choice theory is to apply the same economic approach to politics as economists apply to the actions of consumers and producers in the market. Under the economic approach in general, West notes, a key assumption is that

> new legislation cannot abolish the problem of scarcity; all it can do is to rearrange our institutions that seek to resolve it. Neither can new legislation liquidate the social conflict that accompanies scarcity; all it can do is to change its pattern according to the prevailing circumstances of political power. Generally, most economists, by nature of their trade, have for a long time espoused this non-romantic attitude to lawmaking and lawmakers.
>
> (West, 1994a, p. 295)

That is the basic economic approach, applied to politics in general too. But, curiously, when economists turn to education, West notes, a 'different attitude seems to predominate'. Here,

> there seems to be general agreement that legislation can do, and has done, much more than merely reallocate. A widespread belief seems to prevail that in this case the effect of legislation has been

much more than marginal; that without it very few educational resources would exist; and that, in consequence, society would be engulfed in crime, ignorance, and economic catastrophe.

(ibid.)

West notes the curiosity that economists 'seem to have been much less demanding in terms of evidence when faced with popular histories of the evolution of the public school system' than they are with other 'historical claims', say about 'the special achievements of . . . agricultural or labour legislation'. In particular, West notes that

> views seem to be especially inflexible about the *particular pattern of legislation* that happens to have evolved. For instance, although there are possible alternatives to a nationalized school system, alternatives that might redistribute income and protect the poor more effectively, there is a widespread reluctance to discuss their relative merits.
>
> (ibid., pp. 295–6; emphasis added)

Indeed, West argues that economists often seem prepared to justify 'parts of our inherited educational legislation by arguing that originally they must have been built upon the basis of "scientific" propositions in welfare economics' (ibid., p. 296). He gives the example of compulsory education laws. These, he notes, 'are sometimes considered to have arisen as the logical outcome of the recognition of external benefits in education' (ibid.). But this kind of view

> betrays excessive rationalisation . . . In other fields, economists are quick to recognise that we do not have an 'ideal' political process and that instead of problems being resolved according to 'optimal welfare criteria', they are usually settled crudely according to the distribution of political power.
>
> (ibid.)

And the key issue for West, now bringing in the assumptions of public choice theory to education legislation, is as follows: 'Since it is typically assumed that self-interest motivates representative politicians no less than others, it is clear that normally it must be only by coincidence that political decisions will truly reflect the economist's "ideal" welfare prescriptions.' (ibid.). So has such a coincidence occurred in educational legislation? In his first exploration of applications of public choice theory, he looks at the case of American schooling, and whether the rationalist explanation of the genesis of 'three particular features of it' – its 'universal, free, and compulsory' nature (ibid.) – satisfactorily explains what emerges, or whether another perspective might give a more adequate explanation.

What are the principles of public choice theory that West uses? The key point is to challenge the common perception that politicians operate out of concern for the public good, rather than out of self-interest. Economists generally work with the profit maximization hypothesis, 'based on the assumption that the strongest or most common motive is self-interest' (West, 1968a, p. 15). Public choice theory applies this assumption to politics too, 'to the actions of voters, governments, public agencies, so-called non-profit making organisations, and to all aspects of political and public activity in general' (ibid.). That is, the profit maximization hypothesis is 'extended to apply to those in the political process also', where profit is translated into things like power, prestige 'or mere political survival' (ibid.).

In other words, public choice theory explicitly treats 'political and economic man as one and the same. Man is now assumed to be an egoistic, rational, utility maximizer in both settings' (West, 1992a, p. 595). One implication is that 'it is no longer adequate for economists to assume that progress consists simply in persuading some government to accept their analysis and implement appropriate advice', for 'benevolent government' cannot under this analysis be thought to exist: The political machinery is seen, in fact, largely as operated by interest groups, vote-maximizing politicians and self-seeking bureaucracies. Moreover, the theory implies that economists cannot simply assume that 'by exposing market imperfections' they therefore have shown the need for government intervention. For they have to take into account that 'government failure', under the theory of public choice, can also exist. (ibid.).

In particular, public choice theory leads to predictions about the behavior of government bureaucracies. The theory is

based on the hypothesis that members of any government bureaucracy behave so as to maximise, and continually expand, its budget.
This is due partly to the fact that the heads of bureaus cannot keep
the profits that accrue from efficient operation and thus have not
incentive to operate efficiently. Also the size of personal salaries
are [*sic*] geared to the degree of 'responsibility' and this in turn is
related to the quantity of resources supervised. Steady expansion of
the budget therefore is the most conducive to promotion and salary
advance.

(West, 1975b, p. 63)

West suggests several corollaries to the profit maximization hypothesis: First, since it is postulated 'that every government seeks to maximise political support, it follows that in order to do this it has to
be constantly informed about the wishes of the majority of voters'.
Second,

in the real world, the existence of uncertainty creates barriers to
communication. On the one hand, it is costly for government to
keep constantly in touch with voters; on the other hand, the electorate is not fully aware of all the issues. Such a situation is favourable
to the emergence of special interest groups claiming that they are
representative of the popular will. Propaganda put out by them will
serve to create real public opinion at the same time that it attempts
to persuade government of the existence of such opinion.

(West, [1967a] 1994a, p. 315)

Third, 'producing political influence is a particularly costly operation', so 'the costs will be assumed mainly by those who stand to gain
most from it' (ibid., p. 316). He gives as an example:

[T]he individuals who work in a service that is provided by government can afford to bring greater than average influence to bear
upon government policy since their incomes will be particularly
responsive to it. In contrast, the consumers, having interests that
are spread over many products and services, cannot so easily afford
to buy influence over the supply of only one of them.

(ibid.)

This point for West about the inequality that arises in the political system is very important:

> [T]he communication to parties or government of the opinions of individual members of the electorate is not costless and it is at all times surrounded with uncertainty. We should expect consequently that those parts of the electorate that can best afford the costs of political lobbying would receive above-average political attention. Since the suppliers of particular services have more to lose than consumers from insufficient representation (because their incomes are directly dependent upon the outcomes) we can expect the organised administrators, teachers and local authorities to use conspicuously elaborate organisation or political pressure to lobby parties and governments, to attempt to 'create' public opinion and to 'speak for it' when it is not itself sufficiently articulate.
>
> (West, 1968a, pp. 17–18)

Four points must be made to clarify the discussion here: First, while it is beyond the scope of this current volume to explore any of the criticisms of public choice theory in detail, briefly there appear to be two major set of criticisms of the approach. One is that the public choice approach is ideologically driven, dominated by those of a libertarian or classical liberal frame of mind:

> Ideologically, many of the theorists are accused of selecting for study only those shortcomings of government which suggest reducing it rather than improving it; or else they merely search government for instances of corruption or unproductive gain-seeking and generalize them as the nature of all democratic government.
>
> (Orchard and Stretton, 1997, p. 410; see also Devine, 2004)

However, while it is undoubtedly true that many of those who are attracted to public choice theory – including of course West – are of a particular philosophical or ideological persuasion (for example, in favor of minimal state intervention), this does not seem enough to damn the theory. For it is just as true that many attracted to other paradigms of research – for instance, those looking at 'market failure' – may also be of the opposite philosophical or ideological persuasion. The key issue is whether researchers – whether working under the assumptions of public choice theory or any other research paradigm – allow their emotional, political or ideological persuasions to sway the *conduct* of their research and the *presentation* of their research findings. In a popular textbook for educational researchers, for instance, Borg and Gall, cognizant of this danger, suggest that being 'emotionally involved' in one's research topic is undesirable: 'You should try to avoid working in such areas whenever possible' (1989, p. 179). This seems to be going too far, missing out on an important area of satisfaction, which is precisely in working on issues to which one *does* have emotional or political commitment. Nevertheless, the important point is raised that researchers should be aware that their emotional or political commitments can cloud their research judgments – and that this is nothing to be ashamed of; it merely means that measures should be used to try to minimize this effect. In brief, if researchers adhere to tenets of scientific research – articulating their assumptions, making predictions based on these, testing these against the evidence using proper statistical methods, and not being afraid to find and publicize evidence that goes against their assumptions – then this danger can indeed be minimized.

A second, more substantial criticism is about the assumptions themselves of public choice theory. Some even argue that it is 'immoral' to claim that those working in 'public service', in government or the civil service, should be driven by the same base motives of self-interest as those in business and markets. Voters, legislators and political agents, it is argued, *will* act in the public rather than in their own private interest (Lee, 1988; Devine, 2004). But prior to Adam Smith's discussion of self-interest in *The Wealth of Nations*, it was also assumed that merchants were in large part motivated by the public interest, rather than their own self-interest. Smith introduced a new way of examining the actions of traders by bringing in the assumption of self-interest, and, it is widely accepted, transformed our understanding of economics as a result. Public choice theory aims to do this in the area of the political arena, too. Buchanan believes that it would be an illusion to assume that those acting in the public interest become 'saints' once they are given collective choice roles (Brennan and Buchanan, 1988; see also Kelman, 1987). But, importantly, he also acknowledges that public choice theory is providing an economic model of behavior and does not totally dismiss the possibility that some taking on political roles may indeed act in a manner they believe is in the public interest. West himself takes up these issues. He notes that applying the self-interest maximization hypothesis to education is not meant 'to imply that educators are prompted by motives of self-interest in any greater degree than anybody else' ([1967a] 1994a, p. 316). Of course they might be prompted by other motives too, especially altruism and public service. But '[p]redictions that relate to actual human behaviour require an assumption not about which motives are highest, but which are strongest' (ibid.). And self-interest, in the assumption of public choice theory, is that strongest motivator. So, for instance, if the budget of the education bureau

> can be expected to expand faster with the gradual establishment of a *universal* system of public schooling that benefits the children of middle income parents as well as the poorest, this system will be 'pushed' . . . even if the poorest would do better in a smaller *selective* system wherein all the benefits went to them exclusively.
>
> (West, 1975b, p. 63)

The self-interest of those in the education bureau will in such a case override the interests of the poor.

Third, following on from this, it is not meant to imply that West sees the actions of those in the education bureau as involved in some kind of 'conspiracy theory'. It is not that he believes members of the education bureau deliberately contrive to produce outcomes that are less favorable, say, to the poor – just as it is not the case that operators in the market contrive to bring about the favorable outcomes for society that Adam Smith argued were the result of the working of the 'invisible hand'. On the contrary, in both cases we simply see the outcomes that the operation of self-interest brings, outcomes that are not necessarily intended in any way by the actors involved.

Fourth, the key point is that public choice theory uses the scientific method, in order to set out predictions that can be falsified or, alternatively, corroborated. In other words, as West puts it, 'the best way to attack a theory is not to question the "realism" of its assumptions but to use evidence to refute its predictions' (1968a, p. 15). Some critical commentators do go as far to say that public choice analysis has generated 'inaccurate predictions' (Orchard and Stretton, 1997, p. 423) and that 'research has also discredited the main branches of public choice micro-theory' (ibid., p. 424). But this seems to go beyond the evidence: public choice theory may be thriving precisely because it is generating testable hypotheses, many of which are being corroborated, although, of course, as would be expected with any scientific theory, some are not (see Mueller, 2003, for a comprehensive survey of the field).

But the scientific nature of the approach does bring in a genuine difficulty for West's use of the theory. West himself outlines several hypotheses that emerge from the theory, which he then examines in the light of historical episodes to see how they hold up. For instance, he suggests that public choice theory leads to the prediction that the education 'bureau' – that is, government department – will:

- 'engage in promotional activities favouring its own services';
- 'be increasingly jealous of rival bureaus and other competitors';
- 'sponsor analysis and statistics concerning the services for which it is responsible';
- 'form alliances with supply ... interests', and 'gradually to attempt to exclude all rivals by means other than normal competition.'

(West, 1975b, pp. 63–4)

This does lead to an obvious difficulty for West's method. For, of course, he already knew what happened historically, and so is positing these hypotheses after the event, and clearly informed by his reading of the historical evidence. This could appear rather contrived. It could also lead to the accusation of selective reading of the historical evidence in order to corroborate his hypotheses. It would have been much more satisfactory had West been able to put forward hypotheses and then genuinely explore whether or not they were falsified or corroborated by events as they happened, in real time. This brings us to a fundamental problem with all of West's evidence: he wants to use empirical evidence to explore the economic justifications for state intervention, and against markets, in education. But the only evidence available is historical, because in real time all the countries of which he was aware had near-monopoly state educational provision, and so genuine markets in education were not there to be studied. We shall return to this genuine difficulty with West's evidence base in the final chapter, where I point to present-day evidence, unknown to West, that would circumvent the problems he had interpreting historical evidence. In that chapter, I outline the existence of gen-uine, contemporary markets in education that can provide a firm evidence base for the exploration of the kind of economic questions that interested West, including hypotheses arising from public choice theory.

With these caveats, we now turn to explore how West used the assumptions of public choice theory to illuminate the rise of state education. The major purpose of this chapter is to give an exegesis of West's views on the subject, going along with his acceptance of the basic premises of public choice theory. It is hoped that this chapter will still be of interest to those who do not find these assumptions compelling, providing further reflections on the historical evidence for the emergence of state education. The key argument of West, whether or not one accepts the public choice theory dressing, is that the kind of state intervention that emerged, and which we take for granted today, was based neither on the economic justifications for state education nor even on explicit political statements of intent about what desired system should emerge. Rather, says West, the kind of system that emerged seemed to grow for other reasons, and so an alternative explanation is required.

Education in Nineteenth-Century New York State

Chronologically, West's first writing using the framework of public choice theory was an article on the history of education in New York State, 'The Political Economy of Public School Legislation' (West, 1967a), republished as the new Chapter 17 in the third edition of *Education and the State* (West, 1994a). (All references here are to the 1994 republication.) This important study informs the argument of this book in two ways. First, it shows how, in another historical and geographical context, (near) universal education seems to have been achieved *without* very much state intervention, and certainly not the kind of state schooling we take for granted in the United States today. So, the discussion here reinforces the arguments of West that we have already explored. But second, the questions of *why* and *how* the current system of *compulsory* and '*free*' universal state schooling developed can now be given tentative answers. West explores how the actions of vested interest groups around educational provision contrived to bring about the current system – even though its elements (particularly the compulsory and free aspects) were explicitly *not* part of the original plan, and even ran counter to it.

Throughout, it is clear that West is not saying that this is the only possible explanation of what happened. What he is showing is that the historical facts appear at least consistent with the kind of hypothesis that the economics of bureaucracy would suggest. As we move through this chapter, we explore other hypotheses that might also explain what occurred, and suggest that the economics of bureaucracy approach has considerable strengths.

After the 1776 Revolution, the legislature in New York State very soon attempted to become involved in education. First came the 1795 Act 'for the encouragement of schools'. This Act was operative for five years but was then discontinued. In 1804, a further Act was passed, providing for the interest of a fund from the sale of 500,000 acres of state land 'be appropriated as a permanent fund for the support of schools' (West, [1967a] 1994a, p. 297). The first distribution from this 'school fund', however, was not made until 1814.

In 1811, the state government authorized five commissioners to report on the feasibility of a system of 'common schools', and they duly reported in 1812, informing the draft of the bill that was to become the Act of that year. The report suggested that while public education might not be necessary for a monarchical government, like that of the United Kingdom, it was essential for a republic, because where government was of the people, the people had to be suitably enlightened. But if state aid for education were to be justified, it needed to be established in what ways people were not getting sufficient education for their children. Indeed, the commissioners noted, just as West observed for England and Wales in the early nineteenth century, that schooling was already widespread:

In a free government, where political equality is established, and where the road to preferment is open to all, there is a natural stimulus to education; and accordingly *we find it generally resorted to, unless some great local impediments* interfere.

(Randall, 1871, p. 18; quoted in West, 1994a, p. 298; West's emphasis)

One such impediment was poverty; another geography; in remote rural areas, schools were not being established, unlike in the cities. The commissioners pointed to how in the cities and heavily populated parts of the country, 'schools are generally established by individual exertion. In these cases, the means of education are facilitated, as the expenses of schools are divided among a great many.' However, in the remote rural areas, thinly populated, there 'education stands greatly in need of encouragement', for the simple reason that families were living too far apart from each other to make (private) schooling economically viable: 'Every family therefore, must either educate its own children, or the children must forgo the advantages of education' (ibid.).

So, the 1812 Act can be seen as having an intention similar to Forster's Act in England 58 years later, as a matter of 'filling up the gaps' in private educational provision. What is interesting for West – bearing in mind his comments about the way economists try to ratio-nalize educational legislation – is that simpler and more obvious routes to 'filling up the gaps' – namely, subsidizing poor families, or encouraging suppliers through subsidies to open up in neglected areas – were not addressed, either in the Commissioners' Report or in the 1812 Act. The commissioners went straight, without discussing these possible alternatives, for the solution of 'the establishment of Common Schools, under the direction and patronage of the State' (ibid., p. 299). Even more curiously, even though the commissioners explicitly pointed to the problem of the rural poor as a motivation for state intervention, there was *no special attention* paid to them in the intervention plan. Rather than targeted subsidies to the rural poor, 'a flat equality of treatment was decreed for *all* areas' (ibid., p. 300). Public monies were to be distributed on a per-capita basis according to how many children aged 5 to 15 were in that district, to every one of the new 'school districts', whether it was a densely pop-ulated urban district – where, to repeat, the commissioners had found no problem of lack of schooling – or to a sparsely populated rural one. Each town or district could also raise as much again through a local tax. This raising of additional funding was made compulsory for each district in an 1814 amending Act, as the new superintendent had found that many towns had not levied this tax, and so assumed negligence on their part.

West notes two key points of interest in this Act for his analysis. First, there was no intention within it of providing *free* schooling. Yes, there were subsidies, but, as the commissioners of 1812 reported, 'it is hardly to be imagined the Legislature intended that the State should support the whole expense of so great an establishment'. No, the intention was far more modest:

> The object of the Legislature, as understood by the Commissioners, was to rouse the public attention to the important subject of educa-tion and by adopting a system of Common Schools in the expense of which the State would largely participate, to bring instruction within the reach and means of the humblest citizen.
>
> (Randall, 1871, p. 21; quoted in West, 1994a, p. 301)

Far from education being free at the point of delivery, parents were required to supplement the government subsidies by paying rate bills (fees) 'in proportion to the attendance of their children'. And these parental fees made up a 'substantial' part of the total schooling costs. In 1830, for instance, the fees contributed by parents made up 59 percent of the total required for teachers' wages ($346,807 out of the total sum of $586,520).

Second, neither was there any intention to make schooling *compul-sory*. But without its being free or compulsory, an official report of 1821 noted that schooling had become more or less universal: it was assessed that the total number of children in New York State between the ages of 5 and 16 was 380,000; and the total number of all ages in school was 342,479 – that is, 90 percent of the total. But, bearing in mind the discussion in the previous chapter concerning Foster's parallel estimates, children were likely to have been in school for less than 11 years, hence the claim of more or less universality.

There are few data about private schools at the time. But the Superintendent's Report of 1830 featured a census of the city of New York for 1829, which showed that 18,945 of 24,952 schoolchildren (76 percent) were attending private schools. But in the state as a whole, the superintendent of common schools estimated that there were only 43,000 scholars in private schools, compared to 512,000 in the common schools (that is, only 8 percent of the total enrollment in the private schools). West notes that, as in England, many private schools had opted to become common schools in order to receive the state subsidies.

By 1836, the New York superintendent reported that 'the number of children actually receiving instruction is equal to the whole number between five and sixteen years of age', with children provided for in the common schools and private schools (1836 *Annual Report of the New York Superintendent for Common Schools*, p. 8; quoted in West, 1994a, p. 304). That is, by this time there was universal schooling of the 5- to 16-year age group without this schooling being free (although it was subsidized) and without compulsion – a fact which, says West, 'seems to have been readily acknowledged' (ibid.). Importantly, throughout the 1830s the superintendents argued for the preservation of significant parental fees, because this kept their involvement and energies focused on the schools. For instance, in his 1831 report the New York superintendent was adamant that the case for the sharing of expense between the parents and 'the public' was 'unanswerable' (1831 *Annual Report of the New York Superintendent for Common Schools*, p. 17; quoted ibid., p. 305), and preferable to either full parental fees or total government subsidies. In his report, the superintendent pointed to the case made by Dr Chalmers in the *Edinburgh Review* supporting this 'unanswerable' case. For West, this provides 'an interesting connection with the views of the British classical economists', noting that Chalmers' approval of the Scottish system of partial state subsidies and an important contribution through parental fees had also been the system favored by Adam Smith (West, 1994a, p. 306). The pressing requirement now in New York was to improve the quality of schooling, since universal schooling had been more or less successfully achieved.

However, this approach, curiously, changed in the 1840s with the advent of the Free School Campaign. Official pronouncements now turned against the idea of rate bills (parental fees), 'which were now declared a serious enemy of the system'. West notes that the opposition came mainly from teachers and government officials, who stressed both the 'administrative difficulties of collection' and the 'discouraging effects upon poor families' (ibid.). West agrees that there was a rather cumbersome administrative machinery set up to collect the rate bills (fees), whereby teachers had to wait for up to 30, or in some cases 60, days for their pay after the term had finished, while the funds were collected from parents, some of whom did not pay up straight away, with the matter referred to the trustees and then the district collector. But why then was the remedy proposed not a reform of this cumbersome administrative machinery, 'a reform that was obviously feasible', but the introduction of a 'Free School System'? (ibid., p. 307). This is the crucial puzzle that West tries to explain, using insights from public choice theory.

The Free School Campaign apparently originated in the teachers' organizations, known as teachers' institutes. In 1844, the Onondaga County Teachers' Institute presented a committee report on the subject, which gave three reasons why schools should be free: First, every child has a right to intellectual and moral education: 'it is the duty of government to provide the means of such education to *every* child under its jurisdiction'. This, recall, was argued even though the superintendent had reported that there *was* (more or less) universal schooling provided without its being free. Second, the provision of free schooling would reduce crime: 'It will be found universally true that the *minimum* of crime exists where the *maximum* of moral education is found.' Nowhere did the committee explain what was meant by 'moral education', nor did it mention that moral education might well be successfully provided outside of state schooling, for instance through the Church; nor did it provide evidence for the proposition that education reduces crime, which we have seen in an earlier chapter to be a difficult thesis to defend. Finally, the Free School System would overcome 'the impediment of poverty', so enabling the development of 'the latent talents of the lower classes' (ibid., quoting Randall, 1871, pp. 215–16).

Why did the institute argue for the first and third propositions when there was reported to be (more or less) universal provision without free schools? One possible reason was given in 1845 by the county superintendent of Genesee. He too presented a report in favor of free schools, suggesting that although on paper the system was supposed to cater for all, in fact there were some poor parents who were *too proud* to accept the total relief of payment of the rate bills allowed under the 1812 Act. The suggestion was that 6 percent of children in the common school population of 742,000 were thus being deprived of schooling because their parents refused to take up their free places (West, 1994a, fn. 19, p. 308). If this were the case, then the crucial point is that it was *for the sake of this small minority*, the 6 percent, that free schooling was argued to be required. This, says West, is rather odd as a purportedly rational explanation for what happened next – which is why he is interested in exploring an alternative explanation of what occurred, based on the hypothesis of the maximization of self-interest of those in the producer groups.

The oddity is strengthened – and the suggestion that something more is prompting the moves than simply rational explanation of the benefits of free schooling – when one examines Horace Mann's contribution to the New York Free School Campaign. Horace Mann is widely acknowledged to be *the* champion of American public education. In 1846, as secretary of the Massachusetts Board of Education, he gave a lively presentation to the State Convention of Superintendents setting out the case for free education. Even here, Mann did appear to acknowledge that government needed to intervene in education only when parents were not able to provide for their children. He wrote that parents had an 'all-mastering instinct' that made them willingly take on the need to educate their children; it was only when this failed, if parents 'are removed, or parental ability fails', that 'society, at that point, is bound to step in and fill the parents' place' (quoted in West, 1994a, p. 311). However, the logic of this position was *not* what Mann actually put forward, namely free education for all. Proposing that education should be free for *all* parents was not a way of solving the problem of, as West put it, 'what to do with the *minority* of families that was neglecting to educate its children' (ibid.), for whatever reasons they were doing this.

So what were Mann's arguments for free schooling? They can be seen as an early enunciation of the argument concerning 'externalities', or the 'neighborhood effects' of education. He argued that '[t]he individual no longer exists as an individual merely, but as a citizen among citizens', and that '[s]ociety must be preserved; and in order to preserve it, we must look not only to what one family needs, but to what the *whole community* needs; not merely to what one generation needs, but to the wants of a succession of generations' (Randall, 1871, n. 1, p. 221; quoted in West, 1994a, p. 308). But what was surely incumbent on him to show was that existing educational provision was deficient in general, not just for a small minority of families. However, not only did Mann not attempt to do this, but his evidence for the existence of these supposed externalities of education (as we shall see) was weak and suspect.

So, what other explanations are possible? Here West brings in his discussion of the economics of bureaucracy, and the possibility that it was the self-interested behavior of teachers and administrators, who were key figures in the struggle for free schooling, that led to the proposed changes. West notes that the teachers and administrators had developed their 'own organised platforms' by the late 1840s, and they were 'the leading instigators' in the free school campaign. 'Whilst conventional history portrays them as distinguished champions in the cause of children's welfare and benevolent participants in a political struggle, it is suggested here that the facts are equally consistent with the hypothesis of self-interested behaviour' (1994a, pp. 317–18).

For instance, in support of this hypothesis, West notes that the sole piece of evidence that Horace Mann gave for the need for free schooling, in an early rendition of the theme that education 'was a good public investment because by reducing crime and disorder it reduced public police expenditure and increased output', was from a small survey he himself had conducted of teachers. In his *Annual Report of the Secretary of the Massachusetts Board of Education* 1848 (pp. 48–9; quoted in West, 1994a, pp. 310–11), he noted that he had selected teachers 'from the sobriety of their judgement and from their freedom from any motive to overstate facts'. He asked these teachers 'how much of improvement, in the upright conduct and good morals of the community, might we reasonably hope and expect?', if all the common schools 'be kept by teachers of high intellect and moral qualifications', with all children in these schools for ten months a year, from the ages of 4 to 16? He continued, 'what percentage, of such children as you have had under your care, could in your opinion, be so educated and trained, that their existence, or going out into the world, would be a benefit and not a detriment, an honor and not a shame to society?' (from *Annual Report of the Secretary of the Massachusetts Board of Education* 1848; quoted West 1994a, p. 310).

These teacher respondents replied that such a policy would lead to between 99 and 100 percent success. Mann, it should be noted, also added the proviso that to attract such teachers of 'highest talent and morality' there would have to be substantial increases in their wages. And this was, argues West, surely a key point. Horace Mann, although typically referring to the teaching profession 'as a noble and religious calling', was very much aware of 'the strongest of economic motives' among teachers (ibid., p. 316). For instance, he noted in his 1846 report that although 'We want a profession which understands the laws of the intellectual and spiritual nature of man', this is impossible 'while the salaries and the social consideration bestowed upon teachers, furnish so little inducement to enter the profession', given that 'avenues to greater honour and emolument, constantly opening around, are seducing its members into more brilliant or more lucrative walks of life' (ibid., p. 317). Note that this move from teachers as promoters of the intellectual and spiritual good of man to teachers being seduced by more lucrative options is all contained in the same paragraph of the report! Moreover, Mann noted, some teachers, looking 'for more liberal remuneration ... abandon the service of the public, and open private schools' (ibid.), or that

> [w]hile we pay so inadequate a salary at home, many of our best educated young women go south and south-west, where they readily obtain $400, $500 or $600 a year ... Others of our best educated young women become assistants in academies, or open private schools on their own account.
>
> (ibid.)

So, West points out that it is not going any further than Horace Mann himself is prepared to go in suggesting that teachers 'will promptly be energetic in the political arena if it so happens that the political process suddenly provides one of the easiest routes to economic gain' (ibid.).

Now, even by the mid-nineteenth century, parents 'were already considerably tied to the Common Schools', because much of the finance for them came from compulsory taxation levied on the parents themselves (ibid., p. 318). However, while there were still fees being paid, this allowed parents to make choices, and there are contemporaneous references to parents moving their children from the common schools to the fully private ones. This led to uncertainty within the system, as the fees charged for the common schools were dependent on how many children were in a particular school. There was also the 'problem', as we have seen, of some common school teachers moving away from the state system. So, says West, exploring what might have happened from the perspective of public choice theory, self-interest may have led the common school employees and organizers to campaign for 100 percent subsidies – that is, a free school system – 'in order that the last traces of customer discretion be removed. Teachers in private schools stood to lose wherever the contest was transferred to the political arena since they were in a minority in the profession as a whole' (ibid., p. 321). And the public school teachers were being increasingly supported by the administrative personnel who were emerging, who themselves had a 'direct interest in the expansion of the public-school sector' (ibid.). The self-interest hypothesis suggests that the impetus must be to create a monopoly, thus stopping other competitors from benefiting. The evidence, says West, suggests that this is precisely what happened next.

Indeed, competition from the private schools was apparent in the data collected by the state superintendents: Between 1832 and 1847, enrollment in private schools in New York State increased from 43,000 to 75,000, while that in the common schools increased from 512,000 to 776,000 (ibid.). So, during that period the private school share of enrollment increased from 8.40 percent to 9.66 percent; in other words, the private schools were taking a greater share of the increase in numbers of customers. Something similar was happening in other states, and, very importantly, it was in the

context of competition from the private schools that 'the very strenuous efforts of Horace Mann' (ibid.) reported earlier were made.
Mann made no effort to conceal this impetus: in his report to the
Massachusetts Board of Education of 1849, reviewing what had happened since 1837, he wrote:

> Facts incontrovertibly show, that, for a series of years previous to
> 1837, the [common] school system of Massachusetts had been run-
> ning down. Schoolhouses had been growing old, while new ones
> were rarely erected ... To crown the whole, and to aggravate the
> deterioration which it proved to exist, the private school system was
> rapidly absorbing the funds, patronizing the talent, and withdraw-
> ing the sympathy, *which belonged to* the Public Schools.
>
> (Twelfth *Annual Report of the Secretary of the Massachusetts
> Board of Education*, 1849, pp. 17–19; quoted in West 1994a,
> p. 322; my emphasis added)

Importantly, Mann reported on 'the general indifference of the public' to these changes, suggesting that this decline in the public schools
may well have reflected parental preference for private schools.

The New York State Free School Campaign almost achieved its
goals in 1849, when the state legislature passed an Act establishing
free schools, abolishing the rate bills (fees) and directing the local
districts to substitute funds previously from the rate bills with funds
from direct taxation. But this new legislation, 'far from facilitating the
supply of schooling, actually reduced it' (ibid., p. 312). The problem
was that the new law compelled schools to be open for a minimum of
four months; but many school districts, especially those that were too
poor, were unable to provide revenue through taxation that enabled
schools to be open for *any longer* than four months. However, parents
had been used to schools being open for up to eight months under
the old regime. The law was abandoned in 1851 after 'a torrent of
petitions from all parts of the State demanding a repeal of the Act'
(ibid.).

It is worth noting that by 1849 the fees (rate bills) 'provided the
largest single source of revenue for most rural school districts' (ibid.,
p. 313) – that is, 29 percent of the total expenditure on schools

($508,725 out of $1,766,668), with the remainder being made up of federal funds, town and county taxes, and the school district tax. There was no evidence to show that the majority of families objected to paying fees, and the hostility to the 1849 Act shows the widespread objection to the abolition of fees. The teaching organizations, however, said that because 'the electorate voted for the 1849 Act with a firm majority', this showed that 'society' demanded the change away from fees (ibid.). West says that 'it is clear, from people's immediate hostility to the practical operation of the Act, that the political spokesmen had not presented them with all the issues' (ibid.).

By the 1860s, the rate bills (fees) had become operable only in the rural areas – but West notes that as the annual revenue from rate bills increased (from $400,000 in 1860–1 to over $700,000 in 1876), so too did the private school population increase; excluding Kings County and New York City, for which figures from earlier years are not available, the official statistics show an increase in private school enrollment from 48,541 in 1863 to 68,105 in 1867. The Free School Campaign won what it was campaigning for in 1867: rate bills (fees) were finally abolished by the Free Schools Act of 1867; this coincided with a decline in private school enrollment, down to 49,691 in 1871.

In the general discussion of public choice theory at the beginning of this chapter, we noted that one corollary of the 'profit maximization' hypothesis for West was that the organized suppliers of public education – the public school teacher associations and administrators – would 'attempt to "create" public opinion and to "speak for it" when it is not itself sufficiently articulate' (West, 1968a, pp. 17–18). West notes that this seems to be precisely what was happening in nineteenth-century America, as the 'special pressure groups' attempted to mold public opinion 'at the same time as they are trying to persuade the government that such opinion exists'. There was '[i]ncreasingly hostile propaganda put out by the protagonists for free Common Schools' against private schools, coupled with 'an attempt to shift the popular image of the public school system' (West, 1994a, p. 324).

West reminds us that the original legislation of 1795 and 1812 had as explicit motives the *encouragement of* education 'in order that the members of the republic become responsible voters, prosperous individuals, and property-respecting, God-fearing persons' (ibid.). There was no suggestion of 'abolishing, hindering, or taking over existing private schools', for such policies would appear to directly conflict with the aim of encouraging education: 'The expressed desire was simply to aid those who were too poor to provide education voluntarily' (ibid.). By the 1840s, however, new ways of justifying public schools against their private competitors began to emerge. The teacher unions 'urged the demise of the private schools and the establishment of free schools on the grounds that the State and the will of the people demanded it' (ibid., p. 325). The Onondaga County Teachers' Institute, which had kick-started the whole process towards free schools as a vehicle to assist *the poor*, now claimed that free schools were especially beneficial and necessary *for the rich*: such children, it was claimed, 'do not generally form those habits of energy or perseverance – steady, unwearied, continuous labor – without which no man can attain eminence' (quoted ibid.). Educated in free schools, however, the children of the rich would realize 'that they are just such beings as the children of the pauper, and that if they would attain greatness they must work with untiring energy and perseverance' (quoted ibid., p. 326, from Randall, 1871, n. 1, pp. 216–17). Or it was argued that private schools were 'unpatriotic' (quoted in West, 1994a, fn. 50, p. 326), or that they were creating 'a distinction in society that ought not to exist in a community of free men, who profess to believe in, and attempt to sustain the principles of republican liberty' (quoted ibid., p. 326). Each of these propositions could of course have been true, and genuinely held opinions of those agitating for free public education; West is not denying this possibility, but pointing to the alternative hypothesis that the system that emerged was also compatible with the self-interest maximization of those in the education producer groups.

Once the Free School Campaign had been won and fees abolished, by 1873 the New York state superintendent was arguing in fact for the complete abolition of support to any private schools, noting that this is what the teacher associations were arguing for:

If all the schools of every grade that the State to any extent supports were associated in one homogenous system, and the appropriations of the State were confined to that system as heretofore recommended by this Department, and *as repeatedly urged by the State Teachers' Association*, there would be no ground for conflict.

(Nineteenth *Annual Report of the New York Superintendent of Public Instruction*, 1873, p. 39; quoted in West, 1994a, p. 327)

There was no sense that competition might be beneficial, for instance by 'spurring most schools into adopting the methods of the best', and reducing inefficiency. Competition between public schools was also seen as an untidy nuisance. In 1850, the superintendent protested against the untidy system of allocating the proceeds of public taxes to a variety of charitable bodies, incorporated societies as well as the municipal schools, which gave parents a variety of choices. But he protested:

> Scholars or parents being thus privileged to select any school they please, it is not strange that some go two miles to school; and that large [school] houses, which will conveniently accommodate one thousand scholars ... have, some of them, but four hundred, and some of them sixteen hundred.
>
> (1851 *Annual Report of the New York Superintendent of Common Schools*, p. 120; quoted in West 1994a, p. 328)

To overcome this problem, the state superintendent repeatedly proposed a very important solution, something that, as we saw in Chapter 2, has since become the mainstay of every public education system – namely, the solution of 'districting' (what we would today call 'zoning'), whereby children were allocated places at their neighborhood school. This system was indeed eventually adopted. The public choice explanation is that this system of zoning overcomes many of the problems of competition for the education bureau, and so is the preferred option. For instance, the state superintendent noted that zoning could not be accomplished 'so long as there are rival organisations of schools, overlaying one another, and each in competition for the same scholars' (ibid.). In his 1849 report, the superintendent was adamant that such preferences of parents were not well founded, that they moved children 'from one side of the city to another, to attend a crowded School, passing half a dozen Schools just as good as the one they had chosen to attend' (1849 report,

p. 125; quoted in West, 1994a, p. 328). Quite why they would expend such effort needlessly is not clear. But in his 1850 annual report, the superintendent at least admits that such movement might be based on perceived differences by parents at least of the neighborhoods in which the schools were located, if not real differences in the schools themselves. West says that the strategy of the administrators

> was to try to focus public attention on what they called the 'inequity' of having schools with superior advantages outside their province (the private schools) while at the same time themselves allowing what were to ordinary people gross differences of quality within their own public system.
>
> (West, 1994a, p. 329)

Here West points to an early version of the 'middle class appropriation of welfare' thesis: through creating zoned schools,

> [a]lthough presenting themselves as champions of the needy, the supporters and leaders of the Common School system do not seem to have given any serious attention to the possibility that the expansion and evolution of it might thus serve to worsen, not improve, the chances of poor children. As subsequent experience has shown, where all pay taxes for the support of such a system, it often transpires that it is the poor who subsidise the middle class. Being more politically active, the latter are more able to obtain and to perpetuate bigger revenues and superior provision for the districts serving their own children.
>
> (ibid.)

The Free Schools Act passed in 1867 led to a decline in private school enrollment, as we have noted. This was reported with satisfaction in the 1871 *Annual Report of the New York Superintendent of Public Instruction*: 'Private schools, always exerting, to a greater or lesser extent, a deleterious influence on the public schools, do not flourish under the operation of the free school system. Most of the academies are unable to compete with free schools' (1871 report, p. 210; quoted in West, 1994a, p. 330).

The year 1867 marked a watershed on the road to state monopoly. Free school places were now provided, funded by compulsory taxation. But there was one remaining route for customer discretion: parents could still withdraw their children from school altogether. In areas where public education was deemed to be inferior, and 'where the new public monopoly removed any hopes of quick improvement', it is likely that 'some parents would want to exercise their remaining freedom by removing their children from school at an earlier age than in those areas where better-quality teaching existed' (West, 1994a, p. 331). But doing this would impact on the public school teachers, given that 'public money was distributed to schools and their staffs in proportion to the numbers in attendance' (ibid.). What would the economic theory of politics predict about the behavior of the public school suppliers under such circumstances? West says that one could predict that the public school teachers would campaign to make schooling *compulsory*, to close the loophole of the remaining parental discretion concerning schooling. This is, says West, precisely what did happen next: 'Serious agitation for compulsory attendance built up very soon after the success of the free school campaign of 1867' (ibid.). He quotes the superintendent of the city of Newburgh in 1870, who blamed the 'laxity and indifference of the parents' for the 'irregular attendance of a large number of enrolled pupils' (quoted ibid.). And the goalposts in the arguments now shifted. Before 1876, it was argued by the teacher associations and administrators that the reason for lack of attendance by some children was that their parents could not afford the rate bills (fees). After 1867, when fees had been abolished but poor attendance still persisted, 'the new contention was that parental indifference was the main trouble' (ibid., p. 332).

However, West notes, there was one major dissenting voice, that of the superintendent of New York himself: in his annual report of 1871, he suggested that it was only very rarely that parents neglected the educational needs of their children, and that for this minority of parents there was already existing legislation, in the Act of 1853, that allowed for *selective* compulsion for such parents. Moreover, the superintendent continued,

It is palpable that the prominent defect, which calls for speedy reformation, is not incomplete attendance, *but poor teaching* ... I speak of the needed improvement in the particular mentioned, in comparison with compulsion, as a means of securing attendance; and I contend that, before sending out ministers of the law to force children to school, we should place genuine teachers in the school-room to attract them ... let the schools be made what they should be in themselves, and it is more than probable that there will be no occasion to send for pupils.

(Seventeenth *Annual Report of the New York Superintendent of Public Instruction*, 1871, pp. 66–7; quoted in West, 1994a, pp. 333–4)

It is an extraordinary revelation for West that the superintendent himself is suggesting that his new near-monopolistic schools were featuring bad teaching, and that *this* was the problem that led to pupil 'truancy'.

The suggestions of the New York superintendent notwithstanding, the teacher associations successfully agitated, and the Compulsory Education Act was passed in 1874. But compulsory schooling too was ineffective at meeting the hard cores of truant cases. By 1890, the superintendent was asking for more powers: 'It is worse than futile to assume that all parents charged with the care of children will send them to school. The great majority will. But unfortunately some parents are idlers, drunkards or criminals themselves' (Thirty-sixth *Annual Report of the New York Superintendent of Public Instruction*, 1890, p. 35; quoted in West, 1994a, p. 335).

In other words, the laws constructed during the nineteenth century did not in fact achieve universal schooling in the sense of 100 percent school attendance. And it is not clear, says West, that the system which was being replaced, one that the government authorities themselves agreed was providing for almost everybody, without any element of compulsion and without the provision of free schooling, was thus any worse. So much for further insights into the provision of the neighborhood effects of schooling, and the economic arguments for justification of the current system.

But West's examination of the history of nineteenth-century New York has also enabled us to see how the system that arose *may* have owed more to the self-interested actions of vested interest groups than to the need for the system to provide universal education for all, particularly for the poorest. The moral of this story, for West, is that economists 'should question how far *their* acceptance of particular instruments of public intervention springs from logical demonstration' of the need for the state, or how far it arises from 'the successful salesmanship of those already employed in government undertakings' (1994a, p. 337).

Erroneous Calculations?

Our second look at West's examination of historical episodes in the light of his reading of public choice theory concerns examples of how the education 'bureau' would, through self-interested behavior, do as much as possible to run down the competition, even going so far as to use, in West's terms, 'erroneous calculations' – what might today be termed giving a false 'spin' on the data.

West gives a couple of examples of this. The first is from nineteenth-century England and Wales, while the second is from New South Wales, Australia. Both show for West how the educational reformers, 'although professing to herald a new social-science approach to legislation', in fact were led to use 'statistical reasoning that, to another and later century, looks to have all the marks of expedient propaganda' (1992a, p. 617). West notes that it is 'consistent' with public choice theory

> that bureaucrats would have a self-interest in presenting the prevailing quantity of schooling in as bad a light as possible. This strategy would strengthen the case for further intervention which would increase both the budget and the importance of the bureau.
>
> (ibid., p. 608)

In at least the first of West's examples, however, we can see an alternative explanation of what the educational reformers were striving for, which suggests that the arguments might not be as clear-cut against them as West implies.

Expedient Propaganda in England and Wales?

The key players in bringing about state education in England and Wales, says West, were Edwin Chadwick and James Kay (later Kay-Shuttleworth). The former was secretary to the Poor Law Commission after 1834, while the latter was assistant commissioner. Chadwick delegated Kay to explore the education and training of pauper children; his enthusiasm and interest for this work led to Kay's appointment as the first secretary of the committee of the Privy Council on Education in 1839, the body that was in effect the first Department of Education in England and Wales.

Now if a department is to extend its influence, it has to demonstrate evidence of the need for what it offers. For the Council on Education, this was originally to provide subsidies for education. The main evidence offered was 'new statistical calculations of "educational destitution"' (West, 1992a, p. 603). Here lie the key 'erroneous calculations', says West, used to influence policy. Kay was also the founder and treasurer of the Manchester Statistical Society (MSS). In this role, Dr Kay was invited as a chief witness to the 1838 Select Committee enquiring into the state of education in England and Wales. An important exchange between Kay and William Gladstone, chairman of the Select Committee and later to be prime minister when Forster introduced his 1870 Education Act, illustrates, according to West, how the statistical data of the MSS were manipulated to further the ends of the education bureau – in effect, implies West, dishonestly. (The quotations from the interchange between Gladstone and Kay are from the UK Sessional Papers 1837–8, paragraphs 100–13; quoted in West, 1992a, pp. 604–6.)

Mr Gladstone first asked Dr Kay the direct question 'Can you form an estimate of the *amount* of deficiency in the means of education in any given district, say, for instance, the district of Manchester?' (quoted in West 1992a, p. 604; my emphasis). Kay, says West, switched this from a question about *quantity* of provision to a question about *quality*, which was, says West, not being asked. Kay replied:

If by education I am to understand what I have previously described, sound religious instruction, correct moral training, and a sufficient extent of secular knowledge suited to their station in life, I should scarcely say that it exists within the limits of my observation.

(quoted in West 1992a, p. 604)

Gladstone prompted, 'You think it is not afforded by any schools at present efficiently?' Kay responded, 'Not efficiently.'

West interprets Kay here as giving a bureaucrat's answer in order to deflect the discussion away from the quantity of schooling – about which, as we saw in the previous chapter, the Manchester Statistical Society was actually rather upbeat – to one about quality of provision, which would reveal the need for state intervention, and hence the expansion of Kay's education bureau. West argues that Kay was an 'enthusiast for large-scale economies in schooling', with 'an almost doctrinaire dislike of small schools, which were usually the entirely self-supporting establishments called common day schools' (ibid.). The large monitorial Lancastrian and national (charity) schools were Kay's favorites during this period. So, argues West, he was very much out to show that the small schools were of low quality and hence in need of replacement. Gladstone 'seems to have been the only member of the Committee to have clearly perceived that Kay was confusing questions of quality with those of quantity' (ibid.). But a more charitable interpretation of Kay's answer would be to accept that he genuinely did believe that education, as he defined it, was not being provided in the vast majority of existing schools. In that case, of course, there was nothing disingenuous in conflating issues of quality and quantity. Kay could admit that there were many *schools* in existence, as the Manchester Statistical Society had found. But he did not have to agree that they were providing *education*, and so could be safely ignored.

West then examines Kay's introduction of the 'erroneous calculations':

Gladstone: 'Separating from your view at present all those considerations which appear to attach *rather to the quality than to the quantity of education*, and looking simply to the question of quantity, can you form an idea of what number of children there are in the town and neighbourhood of Manchester, upon any given population, *that are entirely without education of any kind, however defective?*'

Kay: 'The Report of the Committee of the Manchester Statistical Society states that one-third of the children between 5–15 are not receiving instruction of any kind whatever; and the report also proceeds to state, that the education given in the common day schools and dame schools, and certain other schools appears to be either altogether inefficient or very indifferent.'

In fact, the first part of Kay's answer is not exactly what the Manchester Statistical Society had found. In a footnote, the committee was at pains to spell out that it had 'not drawn the inference which various commentators have attributed to them, that this proportion of the youthful population continued *permanently destitute of schooling* ... The Committee possesses no data for stating what number of children have never enjoyed the advantage of attending school' (quoted from the report, p. 18, in West, 1992a, p. 605). In other words, the Manchester Statistical Society's data reported what was happening at one time, and were not meant to imply that the young people currently not in school had never been in school. But this is what Kay appears to imply to the Select Committee.

The discussion continued, exploring the crucial point of the school-aged population being between the ages of 5 and 15:

Gladstone: 'In reference to the first part of your answer, do you imagine that they have arrived at that statement by calculating the number of children between 5 and 15 in the population, and then ascertaining the number of children who attend schools, of any kind, and given the difference as the amount of deficiency which exists?'

Kay: 'Certainly.'

Gladstone: 'Do you imagine that the average number of children who attend schools in Manchester continue in attendance for anything like the period of 10 years?'

Kay: 'In the Sunday Schools the great mass of the children continue pretty regularly in attendance; and I have personal experience of the quality of instruction conveyed in the Sunday schools of Manchester

which, as far as religious instruction is concerned, may be stated to
be the best instruction which exists of this nature.'

Gladstone: 'But do you think that the generality of the children who
go to school at all in Manchester continue at school, week-day or
Sunday, for anything like so long a period of 10 years?'

Kay: 'I think the great portion of the Sunday scholars do.'

Gladstone: 'Do you think that any considerable proportion of the day
scholars continue at school for 10 years?'

Kay: 'I do not think that any very considerable proportion of day
scholars do.'

Gladstone: 'Then will not the calculation be inaccurate if it has been
upon the supposition, that those who are at school continue at
school from the age of 5 to the age of 15?'

Kay: 'Certainly; it can only refer to the number who were at school at
the period when the calculations were made.'

This is the key issue for West – the basis of his allegations of the
'erroneous calculations'. For Kay has introduced the notion that
the school-age population is from 5 to 15 – that is, a period of ten
years. West argues that this was a totally unrealistic assessment of what
was possible. To answer Gladstone's question properly, says West, we
would need data on the *de facto* school entering and leaving stages.
Such information appeared a year after Kay's evidence. Concerning
Pendleton, Manchester's neighbor, 'a typical town of the Industrial
Revolution' (West, 1992a, p. 606), evidence emerged in the *Report of
a Committee of the Manchester Statistical Society, on the State of Education
in the Township of Pendleton* of March 1838 (published 1839). Here it
was reported, on the basis of careful enquiries, 'that not more than 2
to 3 percent . . . of the juvenile population are at present left entirely
destitute of instruction'; of the school-goers, 'one-third appear to
remain less than three years; one-third from three to five years; and
one-third remain above five years' (p. 74, quoted in West, 1992a,
p. 606). If Pendleton was anything like Manchester, then Kay's answer
to Gladstone, says West, was a 'gross overestimate' (ibid.) of the
educational 'deficiency' of the voluntary system. In other words,
says West, it must be disingenuous to argue that children not in
school for that whole ten-year period in 1834 pointed to serious

deficiencies within the current system – an argument deliberately contrived to show the current system in the worst possible light in order to strengthen the argument for state intervention.

However, a more charitable interpretation of Kay's argument is possible. Perhaps he and other reformers really did believe, for whatever reason (and Kay gave one possible reason – that ten years of Sunday schooling seems to be beneficial), that ten years of schooling was necessary for a young person's development, and so the current system genuinely was deficient when measured against this standard. One can see what West is trying to argue: that using this inflated period of schooling *would* show, unfairly as it were, the current private system to be deficient. But one can also see what West appears to ignore, that the educational reformers might genuinely have believed that the existing number of years in school was not enough, and that improvements, through the state, were necessary to correct this. And of course it is only with the luxury of hindsight that West is able to point to the practical difficulties that emerged in creating a ten-year schooling period: he points out that the Newcastle Commission *some 20 years later* found that children were in school for an average of only around six years; moreover, the compulsory school leaving age was not raised to 15 until 1944, over a century after Kay was giving evidence. But in fairness to Kay, had he known the difficulties he might have been dismayed by this lack of progress towards ten-year schooling, but nevertheless this would not have stopped him advocating it as an ideal to be striven for.

West argues that it was Kay's evidence that swayed the 1838 committee and led to the increasing activity of the government education bureau. Such statistical sleights of hand continued, says West. Most famous, and with perhaps most effect, was W.E. Forster's 1870 bill and the calculations that we have already discussed in the previous chapter. Forster put forward a school age period of 5–13, and on the basis of his inspectors' calculations showed that a quarter of children of this school age were not in school. As we noted, had a more realistic school age period been taken into account, Forster could have pointed to more or less universal provision, and hence there would have been no pressing need for his proposed intervention. But again, we could also now be more charitable towards Forster: if he genuinely believed that a longer period in school was desirable, then his use of statistics could possibly be vindicated. Without a more detailed examination of the motives and intentions of those engaged in seeking to extend the number of years in schooling, we have to return a not-proven verdict: West may be right in saying that his 'erroneous calculations' did serve the interests of the education bureaucracy; but he may be wrong in believing that the statistics were put forward disingenuously.

Australian Spin?

A similar example of 'erroneous calculations' occurred in New South Wales, says West. Now a standard historical interpretation of what happened in the Australian colonies was that the ministerial departments responsible to Parliament had allowed private interests, particularly the churches as well as proprietors, to provide education. But then, reluctantly as it were, the state had to intervene because this voluntary coverage was not wide enough. West proposes an alternative explanation, based on the self-interest of those wishing to expand the educational bureaucracy. He does seem to be on stronger ground in his criticisms of the way statistics were used in the argument here, for they appear to have been used without the nuance shown by Kay in England.

Robert Lowe was the main actor here, and later was to introduce the Revised Code in England when education secretary. He went to Sydney in 1840 to set up a law practice and was appointed to the legislature in New South Wales in 1842. In Lowe's report, the use of the same kind of calculation to show things in the worst possible light is again apparent to West – both in using an inappropriately optimistic school leaving age and, more importantly, in suggesting that those not found currently in school were *never* in school. Lowe's 1844 report read:

> There are about 25,676 children between the ages of four and fourteen years; of these, only 7,642 receive instructions in public schools, and 4,865 in private ones, leaving about 13,000 children who as far as your Committee know, are receiving *no education at all*.
>
> (Griffiths, 1957, pp. 73–4; quoted in West, 1992a, p. 610; emphasis added)

But again, says West, the first problem is in the school leaving age assumption. Few children would have had ten years (ages 4 to 14) of schooling. If the 1851 British Census is a useful point of comparison, then five years of schooling would be a more suitable period to use. But if this figure is used, it is likely that the number receiving no schooling at all *would be virtually zero*. And again, those children who were above the *de facto* schooling age would have been likely to be in school between the ages of 4 and 10, meaning that the admittedly ambiguous phrase used by Lowe (does 'are receiving no education at all' mean only *at this instant in time*, or does he mean to imply, as West assumes, that they have *never* received any education?) was likely to be misleading.

However, this conclusion of 13,000 totally unschooled children was 'relentlessly' pushed by Lowe 'as evidence of the educational failure' of the voluntary system. A few weeks after the presentation of his 1844 report, Lowe related to a special meeting on education:

> Gentlemen, there are thirteen thousand children in this colony growing up without a knowledge of the God who made them, or of the Saviour who died for them. We come forward with a proposition to arrest this evil, to check this plague, to substitute light for darkness, religion for atheism, and we are met by . . . overstrained objections.
>
> (Griffiths, 1957, p. 76; quoted in West, 1992a, p. 610)

Such rhetoric had a big impact on policy in the colony. Further contributions along similar lines were made by William Wilkins, the inspector and superintendent in Sydney, who had been a 'star pupil' of the Battersea teacher training college set up by James Kay in London, and who had introduced the pupil-teacher system to Sydney. In 1854, Wilkins was appointed one of three commissioners to investigate elementary schools and became, says West, their 'dominant spokesman' (ibid., p. 611). The commission's final report was published in December 1855. It too proclaimed the same type of reasoning: It complained that only half of the approximately 50,000 children 'of an age to be in school' – that is, aged 5–14 – were in fact in school. But if the children were in school for five

years, then again it is likely that *all* would have been in school, and
there would have been no evidence, says West, of the need for state
intervention.

The Public Schools Act for New South Wales was introduced
by Henry Parkes, a journalist and politician who had befriended
Wilkins. 'All possible evidence was mustered to show the weakness
of the denominational system, and the earlier arguments of Lowe
and Wilkins were rehearsed to good effect' (ibid., p. 612). The Public Schools Act created a Council of Education, with Parkes as the
chairman and Wilkins the secretary. 'This new government regime
discriminated promptly and severely against denominational establishments' – that is, the church schools, which were in competition
with the public schools. Restrictions were placed on church schools
that were close to public institutions. The capital and maintenance
costs for public schools were met out of compulsory taxation, whereas
for the church schools these all had to be met out of voluntary funds.
The impact on the church schools occurred rapidly: enrollment in
them fell from 55 percent of all pupils in 1867 to 38 percent by
1872.

Again, says West, an 'erroneous calculation was a main cause, if
not the key influence, in the passing of the educational legislation'
(ibid.), at least coupled with Parke's rhetoric. Once more, West seems
to be on stronger ground here, for Parke in his proclamations does
seem to go beyond what the evidence shows. Here is a key extract
from one of his speeches: 'The children under 14 years of age in the
country at the latest date to which our statistics come was 150,845 ...
Of this number there were attending schools 53,452, leaving the enormous number of 97,393 *with no education whatever*' (Griffiths, 1957,
p. 117). The words italicized more strongly imply that these children had never received education, rather than that they were not
in school at that precise time. But some of these children under age
14 were also of course under age 5, so *too young* for schooling at
all. Assuming an equal distribution of children each year, then omit-
ting these children we arrive at 92,828 aged 5 to 13, a span of nine
years. If we assume an average *de facto* school life of around five years,
then the number of those 'with no education whatever' would have
been zero – as older children currently out of school would have

very likely had schooling when they were younger. We need more precise statistics to know what the actual position was. But we can suggest that Parke's claim that nearly 100,000 had no education whatever 'is totally invalid'. But this 'erroneous statistic nevertheless was paraded at every opportunity' (West, 1992a, p. 613). Here are some examples:

> I think then I have made out a case for interference. If we are here with a population little over 400,000, and if one-quarter of the whole are children in a state of educational destitution, with no provision at all for their instruction, I think it will be admitted that I have unanswerably made out a case for interference ... No higher duty can engage the ability of Parliament than supplying these hundred thousand unhappy children with the means of instruction.
>				(Griffiths, 1957, p. 117; quoted in West, 1992a, p. 613)

And again:

> The voices of a hundred thousand children appeal to you and implore you not to allow any secondary consideration to impair your generous exercise of power in saving them from neglect and ignorance ... They will come after us in the field and in the workshop, in the school and in the church, in the judgment seat and within these walls – a mighty wave of intelligence that must receive its temper from you, but whose fire you will not be here to control.
>				(Griffiths, 1957, p. 120; quoted in West, 1992a, p. 613)

These quotations bring to mind how some development experts argue today for greater state and international agency intervention in education in developing countries. In the last section of the last chapter, we shall explore how these also may be based on parallel 'erroneous calculations' when we consider West's relevance for today. Most significantly, rather than rely on historical evidence to interpret what actually was going on, I shall point to contemporary evidence that could be used to more satisfactorily explore the relevance or otherwise of West's preferred public choice theory approach.

The Crowding Out of Private Schools in Nineteenth-Century England

The final application of public choice theory we shall consider is West's argument about the 'crowding out' of private schools in nineteenth-century England (West, 1975b). A key point here is that West is not concerned with exploring the *rights and wrongs* of the crowding out of private schools that took place. He notes that both Horace Mann of England and Horace Mann of Massachusetts were in favor of all children going to public schools, because of the require-ment for 'social cohesion' (ibid., p. 71), an economic justification for state intervention that we have already examined. So, West is not dismissing these 'higher-order' intentions from the key players and suggesting that only self-interest played a role. Instead, what he is interested in is a twofold enquiry: First, he asks, was the outcome of the crowding out of the private sector something that was planned for in the legislation? West says that it certainly was not. For in 1870, the *explicit intention* in Parliament was the opposite of what occurred, as W.E. Forster in presenting his bill repeatedly emphasized that 'we must take care not to destroy in building up – not to destroy the existing system in introducing a new one' (*Newcastle Report*, 1861, vol. 1, p. 95; quoted in West, 1975b, p. 72). Similar sentiments had been expressed in Parliament throughout the nineteenth century. If this were the intention, then why was the private system crowded out? West finds a plausible explanation in the economic theory of bureau-cracy: 'The actual events, it seems, were much more the consequence of discretionary *bureau* behaviour' than of the will of Parliament (ibid., p. 72).

Second, West seeks to ascertain whether the system that actually arose – including the crowding out of private schools – in the nine-teenth century was 'optimum' in the sense of leading to an increase in total expenditure on education. For if it did lead to such an increase, then this would lend support to the more usual explanation of what occurred as being explicable in terms of the 'higher motives' of those engaged in the educational bureau. They were concerned to increase total expenditure on education, and used their power to do so. On the other hand, if it did not lead to such an increase – and if it in fact led to a decrease – then West might be right in exploring the alternative explanation in the self-interest maximization hypothesis of public choice theory.

West goes back to the origins of the Education Department in England and Wales in 1833. He notes from the beginning an initial encroachment on private schools. First, there was partial 'takeover' of private schools. The Committee of Council encouraged private schools to receive public funds 'in exchange for their agreement to regulations and to inspections' (ibid., p. 66). Second, the Committee of Council produced official statistics showing the alleged educational 'deficiencies' after the 1840s, as we have seen. These, says West, 'were based on an unexplained target school population of one in six of the total population, a target that was not reached by any other country and was conceded to be impracticable' (ibid.). In *Education and the Industrial Revolution*, he adds that it has not been reached even today (2001a, p. 222). These allegations of deficiencies 'nevertheless prepared the ground for further public growth' (1975b, p. 66).

Third, the Committee of Council brought teachers into its ambit, and made their interests increasingly coincide with its own. In 1846, it introduced the pupil-teacher system into private schools, provided that they accepted public supervision.

> An elaborate scheme emerged outlining the role of the pupil-teacher, the examination he had to pass, the amount of instruction to be given by the principal teacher, and the stipends to be payable by the Committee of Council. Payments were . . . relatively attractive to all concerned.
>
> (ibid.)

Importantly, headteachers also had their incomes augmented 'by a special Departmental grant dependent on the examination success of the pupil-teacher' (ibid., p. 67). For West, the key point is that the 'interests of the school masters and managers were thus engaged quite effectively' (ibid.).

Fourth, West notes that the churches were being restricted in their own ability to 'fill in the gaps' in education – something that he says an '[e]ducation bureau that aspired eventually to monopolize education' would be keen to ensure. Many of the 'gaps' were being filled without anyone's assistance, in any case, says West, simply through the poor's increasing income. However, there were some educational deficiencies 'concentrated in the lower income families and in the poorer areas generally' (ibid.). But the churches were restricted in what they could do in these areas because it was made a condition for them to receive government building grants that 'an equivalent sum should be contributed by local proprietors or local voluntary help from persons living within four miles of the parish'. In the poorer parishes, such 'volunteer wealth' was usually lacking, hence the churches were unable to take advantage of these public grants. However, if the more prosperous churches tried to offer help, they were stopped by the Committee of Council, which said that 'they were not allowed to use any portion of the public grants to be transferred to poor neighbours' (ibid.). There were also strict building codes insisted upon by the Committee of Council in the 1840s, with 'precise regulations about the width of the rooms, ventilation and materials used. Later in the century new Departments found fault with earlier requirements and expensive changes were insisted upon' (ibid., fn. 13, p. 67).

Then came the 1870 Act, with, as we noted, its explicit intention, voiced in Parliament, of 'building up – not to destroy the existing system in introducing a new one' (*Newcastle Report*, 1861, vol. 1, p. 95; quoted in West, 1975b, p. 72). As we have noted, Forster used his 1870 legislation to set up a new type of school, the board school, supplied by school boards, to fill in the gaps in the voluntary system where necessary. But these board schools became the main way for the Department of Education to expand its domain of influence, argues West. He looks at the impact of these schools on two types of schools: the wholly independent private schools, which received no subsidy at all, and the subsidized denominational or church schools. We shall look at the latter as an example.

Those who ran subsidized private schools were promised by Forster that they would not be put at any financial disadvantage by his new board schools; but in fact they were. Initially, when Forster's bill was introduced, on 17 February 1870, the school boards were able to use the rate funds to assist the church schools, but this provision was soon dropped. School boards could fund the new board schools through new local rates (property taxes), but these were not allowed to be used for the church schools. To offset this disadvantage, church schools were to receive a central government grant, but this was worded in a rather loose form in the legislation. 'Gladstone, who first introduced [this compromise] on June 16, 1870, confidently announced that this matter did not need positive legislation but could be handled later by a Council Minute' (West, 1975b, p. 68). He was pressed by various people to make it a matter of legislation but consistently refused, saying that there was a gentleman's agreement from the British House of Commons, a 'gentlemanly' institution, that this additional central government grant would be up to a maximum of 50 percent of the earlier grant. This did in fact happen, but all the conditions that had to be met were also raised, so in effect it was impossible to achieve: Attendance requirement for students was increased by up to 50 percent, and the length of time at school specified. Most significantly, 'the grant for any *year could not exceed the annual school income derived from voluntary contributions, school fees, and any other sources other than the Parliamentary Grant*' (ibid., p. 69). But the poorer voluntary schools were not able to provide sufficient funds to enable them to reach the extra 50 percent.

> This situation not only led to severe hindrance to the continuation of church attempts to build new schools in the poorest 'gap' areas . . . there were now difficulties faced by existing voluntary schools when neighbouring board schools began to compete for students.
>
> (ibid., p. 70)

I have already outlined one example in the previous chapter of how existing church schools were finding it impossible to compete with the reported 'menace' of the board schools.

While Gladstone had promised a 50 percent increase in grant for the church schools to ensure equality with the new board schools, in fact the increased grant that schools were able to access was only about 25 percent. Political agitation from the churches eventually led to Lord Sandon's Act of 1876, which 'did something to remove the financial plight of the church schools' (ibid.). However, in 1878 the

Department did something that was to pose a huge obstacle to the non-board schools. It 'now took it upon itself to establish the rule that *where school boards existed*, they had the first right to supply the deficiencies of the gaps' (ibid.). But these gaps were a 'continuous phenomenon', given the growing population.

> Where the school boards accepted the responsibility to supply these growing needs after 1887, as they invariably did, additional private school accommodation was officially deemed unnecessary. New proposed voluntary establishments were now *completely* ineligible for any subsidy, and this by *administrative* (bureau) decree.
>
> (ibid., pp. 70–1)

Thus, the crowding out of the private schools happened, even though this was not given as any explicit intention of the legislation. But did it have a beneficial impact on total educational expenditure? For critics of West's approach could clearly claim that the interventions were in fact beneficial since they led to improvements that would not have been possible without them; most notably it might be assumed that the interventions led to an increase in overall expenditure on education, which would be a positive outcome. West examines the evidence and suggests that what actually may have occurred was the paradox that increased state funding of education actually led to a net *decline* in total expenditure on education.

West first gives an example of how this is theoretically possible, using the argument of Professor Sam Peltzman. The key to exploring how more government expenditure can lead to an overall decline in expenditure is to note how public aid was offered after 1870 (in comparison to how it was offered before). The method used was that of 'subsidy in kind': Here, those who want public aid have to accept a roughly homogeneous quantity of education from the government-provided institutions (the board schools). Say this is $£x$. But if a family wants a larger quantity of education, say $£x + 2$, then it has to 'forfeit the public aid altogether' (ibid., p. 73). However, rather than forfeit the 'free' public education, they might accept the $£x$ worth, even though they would have purchased $£x + 2$ if the government had not intervened.

This 'subsidy in kind', the method post-1870, can be contrasted with the 'money subsidies' that occurred in the period 1833–70. This earlier system allowed for direct government rebates, which allowed schools to lower their fees. This method, argues West, would lead to *higher* levels of total expenditure. Suppose that the socially desired level education in 1850 was one costing 4 pence. Government now offers a 'subsidy in kind' of a third of the price of education, with the aim of ensuring that all can get the socially desired level (a schooling costing 4 pence). First, those families that could afford to pay 6 pence would not then reduce their expenditure to 4 pence to take advantage of the subsidies. In fact, they would now be able to attend a school that previously had charged 9 pence, which would now cost only 6 pence after the government subsidy. Indeed, says West, the family could see that by changing to a school that now charged 8 pence, the family could benefit from a 1 shilling (pre-subsidy) school – that is, they could double their benefit by extra expenditure of only 2 pence. The important point is that 'in so acting, public aid is not forfeited, the family is more encouraged to increase its expenditure too' (ibid., p. 74).

West provides an economic abstract model to show the possibilities here, as in Table 4.1. He considers a ten-parent community. Two of the families are very poor, with an income of 100 shillings per annum, while six are of middle income (200 shillings per annum) and two are rich (with an income of 300 shillings per annum). The poor families are spending 10 shillings per annum on education before the government intervenes, while the middle-class families are spending 20 shillings and the rich families 30 shillings per annum. Under this total private system, the 'national' expenditure on education is 200 shillings.

However, a paradoxical situation emerges when government provides 'free' a schooling worth 12.5 shillings (and further, we assume that there are no excess costs in doing so). The two poorest families will obviously accept this; their 'educational consumption' increases, and so they will be better off. The middle-income families, however, will be in a quandary. If they persist with their 20-shilling private education, then they give up the right to have their 12.5-shilling education 'free', in which case 'a decision to forgo this "gift" is an opportunity

Table 4.1 The Peltzman effect on educational expenditure

Number of families	Income pre-family (shillings)	Value of each family's education purchased before intervention (shillings)	Total education expenditure before intervention (shillings)	Value of each family's education consumption after 'free' education provided worth 12.5 shillings	Total public expenditure after intervention	Total private expenditure after intervention
2	100	10	20	12.5	25	–
6	200	20	120	12.5	75	–
2	300	30	60	30	–	60
Totals			200 (all private)		160 (100 public, 60 private)	

Source: West (1975b, p. 75).

cost. It is conceivable that it will judge the continuation of the private schooling not worth such cost' (West, 1975b, p. 74). So, West makes the assumption that all six of these middle-class families will choose subsidized schooling instead. The two richest families, however, will have their intensity of preference for the more expensive private school maintained, and they will not consider the new opportunity cost of forgoing public education 'sufficiently high enough to transfer' (ibid.).

So, in this model, after government intervention the national expenditure on education *could fall* from 200 to 160 shillings. Some families – in this case, the majority – could move to a lower-valued education (from 20 to 12.5) *because of the subsidy*. Most importantly, after intervention the public funds are not actually targeted on the poorest families, which need them most. One hundred shillings worth of public funds is used, but only 25 percent of this is targeted to the poorest families! 'The remainder is going to the middle income families who do not need [it]; for they can be relied upon to purchase 20 shillings worth privately; and this is above the social minimum of 12.5 shillings' (ibid.). Very importantly, although the *national* expenditure on education is *falling*, the size of the *public* sector is *increasing* – and it is this that plays the 'dominant role in the economics of the "strong" bureau; the key maximand is the size of its budget, not national expenditure' (ibid., p. 76).

All this is theory. What of the facts? Do they support the possibility of actually lower national expenditure on education after the intervention of 1870? West focuses on evidence from 1882, a year 'sufficiently distant from 1870 to allow the new "subsidy in kind" system in England to have settled down' (ibid.). It is, moreover, two years after universal compulsion was established, and there are good figures available from the Annual Report of 1882. The details of West's argument are somewhat technical, but in brief it is as follows: West estimates total expenditure on primary education of about £10 million in 1882. The gross national income for England and Wales is about £940 million, hence his estimate of educational expenditure at about 1.06 percent of national income. He also estimates that in 1858, the percentage of national income spent on education would be about 1.10 percent, while in 1833 it would be 1.00 percent. In order to compare these

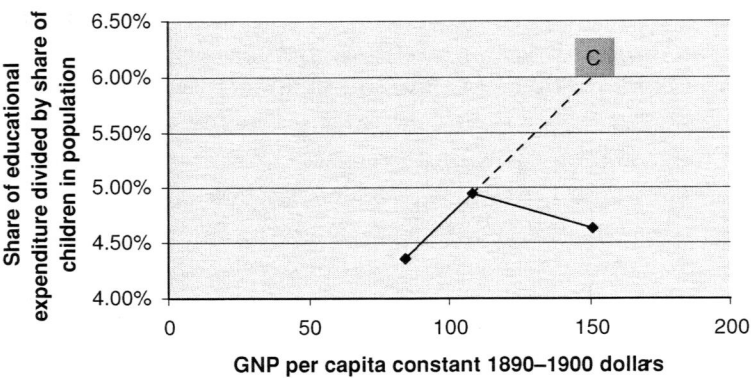

Figure 4.1   The Peltzman effect for expenditure in education

figures, West computed data that enabled him to construct Figure 4.1, which plots the share of educational expenditure in England and Wales divided by the proportion of children in the population (on the *y*-axis) against the GNP per capita (in constant 1890–1900 dollars).

This gives an upward- then downward-sloping line. Now, crucially, if we were to see no 'Peltzman effect' – that is, no effect of declining overall expenditure even though there is increasing public expenditure – we would see a fully straight line. So, we can posit a point C that would carry this as a straight line; in other words, for the GNP per capita at constant dollars of $151 (as in 1882), the share of educational expenditure divided by the share of children in the population should have been nearly 6.00 percent rather than the 4.63 percent actually found. But to reach this point C, West estimates that we would require a figure of £12.7 million total expenditure for 1882 – that is, £2.7 million more than was actually estimated, as above.

What this means is that the amount of educational expenditure that has been 'displaced', or 'crowded out', by the intervention of the state by 1882 is 27 percent of the actual expenditure on education. In other words, what West is suggesting is that the evidence from nineteenth-century England and Wales shows that the crowding out of private education that occurred led to a *decrease* in the total national expenditure on education compared to what might have been the case had the private schools not been crowded out by the actions of government – that is, if the method of intervention by government had not changed from the 'money subsidies' prior to 1870 to the 'subsidies in kind' that followed the 1870 Act.

But then we can return to our questions raised at the beginning of this section. What explanation can we give for this change of subsidy? It had the impact of crowding out private schools and, crucially, of reducing overall expenditure on education. It did, however, lead to an increase in government expenditure on education, and a dramatic increase in the power of the education bureau. Given all this, West suggests, the explanation offered by the economic theory of bureaucracy, that the changes occurred because of the self-interested actions of those in the education bureau, would seem to be strongly supported. Under this interpretation, it was not for the benefit of the masses, especially the poor, that the department of education expanded its brief. The changes arose instead as a result of the promotion of the self-interest of those officials and teachers under the state system. Its impact, whatever the higher-order intentions of those putting forward the changes, was detrimental, not beneficial, to the interests of the poor.

Chapter 5

A Framework for Policy

The Context: Economic and Historical Arguments

Having explored the economic justifications for state intervention in education and having searched for historical evidence to support and challenge them, in *Education and the State* West sets out an abstract model to show the limits of justified state intervention. In doing so, he creates a framework by which we can judge both the efficacy of extant state intervention in education, and possible reforms to it. Here I outline the model and point to some of the challenges it faces, particularly from the perspective of coherence with West's own critique of state intervention.

What are the justified limits of state intervention that are suggested by West's exploration of the economic arguments and his historical excursions? Concerning the protection of minors principle, West suggested that the major justified state intervention would be targeted at parents who were shown to be failing in their educational duties; his historical evidence suggested that this might be only a very small minority of parents. That is, this principle would lead at most to *selective compulsion*. However – and it is a major limitation of his discussion – West did not satisfactorily answer the question of what ignorance children needed protecting from, and so, as a possibility, a further area of state intervention could be *regulation of the curriculum (possibly through regulation of assessment)* in areas such as education for democracy and social cohesion. Importantly, state regulation of the curriculum would not imply that such a curriculum would need to be carried out in schools (let alone *state* schools); following John Stuart Mill, West would appear happy for compulsory examinations (if these were justified) to test for knowledge and skills acquired *anywhere*, such as through the home, television, radio or other media.

Concerning the neighborhood effects or externalities of education, similar considerations arise. As far as the reduction of crime is concerned, for West, universal state schooling was certainly not implied as a solution for this neighborhood effect, but again, selective compulsion might be required. Moreover, areas of the curriculum again might need to be regulated, perhaps to make sure that functional illiteracy was overcome (as this was linked to higher crime rates). Similarly, education for democracy, social cohesion and equality of opportunity would only require at most targeted compulsion and a regulated curriculum to ensure a minimal level of education for all. Education for economic growth did not appear to add anything to these justified requirements for state intervention.

West's 'Market Model' for Education

On the basis of these considerations, West sets out his 'educational model in political economy', henceforth dubbed his 'market model', by conducting a thought experiment, assuming that we are 'about to establish our state intervention policy for the very first time and under explicit conditions' (1994a, p. 247). West makes four explicit assumptions, together with the implicit simplifying assumption that *schooling* is the major educational vehicle in the society under consideration (we shall relax this assumption shortly). First, he assumes that state education has not yet been established in the country; second, that 'taxation is therefore correspondingly much lower', so families 'have more disposable income in their purses' (ibid., p. 248). Third, he assumes that only 5 percent of families (50 out of every 1,000) do not send their children to school, while the rest do – using figures approximating to those provided by the Newcastle Commission in England and Wales, as discussed previously. Fourth, he assumes that in this society, these 95 percent of families are sending their children to school for a minimum (not average) of eight years (ibid., p. 249). It is not clear why he assumes this, except that it fits in with what he says government will require for the minimum schooling requirement (see below). Presumably he is thinking in terms of a more advanced society than Victorian England, where, because of increased wealth, the 'galloping horses' of private provision had continued, and parents were using this to a larger extent than was actually found in late nineteenth-century England.

Given these assumptions, he asks us to imagine that

> a campaign has for a long time been organised by a pressure group, on which the teaching unions are well represented, in order to complain that because education is not yet universal ... and because some parents are sending their children to inferior schools, government intervention should immediately take place.
>
> (ibid., pp. 248–9)

This campaign succeeds, he says, in getting government to realize that it must intervene in education in some way. The state lays down the 'minimum education' in terms of *time* in school; that is, eight years' schooling – which is being met by 95 percent of the families already, by assumption. But 'the state is not satisfied about the quality of some existing schools', so it sets 'minimum standards' and policing (inspection) arrangements for all schools (ibid., p. 249). West does not outline what these minimum standards might be, although presumably they will incorporate the curriculum needed to provide the required externalities, such as education for democracy and social cohesion, that I have suggested above. It may also be the case, says West, that there is an information problem with parents not having sufficient information to judge the quality of the schools on offer. Here he says the solution is that 'the state can *temporarily* establish agencies to provide them with ... information both on the standards available and on the minimum standards that the state recommends' (ibid. emphasis added). We shall explore later what difficulties the italicized word might create.

West suggests that what will happen now is that, with parental free choice,

> pressure will be brought to bear on the least satisfactory schools so that they are constantly prodded into matching the services of competitors threatening to attract or already attracting their clientele. In these conditions there would be every reason to expect efficiency in schools to continue rising until they all exceeded and

made superfluous the minimum standards originally specified by the state.

(ibid., pp. 249–50; emphasis added)

West continues: 'Beyond laying down minimum standards and the establishment of an inspectorate', any further intervention (that is, justified state intervention) would need to be considered carefully as being in three distinct steps: first, 'the provision of legislated compulsion'; second, 'covering the costs of education by government' – that is, government finance; and third, 'the actual provision of education by government authorities' (ibid., p. 250). That is, he has distinguished regulation (preliminary and first step), finance (second step) and provision (third step). He notes that he agrees with 'Professors Milton Friedman, A.T. Peacock and Jack Wiseman' in their arguments, as we noted in Chapter 1, that have been supported throughout his work, 'that the third of these steps (state schooling) is not a necessary one'. However, he says he will 'go further than these writers in outlining qualifications upon the other two' (ibid.).

The key question we need to examine, he says, is what the circumstances are of the (assumed) 5 percent of families who are not sending their children to school. Some proportion of these, say 2 percent (of the total families), will be responsible, but too poor to pay for their children's schooling. For these families, the aim of government should be 'direct alleviation of the root of their problem and relieving their poverty' (ibid.). This could be done in many ways, including reducing taxation – that is, 'discovering to what extent the poverty is due to the existence of government itself' (ibid.). For it may be that poor families are paying more through (regressive) taxes than they benefit in terms of schooling. Reducing such regressive taxes may in itself be enough to allow these 2 percent of families to 'buy education for their children'.

But suppose that this didn't work, or that existing taxation was 'deemed to be equitable'. If so, then the state has a role to intervene 'by the provision of *direct money grants*' to ensure that they can do what they wish for their children. He suggests using the income tax system for this purpose, with *negative* income tax – that is, tax credits – given to the neediest (ibid., p. 251). He prefers such a negative income tax system, which delivers cash to the poor, rather than, say, a system of targeted education vouchers, because 'the basic administrative apparatus is already established and well tried' (ibid., p. 252). He also argues that it will overcome some of the problems of giving the authority over administration of education vouchers to an education department. This argument is of importance to the discussion here:

> [T]his method will be more efficient because the authority will be making disinterested judgements and it will discriminate on the basis of a less ambiguous set of rules which are based on the measures of money costs and money incomes. In contrast an Education Department in charge of subsidising or providing schools will always be tempted to be more and more generous in its ideas of the cost of a minimum education. And if its own notions are to be the chief criteria, it will constantly be subject to pressure by new candidates to revise the definition of poverty so as to let them qualify for subsidies or other aid.
>
> (ibid.)

This will lead, says West, to a cumulative process, as he has described historically, whereby the education *of all* will progressively be taken over by the state. We will query this approach below.

West then moves on to discuss those who are too poor but who would not provide educational opportunities of an adequate standard even if they had the funds. These families need funds *and* 'selective compulsion'. Here, West draws a parallel with the approach to the protection of children from physical neglect. In those cases, the state

> has means to see to it that no family is without the purchasing power necessary to feed and clothe a child to a certain standard. The total apparatus of protection is then strengthened by the provision whereby health visitors are allowed periodic access to children in their own homes. Such persons have the duty to report clear cases of parental neglect. They can appeal to Child Abuse Laws to instigate what amounts to legal compulsion of the parents.
>
> (ibid., p. 253)

Educationally irresponsible parents thus require additional regulation and funding – which could either be of the negative income
tax kind, or through vouchers to be redeemed in any school. Why
not universal compulsion? West suggests that there is no reason to
suppose that the latter would be more effective than the former. 'If
there were such an argument it is surprising that, in the case of health
protection, which is needed to prevent damage likely to have equally
serious consequences to children, we use the least efficient available
form of compulsion' (ibid., p. 254).

Finally, there will be those who are rich enough but who do not
have the desire to provide educational opportunities for their children. These families require selective compulsion (more regulation)
but no additional funds. 'To some economists, the addition of this
assumption about the possible existence of "rich" but negligent parents ... is so important as to swing the balance in favour of *universal* provision ... of state finance, that is, the provision of universal
vouchers' (ibid., p. 255). This, he says, is the argument of Peacock
and Wiseman, 'that the state, having made education compulsory,
cannot escape the obligation to provide all the necessary finance for
compulsory education' (ibid.). West points to Peacock and Wiseman's
argument from *Education for Democrats* (Peacock and Wiseman, 1964,
p. 28) that

> there is no operational way to distinguish the families upon whom
> financial assistance should be concentrated, if the criterion is the
> amount of education that would have been bought in the absence
> of compulsion. A means test, for example, would meet the need
> only if there were a high correlation between means and demand
> for education, and if this were so many of the problems of education
> policy would be much simpler.
>
> (quoted in West, 1994a, pp. 255–6)

But Peacock and Wiseman are at fault, he claims, for having accepted
that universal compulsion is preferable to the selective compulsion.
But West says that there

> is no more reason for announcing to *all* parents that education is to
> be formally compulsory and 'free' because of the possibility of a *few*

negligent parents, than for announcing that for the same reason
child feeding is to be formally compulsory and 'free' too.

(ibid., p. 256)

We accept that the way we protect children from malnutrition is
through selective compulsion and selective funding. Why not in education? 'To bring into existence the vast, costly and cumbrous machinery of state administered finance for the "benefit" of 1,000 families,
just because of the shortcomings of less than 50, would be inappro-
priate' (ibid., p. 257).

In short, West's 'market model' is that the following would be
enough to satisfy the economic arguments – both the protection of
minors principle and the arguments for neighborhood effects – for
state intervention in schooling:

1. Regulation: Through the Education Department, the state sets
   and regulates minimum standards of schooling and sets up an
   inspectorate to police these standards;
2. Funding: Through the Income Tax Department, liaising with the
   Education Department, the state provides funds to those families
   who are too poor to provide schooling for their children (after
   ensuring that inequitable taxation is removed); and
3. Regulation: Through the Education Department, the state selectively compels families to partake of schooling who otherwise, without compulsion, would not do so for their children.

If we drop our simplifying assumption about schooling, and write
about educational opportunities more generally, then West's market
model might look like this:

* Regulation: Through the Education Department, the state sets and
  regulates minimum education standards and sets up an inspectorate to police these standards, perhaps through compulsory
  examinations to assess educational standards however they are
  achieved;
* Funding: Through the Income Tax Department, liaising with the
  Education Department, the state provides funds to those families

who are too poor to provide educational opportunities for their children (after ensuring that inequitable taxation is removed); and
* Regulation: Through the Education Department, the state selectively compels families to partake of educational opportunities who otherwise, without compulsion, would not do so for their children. This might be more difficult to administer than in the schooling case, as the methods of obtaining education are more diverse. Nevertheless, the difficulties might not be insuperable (vide the way that the 1944 Education Act requirement for parents to show that they are providing adequate education for their children if they 'home-school' is policed).

That is, in West's market model there is no need for state *provision* at all, the only *funding* is for the poor, and *regulation* is only in terms of the minimum standards and selective compulsion for those who would not partake of educational opportunities. For the great majority of people, West argues, state involvement in education is required only in terms of regulation, which he sees as being rather minimal.

Reflecting back on the discussion in Chapter 1 on the influences on West, we can see that this model suggests a far lower state involvement than the systems proposed by Friedman, and Peacock and Wiseman, and also even undercuts the kind of state intervention that Adam Smith proposed. But West has justified his model in terms of historical evidence – including, in terms of going beyond Smith, using evidence from Scotland that showed it was the private sector, rather than Smith's preferred (public) parochial schools, that had succeeded in meeting the educational needs of the growing population.

Moreover, the model should also be appropriate to provide a framework for reforms for today too, relevant for reformers who are seeking to 'roll back' the state in education. West's model depends on the assumption that the vast majority of families will be competent to choose. But what, he asks, about *present-day* families? Suppose the government were to progressively get out of education and return cash to families. Would parents then spend this extra money on education? Some commentators would argue that parents could not be trusted to buy the 'normal' amount of education once the state gets out. This may be because the vast majority of parents will be irresponsible – but why would they be so much more irresponsible than their Victorian forebears? Perhaps they would be, but as a consequence of the welfare state, including in education – but then West believes that getting rid of the welfare state in education could lead to the restoring of the family responsibility (ibid., p. 262). However, he also notes that we consider that parents are responsible enough to vote for a government that decides how educational welfare is allocated, so why would we suggest that they are not responsible enough to make those decisions for themselves? (ibid.).

So much for the 'market model' that West proposes. Two points must be made. First, he is emphatically *not* advocating *universal* education vouchers – the type of vouchers proposed by Milton Friedman, as we saw in Chapter 1, where all parents are given vouchers to spend at the school of their choice, funded out of taxation. (He is not even advocating *selective* vouchers, apart from for what he envisages will be a very tiny minority of parents, those who are poor *and* irresponsible – for the poor and responsible will instead be given cash through tax credits.) What West proposes is very different: the vast majority of parents funding their children's education through their own resources. In later work, as we shall see, West was to write about voucher reforms in education. But it is clear that the market model he prefers was a far more radical solution than that.

Second, however, a major problem with West's market model as it stands is that it does not seem to take into account his *own* discussion of the way states operate, including his discussion of the economics of bureaucracy, as outlined in the previous chapter. It is true that the market model was first proposed in *Education and the State*, written before West had taken public choice theory into account. However, the revised publications in 1970 and 1994 could certainly have taken this theory on board, but West chose not to revise his model accordingly. Because of this, there is something rather unsatisfying about West's conclusions here – for they do not appear to fit comfortably with his own interpretation of the historical and economic evidence.

For instance, West puts forward an education department, complete with inspectorate, in his market model. Under West's assumptions, it has what he thinks are rather minor roles, but when they are spelled out in terms of our discussion in this book, they seem anything but. They involve the setting of educational standards that take into account the requirements for education for democracy, social cohesion, reduction of crime, etc.; inspection to see that these standards are reached by all (inspection either of all schools, in his simplified model, or of how all children obtain their education through whatever means in the more complex model); and where it finds these standards are not being reached, locating parents who are not satisfying these standards and passing on their details to the income tax department, and locating and policing specifically those who are too poor *and* negligent, and allocating and policing selective vouchers for these.

Indeed, we might conclude that the roles that West gives his education department are *much larger* than the roles that the embryonic education department had in the nineteenth century (when it was required to inspect, in quite a minor way, schools only, and issue small subsidies). Yet the importance of West's work is to show that, out of these relatively inconspicuous beginnings, the education bureaucracy was to grow larger, to eventually create a universal state schooling-system – with all its, for West, undesirable and destructive implications. This is particularly so as we note that West's model explicitly assumes that some agency in collaboration with the teacher unions is seeking to bring about state intervention. (And we note that he saw some of its interventions as being only *temporary* – but that too was what West suggested was behind government intervention per se in the nineteenth century, so it is not clear why he assumes that his temporary measures will be any less permanent than those brought in then.)

Moreover, as I noted earlier, *W.E. Forster himself* only proposed *rather minor interventions* in education in 1870 in order to fulfil the goal of universal provision. But the school boards increasingly came to dominate provision; they had their own incentives. In other words, the kinds of state intervention brought in by Forster himself were not a million miles away from the kinds envisaged by West in his idealized market model; indeed, they appear far less intrusive, given the regulatory requirements discussed. So where lies West's optimism that his own framework would also not become distorted in similar ways?

The slightly unsatisfying aspect, then, of West's market model is: what would stop West's 'education department' expanding and developing in much the same way that Forster's did? (This question is raised whether or not one has accepted the assumptions of the public choice theory critique in the previous chapter. The fact remains that Forster's initial interventions expanded into the state near-monopoly we see today.) Indeed, West himself notes, in the conclusion to his second edition of *Education and the State*, that today's education system is far from the one intended by Forster: 'indeed he would presumably now be urging reform to recapture the real vision of his original scheme, a scheme which really could fill the gaps in education – even those as serious as today's' (West, 1994a, p. 291). It is hard to see how the politicians putting forward West's scheme would also not suffer similar disillusionment. There might still be the self-interest of bureaucrats operating to expand their empires and stamp out competition. Why would anything or anyone be able to stop them?

All this suggests that if West's historical discussion and his entire repertoire of economic techniques are brought to bear, including public choice theory, then one should be much more skeptical of the possibilities of even his rather limited state intervention not to get out of control. Let's dub this 'West's Market Model Conundrum'. There would seem to be at least three possible responses to it.

The first, for reasons that will become apparent when we come to examine the reception and influence of West's work, might be termed the 'Halsey Response'. This response would say that the conundrum in fact is a *reductio ad absurdum* for West's whole position, proving that he has been misguided in his approach all along. If the logical outcome of his work is in effect a contradiction of all he has been trying to show – in his very argument for only minimal state intervention, he ends up with the basis of massive state intervention – then this shows the absurdity of his position. We have explored some of the criticisms of West in earlier chapters and will do so in the next chapter, and I leave it to readers to judge whether or not they have been successful, and whether this response is a valid one.

The second response we might call the 'Churchill Response'. Winston Churchill famously remarked that democracy is the worst of all systems of government, apart from every other one that's ever been tried. This response would observe that, yes, there are dangers with any type of government intervention. The state has a voracious appetite for intervention, and as soon as any small amount is permitted, you are on the slippery slope to more intervention. But rather than despair, what is required is as many checks and balances as possible to ensure that we have the *least bad* system possible. This might, for instance, bring in the power of parental choice of schools or other educational opportunities through a strongly pro-market voucher system, allowing all types of providers into the supply of educational opportunities, including for-profit providers, which might act as a counterbalance to the power of the government. Of course this would be the worst of all solutions, apart from all the alternatives. We shall explore some possible voucher proposals below and outline how they might fare in terms of West's discussion.

The third response is one we shall call the 'Rothbard Response', after the economist Murray Rothbard, who made a point of criticizing West for not being radical enough. Rothbard notes approvingly that West's work will lead to a 'long-needed consideration of the idea of moving toward an educational system that will be free from governmental control and governed solely by the choices of parents on the free market' (Rothbard, 1976, p. 102). However, Rothbard believes that West does 'not go far enough' and that his analysis 'is deeply flawed' (ibid.), because he still allows for some state intervention in education. Trust the parents, Rothbard would say, trust the 'invisible hand'; it will deliver all that society requires from education. The solution to the Market Model Conundrum is simple: do not permit the state to be involved in education at all. Only in this way will the dangers of even minimal state intervention be avoided.

But would such a radical solution be able to bring about the desired externalities of education and satisfy the protection of minors principle? If it could not do so, then, no matter how desirable it might seem as a way around West's conundrum, it would fall short on delivering required social outcomes of education, and hence could not be *justified*, in terms of the arguments of this book. Elsewhere, I have explored these arguments further and suggested that the pure market model that West may be hankering for, and that Murray Rothbard espouses, could in fact be capable of satisfying equality of opportunity, education for democracy and social cohesion, and other desirable externalities of education, or at least of satisfying them to the extent that is possible under state education (see Tooley, 1995, 1996, 2000). If these arguments pass muster (and they of course have their critics; see, for example, Brighouse, 1998, 2004; Swift, 2003), then the third response to the conundrum could be a feasible one. However, the details are beyond the scope of this current volume. Instead, we shall assess what West's own position might have been to the solution of this conundrum.

In the preface to the first edition of *Education and the State*, the IEA's editorial editor, Arthur Seldon, might be seen to suggest that West's position was to explore educational vouchers as a route towards pure privatization of education: Seldon writes that West

> takes further the proposal that a choice between competing state and private education could be made practicable by a system of vouchers proposed originally by Professor Milton Friedman . . . and developed by Professors A.T. Peacock and Jack Wiseman . . . [West] considers whether the voucher should be regarded as *a temporary device for returning taxes to tax-payers until reconstruction of the fiscal system can more effectively make possible a choice in education by reducing taxation.*
>
> (Seldon, 1965, p. xi; emphasis added)

Professor Mark Blaug, in his critique of *Education and the State*, seems to be suggesting the same: Initially Blaug observes that West's historical and economic analysis 'is only supporting material' for a (universal) voucher proposal, with 'tax financed "education vouchers" to all parents, redeemable at any "approved" school whether privately or publicly operated, and capable of being supplemented out of the parents' own resources if they so desire' (Blaug, [1967] 1970, p. 23). But this itself is 'only proposed as a stop-gap until such time as all education is paid for directly by parents. *The ideal towards which we ought to be striving, the author argues, is a 100 per cent system of private education*' (ibid.; emphasis added).

West himself could also be seen to be taking such a position in some writings. For instance, in a debate with Professor Henry Levin (Levin, 1991a, b; West, 1991a, b), he notes how odd it is that Levin looks only at a publicly funded education voucher system, even though Levin's argument is ostensibly about education markets: 'He does this presumably because he believes the voucher is the only alternative method available for getting back towards a market system from the present reality' (West, 1991a, p. 162) – whereas West in that debate explores how a genuine market in education might operate, where parents pay fees and there are no government schools, etc.

Perhaps the clearest statement of such a position is found in a paper West published in 1994 (the same year as the revised *Education and the State* was also published) in *Economic Affairs*. Here, showing his philosophical preference for a real market in education, West notes that some of 'the more radical of reformers of education' – he references Lewis Perelman's *School's Out* (1992) as an example – are now demanding what is in effect a return to the 'fluid, heterogeneous and competitive educational scenario' (West, 1994b, p. 15) that existed before government involvement in 1870 (in England and Wales). This is premised on the argument that the 'choice of school movement' – that is, the movement dedicated to vouchers and similar, especially in the United States – is 'to a large extent misinformed. What is needed is choice in *education*', not schools:

> School choice has not and will not lead to more productive education because the obsolete technology called 'school' is inherently *inelastic*. As long as 'school' refers to the traditional structure of buildings and grounds with services delivered in boxes called classrooms . . . 'school choice' will be unable to meaningfully alter the quality of efficiency of education.
>
> (ibid.)

West concedes, it is true, that 'this argument is extreme', but, crucially, that 'it contains a substantial truth'. For '[g]enuinely free markets are unpredictable in their unfolding . . . organisations as well as in their offerings of completely new curricula with which they constantly

surprise us' (ibid.). Most importantly, if government had not intervened in 1870, then we would have had, says West, 'precisely the
setting necessary for the emergence of a truly dynamic and innovate
education market in the 1990s' (ibid.). And he concludes:

> *It is unfortunate* that this market was destroyed by the combined
> action of politicians, bureaucrats and rent-seekers, actions that not
> only reduced the potential quality of education but also imposed on
> citizens enormous financial burdens, especially in the deadweight
> costs of taxation.
>
> (ibid.; emphasis added)

The italicized remarks suggest that West is thinking that a purely
privatized system of education – that is, aligning himself with the
Rothbard Response to the Market Model Conundrum – is philosophically the one to be preferred. But earlier in the same article, he
had noted that it may now seem 'impossible to return to a world of
almost negligible state involvement in education' (1994b, p. 12). State
intervention is an unavoidable reality. However, since the current system – and in particular the 'rent-seeking' (that is, 'the extraction
of privileges from government') that accompanies it – 'depends on
differences in the volume of information about education possessed
(a) by the suppliers (teachers and officials) and (b) by the voters at
large, *the equilibrium could eventually change*, at least at the margin, as
parents, families and members of the general public became more
informed' (ibid., p. 13; emphasis added). That is, it is possible that we
could move, at least at the margin, towards a more favorable system,
with more power to the consumers of education, counteracting the
power of the state education suppliers.

That is, West's considered verdict might be that the Churchill
Response is the appropriate one to take to his Market Model Conundrum. Accepted as a political reality is that there will be state intervention; but with voucher-style reforms, this could lead to a more
favorable situation over time. For as change occurs, albeit slowly,
and consumers become even better informed through the process
of choice, the political equilibrium could further move away from
favoring the suppliers to the consumers, and move further towards

the market solution. In West's response to Rothbard himself, in 1975, he appears optimistic that this was the preferred route for reform. He writes:

> What kind of world does Rothbard seek? He says explicitly that it is one of zero intervention in education ... Yet if he reads my essay once again, he will see that the argument is pointing substantially in his direction ... My essay predicts or outlines a 'solution' that is not as revolutionary as Rothbard's, but it would benefit all parties within the realistic assumption that 'we start from here' with existing inequalities. Rothbard must come to terms with political realities; he should consider whether half a loaf is not better than none at all.
>
> (West, 1976d, p. 114).

West on Vouchers

West's market model set out a radical prescription for very little state intervention. However, in later writings West was also to explore less radical 'market' solutions, including tax credits, proposals for loan schemes, and, especially, education vouchers. The principles underlying each of these reforms are similar: they are based on a dissatisfaction with the current justifications for state intervention in education and a reflection on the current inadequacies of state provision. They are offered as an alternative that will help improve educational standards and lower costs through competition, and to extend access and provide choice. In this section, we explore West's discussion of education vouchers only, as an example of the reforms that he considers. For this summary of his views, we turn to his mature and considered reflections on the subject in an article for the *World Bank Research Observer* (West, 1997a).

West begins with a definition: 'A tax-funded education voucher in the broadest sense is a payment made by the government to a school chosen by the parent of the child being educated; the voucher finances all or most of the tuition charged' (1997a, p. 83). Notice that this is a broader definition than others, including West himself, had considered earlier; the difference, although subtle, has important implications. For instance, Peacock and Wiseman's definition makes it clear that the voucher is something to be *given to parents*, who then *spend* it at the school of their choice: 'Parents would be left to "spend" the vouchers at private or unsubsidised state schools of their choosing, subject only to general certification' (Peacock and Wiseman, 1964, p. 35). While not rejecting this as a possibility, West's broader definition now allows a system to be counted as a voucher system if, in some way, 'funds follow the child' to a school of parental choice; there is no necessity of the parents actually having to take a piece of paper, as it were, to the school of their choice in lieu of fees. As West outlines, 'The tax-funded payments can be made directly to parents or indirectly to the selected schools' (1997a, p. 83). West does not explore here whether this might have different *psychological* implications for parents and children.

However, such implications are implicitly what he did stress in *Education and the State*, where he argues for the advantages of his idealized market model as against a system of universal vouchers: although a voucher system does promote 'choice and . . . competition' (West, 1994a, p. 283), he suggests that choice and competition would be 'even keener' if parents were to spend their own direct cash rather than use a (tax-funded) voucher:

> It may be for instance that the psychology of consumers is such that they are much more alert when they are spending their own money directly than when they are 'spending' a government voucher only. In other words many spenders of vouchers may still be under the illusion that the money to finance them could not possibly have come from taxes paid by themselves and may therefore be taking less trouble in seeing that they are spent as wisely as personal income.
>
> (ibid., p. 284)

It would be even worse, West implies, if parents did not even have the luxury of *spending* the voucher, but had funds transferred 'behind their backs' to the school they chose.

We have noted earlier how West defends the market system against universal state provision on the grounds of promoting equality of opportunity. This is also one of his important arguments for vouchers: 'One of the arguments for vouchers is that they enable families to break through these obstacles [that is, zoning of schools that allows middle-class parents access to better schools] to give equal opportunity a genuine chance' (1997a, p. 84). Indeed, the promotion of equality of opportunity is one of the four principles that make up the rationale for voucher systems, the other three being 'consumer choice, personal advancement' and 'the promotion of competition' (ibid.).

Regarding the first, under consumer choice (that is, parental choice, because parents act in proxy for their children), 'government serves the consumers of education ... rather than the suppliers of education – schools' (ibid., p. 85). The second principle of personal advancement rests on 'the conviction that people want to shape their own destinies' (ibid.). For West notes that being able to choose and decide 'stimulates interest, participation, enthusiasm, and dedication' (ibid.). The third principle looks to stimulate competition among the educational suppliers, to break the near-monopoly of state provision: vouchers challenge state schools to compete 'with each other and with private schools – through reducing costs, increasing quality, and introducing dynamic innovation' (ibid.). As funds follow the student, and schools have no other government funds available, 'each school is thus in competition with every other school for students. Good schools attract many students, redeem many vouchers, and prosper. Inferior schools, avoided by parents, are stimulated to improve or must close down' (ibid., p. 86).

These three principles, says West, lead to the promotion of equality of opportunity as 'a logical outcome', based on the objective 'of increasing access to private schools', particularly embodied in schemes that allow 'selective' or targeted vouchers to give low-income families access to private schools (ibid., p. 85). The key problem, he notes, is the poor educational opportunities provided for the lower quintiles of the population; it surely is a priority to enable such families to access higher-quality education, which studies have shown to be available in private rather than public schools, he suggests.

A key advantage of vouchers, for West, is that they break the zoning that is prevalent under any other state system of education: under a voucher system, 'children are not assigned to schools by attendance

zones or any other criterion of the school system'. Instead, parents
are able to choose a school from any of the eligible schools, public
or private (ibid., p. 86). He does note the wide variety of 'regulatory
rubrics' under which voucher systems could or do operate, including
government inspection of eligible schools; teachers in eligible schools
requiring government certification; universal vouchers or those targeted only at the neediest families; systems with variable-size vouchers
in inverse proportion to income or wealth; and vouchers that do or
do not allow 'top-ups', where parents are allowed to increase the
funding of their children. He also notes that some voucher schemes
provide access to public schools only, others to both public and private schools; but it is clear that those systems that do not allow access
to private schools will not bring about the full benefits he proposes.

West argues that schemes of 'open enrollment', where choice of
school, usually over a wide geographic area, is available to any parent but within the public system only (such as the scheme currently
in operation in England and Wales), do not in fact satisfy one of
the key principles for voucher systems, namely competition: 'In practice . . . disproportionate applications to enrol in a popular school lead
administrators to declare it to be full. Unpopular schools, therefore,
are not faced with serious costs of undercapacity and typically continue to survive such weak competition' (ibid., p. 87). He also notes
the interesting case of charter schools, as in the United States and
Canada, which are 'decentralised and fairly autonomous institutions
that operate under contract or charter to an authorised public body'
(ibid.). Although these partially respect the voucher principles –
for funds follow the child, and schools can go out of business – as
other private schools are not allowed to receive these funds, the full
benefits of vouchers are not realized.

West gives details of voucher systems that satisfy many of these principles, operating in 20 countries, states or provinces around the world.
These include targeted voucher schemes in Bangladesh, Colombia
and Puerto Rico aimed at low-income families or girls, allowing the
vouchers to be used at public or private schools. They also include
universal schemes in Sweden and the Netherlands, and schemes targeted at over 15-year-olds in Japan. Finally, there are several examples
from Canada and the United States, including the key example of

Milwaukee in the United States, which, while accepted as small-scale, is important because 'it is the only source of hard evidence on the effects of vouchers in the United States' (ibid., p. 92), thanks to the detailed evaluation reports of Professor John F. Witte. In particular, West suggests, there are 'unambiguously positive' findings on several fronts, including the following: the vouchers genuinely are serving the poorest of the poor; the vouchers do not appear to lead to 'segregated and antisocial' schools; voucher schools do not appear to 'skim off the "cream" of the student "crop"'; and there is high parental satisfaction with the scheme.

Disadvantages of Vouchers vis-à-vis the Privatized Alternative

We shall come in the next chapter to objections leveled against voucher systems by some critics. But for a critical discussion of West's ideas, what is important for us is to explore the consistency of his approach. To what extent does he see vouchers satisfying his market principles? What are the objections leveled against a voucher system *by West himself*? And how does his discussion of vouchers illuminate the problem of the Market Model Conundrum?

We have noted one of what West believes are disadvantages of vouchers vis-à-vis a truly privatized alternative already from *Education and the State*: that of the psychology of parents. A second is also raised in *Education and the State*, where West notes that it is under the vigorous competition of a genuine market, rather than a voucher system, that 'costs can be expected to fall'; this would be difficult in a voucher system, for these would inevitably be set at 'a fixed amount that must be spent'. Even if the amount was fixed at intervals, to take into account the reduced costs brought on through competition, still 'the authorities will always be several steps behind' (West, 1994a, p. 284).

A third issue concerns the rather technical but nonetheless important issue of the 'deadweight costs of taxation'. This is an important difference between fully private and publicly funded schooling – irrespective of whether the latter is in public schools or via funding for vouchers. The 'free' education provided in the publicly funded system is of course funded from somewhere: through taxation. But taxation brings about additional costs, namely what economists call 'welfare costs'. These 'welfare costs' are involved in the raising of all public funds, 'especially so' for education, 'where revenues that fund it normally come from a wide variety of sources including property taxes, gasoline taxes, income taxes and excise taxes'. These taxes cause 'well known distortions in the allocation of goods and services and of the inputs producing them'. The outcome is that any publicly funded education system, in contrast to a fully private one, 'is faced with an important extra cost, or "excess burden"' (West, 1991a, p. 162). West refers to estimates of this welfare cost of taxation from the mid-1970s as about 36 cents in the dollar. Furthermore, West notes that 'it is generally accepted' that the welfare cost of taxation 'increases exponentially with a given increase in the share of government in GNP' (ibid.), so the estimates for the mid-1970s need to be revised upwards, given the growth since. Also, these estimates ignore the 'welfare costs of tax evasion', so the figure is again even higher than the estimate above.

Such costs must be taken into account in any discussion of the relative benefits of publicly funded and private systems. So, a publicly funded voucher system will be more costly, in this sense, than a fully privatized system, and this must be marked as a negative argument concerning vouchers.

Fourth, West points to some of the concerns about voucher systems that are sometimes leveled, and notes that while it may be true that they could be problems under such a system, they would *not* be problems under a fully privatized system. He notes the argument of Henry Levin (West, 1991a, p. 153), for instance, that explores the mechanisms of a voucher system proposed for California. In this 'hybrid' system, says West, 'because of the necessary "doctoring" by government agencies' (ibid., p. 162), 'Levin is able to parade a whole host of additional costs that a *pure market* system would avoid' (ibid., p. 163; emphasis added). For example, Levin says that a fair voucher system will need 'special transport allowances ... because these will be necessary to allow poor families to escape from their immediate neighbourhoods in order to select what they see as the best schools' (ibid.). So, this pushes up the relative costs of a voucher system vis-à-vis a 'normal' public school system. But this kind of thinking, says West, is simply posited on the status quo of state education, where you have 'heterogeneous standards across fixed and non-competing zones (exclusive territories) wherein the low income groups typically receive the worst of the offerings' (ibid.).

West's further remarks are interesting because they reveal the difficulties he might have in coming to terms with whether voucher systems can overcome some of these disadvantages: 'An *immediate* switch to a voucher system from the present situation would certainly prompt poor families to look to spend their vouchers outside their inferior public school zones'; thus, he concedes there might be these problems. But he says:

> In a long established *bona fide market system*, however, this problem is usually resolved. A *free market* can ultimately result in schooling that is typically close to the child's home and provide efficient schooling in the geographical locations where it is most demanded.
>
> (ibid.; emphasis added)

Some evidence to reinforce this advantage of free markets will be offered in the concluding chapter. But note in this context that West has switched from talking about the problems under a voucher system to their resolution under a *free market* system – and he is clear, as we have seen, that this is distinct from a voucher system. Would these same advantages occur in a voucher system too? It is possible, but only if a specific type of voucher system were allowed – with free entry for all sorts of suppliers, including for-profit providers, a liberal regulatory regime, and vouchers easily transferable to private as well as public schools. But it is easy to see how many of the types of voucher systems not featuring these components would not make it possible, and hence that these hybrid systems would not bring about the desired benefits for the educational market.

Moreover, another substantial ancillary cost Levin introduces in the voucher system concerns the problem of information about schools. Levin had argued that 'available methods of providing appropriate information on a large number of educational alternatives to a wide variety of audiences in a constantly changing situation as new schools open and others fail are likely to be costly and problematic' (1991a, p. 144). But without such information, the whole notion of the advantages of parental choice breaks down – and it is likely to be the most disadvantaged parents, says Levin, who will be ignorant of the school choices available, and so most likely not to be able to take advantage of the voucher system. Here, West says, Levin 'reveals a lack of commercial imagination concerning the ability of a *dynamic market* to spread information about quality and prices' (West, 1991a, p. 163; emphasis added). He continues:

> Experience of making several choices in the *market system* of education is itself a most important source of information. Conversely, the reason why parents in a public system lack knowledge of alternatives is because such a system deprives them of meaningful choices.
>
>   (ibid.; emphasis added)

But again, West is here pointing to the virtues of a pure market system rather than a voucher system, and exactly the same comments as those above apply to this conclusion: only in a very particular kind of voucher system, which allowed the 'dynamism' of markets to operate, would these virtues be realized. In other voucher systems, it is easy to see that Levin's criticisms might be entirely justified. It would all seem to depend upon what type of voucher system could be instituted – whether it would have the advantages of the genuine market, or simply have the disadvantages that critics ascribe to it.

In fact, this does seem to be West's considered conclusion. He appears ultimately *agnostic* about whether or not voucher systems will bring about the virtues contained in his abstract market model. For instance, he concludes his 1997 World Bank article as follows: 'It is too early to reach firm general conclusions about the effectiveness of vouchers. There are only twenty entries in the table, and these show a wide variety of design' (1997a, pp. 100–1); many of them clearly did *not* exhibit the features of the more market-oriented design that might have the advantages to which West has pointed. 'Those who fear that government regulations associated with vouchers will ultimately strangle the individuality of private schools' may be correct in arguing 'that this may yet happen' (ibid., p. 101). But, importantly (and here West reinforces the notion we met earlier, that introducing vouchers will have an impact on shifting 'the equilibrium', as we put it above, away from the interests of the state education system and towards consumers): 'Nonetheless significant numbers of families are now obtaining positive firsthand experience with private schooling through voucher systems. This phenomenon alone could well alter the political climate in their favor' (ibid., pp. 100–1).

This, I suggest, seems an accurate reflection of West's final position. From my reading of his work, it is clear that his preferred, ideal solution is a fully privatized education system. However, when he elaborated his own 'market model', it contained concessions towards some minimal state intervention, perhaps in order to satisfy potential critics. But these concessions led to the difficulty of a potentially expanding state sector, here dubbed 'West's Market Model Conundrum'. If West's economic analysis, including his economics of bureaucracy discussion, is brought to bear on his proposed solution, it is hard to see what might stop even a minimum state intervention growing into something much larger, just as we saw happen with Forster's 1870 Act. In his considered discussion of vouchers for the *World Bank Research Observer*, what West is suggesting is that vouchers could be an important step in raising awareness among the public – particularly the poor and disadvantaged – that there is an alternative to blanket public provision of education. Once sufficient awareness of the private alternative is raised – even in the emasculated form that characterizes voucher systems currently in operation – this will help take us towards a 'tipping point' in favor of greater privatization, and towards the system that West ultimately believes is justified. This may be the key insight that West brings from his discussion of public choice theory, applied to the evidence of history, and in the light of the economic justifications for state intervention in education.

Part 3

The Reception and Influence of West's Ideas

Chapter 6

From Libel and Ridicule to Transatlantic Influence

Reception: The Libel Case

West's first book did not go unnoticed; *Education and the State* provoked a sharply polarized debate. *The Teacher*, on the one hand, described it as a 'polemic' written from 'Dr West's stagnant little academic backwater' (2 November 1965). *The Times Literary Supplement* said that West gave the 'impression of an ill-tempered Chesterton on an off-night ... Mr West has asked the wrong questions' (27 January 1966). The *Local Government Chronicle* held that 'Dr West and his colleagues have turned up an academic cul de sac', with a book that held not the 'slightest relevance to educational finance' (20 November 1965).

On the other hand, the *Sunday Times* described *Education and the State* as 'perhaps the most important work written on the subject this century ... Any rich benefactor ... could hardly do better than to present Dr West's book to every Member of Parliament'. It went on: 'Dr West, by turning orthodox doctrine inside out, has effected a Copernican revolution' (*Sunday Times*, 21 November 1965). *The Times Educational Supplement* supported this line, judging that 'Few books more worth serious attention by educationists have come out in the last few years.' *Education and the State*, it suggested, is a

> remarkably able and lively critique of the system and principles under which education is provided by the state ... Dr West is one of those rare and invigorating spirits who asks us to glance freshly at what we take for granted and then consider whether it is defensible.

It continued, 'If working-class parents were prepared to back the choice they then possessed with money, why should they be presumed unfit to choose today when they are so much richer?' (quoted in the *New Statesman*, 10 December 1965, p. 925). *The Times* noted that West's historical argument raised the question

> why the state, in preference to individuals, should provide the bulk of a country's education ... as more people are critical of the deficiencies of state schools and frustrated that for those with even moderate incomes there is no way of opting out it becomes increasingly important that alternatives should be politically voiced ... The most promising proposal put forward so far is that of the education voucher.
>
> (*The Times*, 17 November 1965)

Nor was the discussion confined to the United Kingdom: The *Economic Times of India*, Bombay edition, argued that *Education and the State* 'deserves to be read ... it is undoubtedly worthwhile for policymakers, even in the socialistic political culture of India, to be aware of a line of argument which undoubtedly stems from a totally different historical situation' (31 January 1966). Another reviewer noted:

> At a time when the private sector in education in India is threatened with extinction ... Dr West furnishes a powerful armoury of arguments against Statism in education. Conditions in India differ radically from those in England, but to us as to those in that distant island the same choice between freedom and totalitarianism in education has been presented.*

But it was a review in the *New Statesman* (24 December 1965, p. 1003) in rather intemperate language by Dr (now Professor Emeritus) A.H. ('Chelly') Halsey of Nuffield College, Oxford, that suggests how profoundly the ideas upset the prevailing intellectual apple-cart: 'Of all the verbal rubbish scattered about by the Institute of Economic Affairs,' Halsey began, 'this book is so far the most pernicious.' Halsey continued, 'One deluded right-wing reviewer [that is, the reviewer for the *Sunday Times*] 'has referred to it as a Copernican revolution in the

---

* Book review, unknown Indian source, E.G. West archives.

study of education. This is ridiculous,' he said, not just because West's arguments were 'a crass and dreary imitation' of Professor Milton Friedman's, 'a man whose brilliance in argument is made futile by the absurd irrelevance of his 19th-century assumptions', but because 'if it were a revolution, it would be Copernican in reverse'. West's 'crude version of liberal economics would place the market at the centre of all human institutions'. But 'That the market is not the only human contrivance for rationally relating means to ends is a commonplace to first-year students of economics. It is apparently unknown to Mr West.'

Halsey continued by saying that West knew nothing about psychology or sociology; as for history, 'When it comes to the history of education in the 19th century, Mr West goes beyond tolerable error.' Philosophically, his discussion of 'equality of opportunity' is 'hopeless'. 'What escapes Mr West', Halsey continued, 'is that civilised people like J.S. Mill have always recognised that education should be distributed by criteria other than the capacity and willingness of individual parents to pay'. Far from being an 'impartial enquiry', Halsey opined, West had written

> a gross distortion of the role of the state in education. Choices between beer and skittles may well be left to the market: but education, and the search for equality through education, is too serious a matter to be left to an irrelevant economic doctrine, and least of all to its less competent practitioners.

In 1965, when *Education and the State* was published, West had been recruited by the new University of Kent at Canterbury, England, but was on one year's leave of absence as postdoctoral fellow with Milton Friedman at the University of Chicago, to return to Kent in 1966. Professor Mark Blaug, then of the University of London's Institute of Education, met him in Chicago around the time of these press reviews. He wrote, 'I saw Halsey's scurrilous review in the *New Statesman*. West was pretty upset about it when I saw him in Chicago, and I hardly blame him. Some people do get very hot under the collar about education' (Mark Blaug to Mr Hamish Gray, IEA, 3 March 1966, E.G. West Archives). West was upset, and so was Arthur Seldon of the IEA. Rather than simply accept the insults, the IEA decided to sue for libel. On 22 July 1966, the *New Statesman* published an apology, accepting that Halsey's review went 'beyond the limits of fair criticism by reason of the violent language used and the disparaging references to Dr West and the Institute'. A sober piece in the *Daily Telegraph* of 27 July 1966 reports the outcome:

> Yesterday, after a statement in open court, an unusual action, involving two leading academics was ended with an apology and costs from the *New Statesman* to the Institute of Economic Affairs.
>
> The Institute last year published a book by Dr. Edward [*sic*] West ... Its theme was less State and more parental influence in education.
>
> In the *New Statesman* Dr. Halsey, Head of the Department of Social and Administrative Studies at Oxford, violently criticised the book, Dr. West and the Institute. The Institute held that the attack went beyond the limits of fair criticism.
>
> So the *New Statesman* has apologised handsomely and paid costs. It is consoling that the wider future of education can generate such heat in the Senior Common Room.

In the High Court on 26 July 1966, the magazine made an unreserved apology for its 'unjustified attack' on Dr West and the IEA. Its review, it said, gave a totally misleading impression of West's argument.

This was not the end of the matter, however. By this time, E.G. West had returned to England to take up his appointment as Reader at the University of Kent. Kent was a small new university with about 60 academics in total. The Dean of the Faculty of Social Sciences had recruited West on the strength of recommendations from Professor Lionel Robbins of the London School of Economics but may have been rather regretting it by this time. Charles Rowley was a young lecturer in Economics at the University of Kent, and was to become a close friend of West there. He described the situation like this: 'We were all eagerly awaiting Eddie's arrival. Or at least, I was eagerly awaiting, but most of the people were waiting with real venom and hostility. Canterbury at that time was absolutely packed out with socialists and communists' (author's interview with Charles Rowley, 15 August 2006). The fact that the *New Statesman*, at the time edited by the then-Marxist Paul Johnson, had been forced, unfairly it was felt, to eat humble pie at the hands of this right-wing think tank led, Rowley says, to West's becoming 'an ogre in the minds of most of the faculty; everybody was talking about him, his forthcoming arrival spread right across the campus, and it was dreadful'.

When West arrived, he was the subject of 'virulent hostility . . . Everywhere he went he was targeted'. West had a rather soft, gentle speaking voice 'which was a problem for him in the lecture theater. This is before microphones were used and his voice didn't carry very well, and the students sensed this'. Students would cram his lectures – perhaps at the instigation of West's faculty opponents – and 'shout him down'. On one occasion, West came to Rowley, and told him, 'Charles, I can't go into the lecture theater again.' The students had taken off their shoes and were using these to beat their desks, 'Khrushchev-style', and he could not be heard over the noise. Rowley – 17 years West's junior – accompanied West back to the lecture theater and read the riot act to the students. It made for a difficult time for West. Never able to settle properly at the University of Kent, during the next couple of years he applied for chairs in economics around the United Kingdom, to no avail. Eventually, Rowley helped him to get the chair in economics at Carleton University in Ottawa, where he finally felt respected and able to get on with his work. He remained in this position until his retirement.

A Pivotal Influence on the School Choice Movement

Although West was despised by the Left at the University of Kent and more widely, and hindered in furthering his academic career in the United Kingdom, this did not prevent his *intellectual* influence in effect reverberating around the world, right until the present time. Certainly West's work, in particular *Education and the State*, has come to be seen as one of the most significant rallying points for the school choice movement on both sides of the Atlantic. The most prominent and eminent school choice advocate in the United States, Professor Milton Friedman, presented West with the first Alexis de Tocqueville Award for the Advancement of Education Freedom in 1995. On his certificate, Friedman wrote, 'I am only one of many who has had his

views changed by your pathbreaking work. We want more!' Someone
deeply critical of West, Professor H.J. Kiesling, nonetheless noted that
'West's ideas have enjoyed wide circulation in places where they have
considerable influence upon *present day* policy making' in the United
States (1983, p. 416), pointing in particular to his influence on Milton
Friedman. The Washington scholar and advocate of school choice
Dr Myron Lieberman wrote that *Education and the State*

> is a comprehensive indictment of public education or, more pre-
> cisely, a powerful repudiation of the idea that education should
> be a government service funded by tax revenues. Even propo-
> nents of public education are likely to agree that West's rigorous
> analysis invites a radical rethinking of the rationale that under-
> lies the creation of state-run education and calls for the continu-
> ation of government schools in the United Kingdom and United
> States.
>
> (in West 1994a, p. xvii)

Charles Rowley, West's supportive friend from the University of Kent,
who went on to write in favor of vouchers, explicitly influenced by
West (Rowley, 1969), suggests that *Education and the State*

> is Eddie West's finest work. Its arguments are as convincing now as
> they were thirty five years ago ... Together with West's companion
> volume, *Education and the Industrial Revolution* (1975[a]), it pro-
> vides a devastating refutation of all preceding scholarship from
> the late nineteenth century onwards that attempted to rationalize
> public education provision as a necessary condition for economic
> progress.
>
> (Rowley, 2002, p. 36)

Because of his stature within the classical liberal tradition, throughout his career West was invited onto the academic advisory boards
and editorial boards of many classical liberal think tanks and publications. The list reads like a Who's Who of these think tanks. It includes
membership of the editorial panel of advisers of the Institute of Economic Affairs, London; the advisory board of *Reason Papers*; the board
of advisers of the Pacific Institute of Public Policy Research, San

Francisco; the academic advisory board of the Atlas Economic Research Foundation, Washington, DC; the editorial board of *Policy Report*, the Cato Institute, Washington, DC; the academic advisory board for the Center for the Study of Market Processes, George Mason University, Virginia; the advisory board of the Fraser Institute, Vancouver; the board of academic advisers of the Hong Kong Centre for Economic Research at the Chinese University of Hong Kong; and the academic advisory council of the John Locke Institute, Fairfax, Virginia. He was also an adjunct scholar at the Heritage Foundation, Washington, DC.

West's work has been the subject of considerable international academic debate; I have used some of the critiques of him in our critical appraisal of his work in the previous chapters. Notable debates included that with Professor Mark Blaug, published by the IEA as *Education: A Framework for Choice* (Beales et al., [1967] 1970); debates with Professors J.S. Hurt (1971) and H.S. Kiesling (1983) in the *Economic History Review*; with Professor Michael Krashinsky in Colombia University's *Teachers College Record* (1986); with Professor Henry Levin in the *Economics of Education Review* (1991); with Professor Martin Carnoy of Stanford University in the *World Bank Research Observer* (1997); and with Coons, Sugarman, Friedman, Rothbard and Buchanan in the 1976 publication *Nonpublic School Aid* (West, 1976d). It is clear that to those in favor of school choice, West's work has been seen as the foundation for arguments for many recent policy initiatives, while to those arguing against school choice, or for a more fundamental role for government in education, West's arguments have been seen as the key ones to challenge and oppose. As Myron Lieberman put it, *Education and the State* 'is the single most outstanding intellectual challenge to public education. It is the book the proponents of state-run education must refute or concede the argument'. Clearly, as witnessed by the extensive range of debates, many have attempted to refute his arguments. Whether or not they have succeeded, readers must judge for themselves from the discussion in earlier chapters.

In the remainder of this chapter, we examine two important cases of West's influence, one on either side of the Atlantic. The first is his influence on Milton Friedman, the second on the voucher movement in the United Kingdom.

Influence on Milton Friedman

West and Friedman kept in touch throughout West's early career. As we noted in Chapter 1, West's thesis, and hence *Education and the State*, were clearly in part inspired by conversations with Milton Friedman. When West was Friedman's invitee at the University of Chicago (1965–6), he dropped a line to Friedman enclosing some of the reviews of his book, with a note emphasizing his indebtedness to his colleague: 'Dear Milton, Herewith a sample of the reviews of my book so far. *You see what your influence is responsible for!* Could I have the reviews back when you have finished with them? Sincerely, Edwin West' (E.G. West to Milton Friedman, no date, E.G. West Archives; emphasis added). Milton scrawled back his comments across the same letter: 'Dear Edwin: You should be pleased indeed so to have stirred up the hornets. They must be troubled to buzz as viciously as they do. Halsey's is the bottom. Thanks for showing me these. Milton Friedman'.

Now, as I also outlined in Chapter 1, in 1955 Milton Friedman wrote in favor of education vouchers, satisfied that their justification rested on the 'neighborhood effects' argument (Friedman, 1955, pp. 124–6). Educating a child, he wrote, brings gains not only to the child and parents, but also to others, 'promoting a stable and democratic society'. This justifies a compulsory level of education, which, because compulsory, needs to be publicly funded. Usefully for the argument here, even in 1955 he observes that 'it might be both feasible and desirable to require the parents to meet the costs directly' if these costs were not too great, with 'special provision' for the minority who could not afford them (ibid., p. 125). However, Friedman does not explore this further, because such a proposal was 'hardly feasible' (ibid., p. 126): first, because families varied in their resources; second, because the standard of education required by the state involved 'very sizable costs' (ibid.). These two reasons, combined with the neighborhood effects argument, led him to propose vouchers as a means of enhancing the educational market within the constraints of public compulsion and funding.

However, 20 years later Milton Friedman has become dubious about his earlier position. He wrote:

Over the years, I have become increasingly persuaded that the case for (1) compulsory schooling and (2) government financing of schooling based on supposed externalities is seriously flawed. The flaw is present in my own treatment of these issues in *Capitalism and Freedom*.

(Friedman, 1976, p. 92)

The problem, says Friedman, is 'the failure to distinguish between *marginal* and *average* externalities' (ibid.): if 'private self-interest alone' led the vast majority of parents (say 90 percent or more) to educate their children, then 'there is an *average* externality; I have benefited from other people's behavior though, by assumption, I have paid none of these costs' (ibid.). But if one more child was schooled, 'is it obvious that my benefit would be increased . . .? Is it obvious that this would [say] reduce crime further?' In other words, 'does not the *net* (positive or negative) externality from extra schooling depend on the amount to which that schooling is added?' (ibid.). That is to say,

I have never found any plausible argument for net positive external-ities from schooling that would not be satisfied if 90 percent, to take an arbitrary figure, received elementary schooling – the three R's. I have yet to see a plausible argument for any net positive marginal externality from additional schooling. But if this be so, and if pri-vate interest alone could lead to at least this much schooling – as I believe it is overwhelmingly plausible that it would – then there is no case from externalities for either compulsory schooling or the governmental financing of schooling. There may, of course, still be a case, on paternalistic or redistributive grounds, for government assistance to pay for schooling children of indigent parents, but not for increased government financing of schooling.

(ibid.)

A similar restatement is made in 1980, when Milton Friedman, now writing with his wife, Rose, observe how they are no longer convinced about the 'justification for . . . compulsory attendance' (Friedman and Friedman, 1980, p. 197).

So what made the Friedmans change their minds? They were now aware of research on 'the history of schooling in the United States, the United Kingdom, and other countries' that 'has persuaded us that compulsory attendance at schools is not necessary to achieve that minimum standard of literacy and knowledge'. The research has shown that schooling was 'well-nigh universal in the United States before attendance was required', while in the United Kingdom it was 'well-nigh universal before either compulsory attendance or government financing of schooling existed' (Friedman and Friedman, 1980, p. 197). This evidence challenges the desirability of compulsory schooling laws, and hence, as compulsion was a prime justification for public funding, the *raison d'être* of that also disappears.

And of course it is here that West's influence came in. For the historical work they refer to was E.G. West on the history of public education in New York State (referenced Friedman and Friedman, 1980, p. 186, and discussed in Chapter 4 of the present book) and in England and Wales, and Scotland:

> In Britain, as in the United States, schooling was almost universal before the government took it over. Professor West has maintained persuasively that the government takeover in Britain, as in the United States, resulted from pressure by teachers, administrators, and well-meaning intellectuals, rather than parents. He concludes that the government takeover reduced the quality and diversity of schooling.
>
> (ibid., pp. 187–8, referencing *Education and the State*)

Although still viewing the education voucher as a useful stepping stone, by 1980 the Friedmans are in favor of something more radical: 'We regard the voucher plan as a *partial* solution because it affects neither the financing of schooling nor the compulsory attendance laws. *We favor going much farther*' (Friedman and Friedman, 1980, p. 196; emphasis added). Where they now favor going might be characterized as a move away from the desirability of *universal* vouchers to an emphasis on, at most, *targeted* vouchers:

> Public financing of hardship cases might remain, but that is a far different matter than having the government finance a school

system for 90 percent of the children going to school because 5 or 10 percent of them might be hardship cases.

(ibid., pp. 196–7)

That is, by 1980 they are actually in favor of a more complete privatization of education, with government withdrawing from funding of education and compulsory schooling laws, except for, at most, a small minority of parents who are 'hardship cases'.

The Friedmans have been key players in the school choice movement in the United States, and so we can credit West's influence on their later work. Among other things, they set up the Milton & Rose D. Friedman Foundation, which has had crucial involvement in the research and development for voucher schemes and other school choice reforms across the United States – and was instrumental in the proposals of the first universal voucher scheme there, in the state of Utah, to be discussed in the next chapter. However, it is interesting, then, that even though their views on the role of government were changed by West, they continued to propose *vouchers* as the way forward – something that, as we have seen, West certainly did not do in *Education and the State*; he was ambivalent about vouchers throughout his career. The Friedmans made it clear why this was the case: in *Free to Choose*, they wrote that they would not elaborate on the more radical implications of their position, revised after reading West, recognizing that their new views 'on financing and attendance laws will appear to most readers to be extreme' (1980, p. 197); hence, they 'return to the voucher plan – a much more moderate departure from present practice' (p. 197).

In other words, the Friedmans seem to be adopting what I have suggested might have been West's considered position too in response to whether vouchers could be the way forward: they are valuable, but as a stepping stone to the preferred alternative of a more thoroughgoing privatization of education. Milton Friedman made this more or less explicit in a letter dated 22 October 1975 (Milton Friedman, University of Chicago, to Mr George Pearson, Center for Independent Education, Wichita, Kansas, E.G. West Archives), based on reviewing the material that was to be published as *Nonpublic School Aid* (West, 1976d), including a chapter from Friedman. Friedman wrote:

I have never come down firmly as between a voucher scheme and requiring parents, even if schooling is compulsory, to pay for the schooling of their own children. I may say my ideas in this area have shifted over time and as of the moment I would be much more favorable to abolishing both compulsion and governmental financing than I would have been at the time I wrote *Capitalism and Freedom* ... [However] The case for vouchers remains as a superior alternative to a system of governmentally run as well as financed schools.

Influence on School Choice Policy in the United Kingdom

West was also to have an important influence on policy developments in the United Kingdom. Even though West had moved to North America in 1970, he kept closely in touch with the Institute of Economic Affairs (IEA) in London throughout his life, and was directly involved in education policy developments emerging from there. He was invited on to the 'Planning Board for an Independent University' by Ralph Harris in early July 1969 and remained active in these developments, which were to lead to the only fully privately funded university in the United Kingdom, the University of Buckingham. Moreover, West was to be directly involved with the moves to implement a school voucher system in England, through the IEA and its connections in the Thatcher government of 1979.

Two key players in these moves were Sir Keith (later Lord) Joseph, a frequent attendee at IEA events both before and during the Thatcher governments, and Dr (later Sir) Rhodes Boyson. As this was a particularly important episode in the school choice movement in the United Kingdom, and one that was ultimately unsuccessful, it may be worth looking in some detail at the progress of the movement, the criticisms it came up against, and West's involvement – for his intellectual influence was key. It is a fascinating episode, as it illustrates neatly themes that have emerged in this book thus far, on the economics of bureaucracy and educational reform. The discussion may also be particularly relevant as a preamble to the exploration of the relevance of West's ideas for today, in the next chapter, as the ultimate failure of this movement brings useful lessons.

West's first involvement with Dr Rhodes Boyson came while the latter was the headteacher of the state comprehensive Highbury Grove School in Islington, north London. Arthur Seldon wrote to West that he had sent *Education and the State* to Boyson, noting that '[h]e is the Headmaster of a State school *who has taken to the voucher idea*' (Arthur Seldon to E.G. West, 31 December 1969, E.G. West Archives). A month later, Seldon wrote that 'The Headmaster ... liked the book, of course', and added in a PS, 'I think you would like to meet the Headmaster', whose name was now revealed (Arthur Seldon to E.G. West, 28 January 1970, E.G. West Archives). This meeting was duly arranged, and Rhodes Boyson eventually wrote an 'Appraisal' to the second edition of *Education: A Framework for Choice*, published in 1970. Here Boyson noted the 'movement gaining ground at the moment, greatly helped by the impressive academic studies of the Institute of Economic Affairs [i.e. *Education and the State* and the Peacock and Wiseman paper], to widen choice ..., one hopes, in education' (Boyson, 1970, p. xiv). Boyson explored two alternatives to bringing choice back into education:

> an extension of fee-paying (private or state) education following *either* a cutback in taxation to leave more money to fructify in the pockets of the people and generous scholarships for children from poorer families *or* a state-sponsored voucher system for all.
>
> (ibid., p. xv; emphases added)

Importantly, he finds the former both 'politically possible and educationally perhaps preferable', although the latter 'is probably more technically feasible in the short run and could be a stepping stone to a vast expansion of privately-financed education' (ibid.). In other words, inspired by West, he sees true privatization as the preferable way forward, but accepts that vouchers may be an interim step towards it.

Dr Boyson was elected to the House of Commons as MP for Brent North in 1974, and with the new incoming Conservative government of Margaret Thatcher was made Parliamentary Under-Secretary at the Department of Education and Science in 1979, a position he held until 1983 – in other words, throughout the duration of the abortive voucher discussions.

Behind the scenes, Boyson was active working with Sir Keith Joseph on exploring the possibility for the voucher scheme. And the IEA was active too. The 'intellectual groundwork' for the voucher proposal, says Seldon, had in any case been prepared by the IEA, through, as we saw in Chapter 1, the *Choice in Welfare* series (1963 onwards), Peacock and Wiseman's paper (1964), West's 'now classic *Education and the State*' (Seldon, 1986, p. 13), and the subsequent *Education: A Framework for Choice* (1970d). This intellectual groundwork led, among other things, to a motion in favor of an experimental voucher scheme carried by a majority of votes at the September 1974 Conference of the National Council of Women. Encouraged by this, the cumbersomely named Friends of the Education Voucher Experiment in Representative Regions (FEVER) was set up in December 1974 and embarked upon five years 'of vigorous campaigning' (ibid.), including to packed school hall meetings (which led one local MP 'to declare instant support for the voucher'; ibid.), a local 'referendum' in Ashford, Kent, supporting the idea, and other media broadcasts. In 1976, the Conservative Opposition put forward in the House of Commons a motion led by Dr Rhodes Boyson advocating local experiments with school vouchers, which was supported by all Conservative MPs (with one abstention): 'Henceforth experiments with vouchers became official Conservative education policy' (ibid., p. 14). In 1978, a survey in the county of Kent 'revealed strong parental desire for choice and indicated that the number who would switch schools would not be unmanageable' (ibid.). Throughout this period, Marjorie Seldon, wife of Arthur Seldon and honorary chairman of FEVER, was keeping West fully appraised of all these developments (letters in the E.G. West Archives). With the election of the Thatcher government in May 1979, the 'prospect of political action on the voucher quickened' (ibid.).

West's work was also being forwarded to Sir Keith Joseph (Arthur Seldon to E.G. West, 27 July 1979, E.G. West Archives); Seldon noted, 'The new government is introducing some interesting changes in education policy and it may not be long before we know what they are.' There was a keen sense of anticipation that some of the ideas that had been mooted for some time would soon be coming to fruition. From the House of Commons, Dr Boyson wrote to West (Dr Rhodes Boyson to E.G. West, 29 May 1980, E.G. West Archives), 'Stay in touch and keep us informed of the work you are doing . . . As you know, we greatly rely upon your work on schooling in Britain in the nineteenth century, Yours ever, Rhodes.'

The early Conservative reforms clearly bore the mark of West's ideas, although they were somewhat modest. From 1980 to 1996, there were to be ten major statutes. The key initial thrust of these reforms has been widely interpreted as seeking to undermine producer domination of education – with teacher unions and local education authorities in particular being the subject of the reforms – bringing in instead consumer choice, 'parent power', greater institutional autonomy and diversity of institutions on offer (see, for example, Harris, 1993). The first reform, the 1980 Education Act, under Secretary of State for Education and Science Mark Carlisle, brought changes to key areas (all advocated by West) of greater parental choice (challenging the zoning policy that was prevalent), provision of information, and some state subsidies for private schools.

It is important to realize that prior to the Education Act 1980, parental choice was widely curtailed. In effect, the local education authority (LEA) told a parent where to send his or her child, and that usually was it. While the 1944 Education Act (s. 76) seemed to offer some parental choice, the courts tended to back the notion that 'LEAs had virtually unfettered discretion' (Harris, 1993, p. 131). The 1980 Education Act was the Conservatives' first tool to bring in greater parental choice. The LEA had to grant parental preferences which parents were entitled to express (s. 6(2)), but only if such choices would not interfere with 'the efficient use of resources', which in practice turned out to mean that schools and LEAs could still successfully object to parental choices.

The second aspect that the 1980 Education Act sought to address was in the provision of information to parents. Section 8 of the 1980 Act compelled LEAs to provide details of their school admissions arrangements, etc. Then the Education (School Information) Regulations 1981 provided for individual schools to publish a school prospectus. This created much controversy right from the beginning, with the National Association of Head Teachers (NAHT) saying that it would lead to 'false judgements' about schools (*The Times*, 8 December 1980), and the shadow education secretary, one Neil Kinnock MP (later to be leader of the Opposition against the Thatcher government), said that these were 'a highly suspect means of assessing the performance of a school' (Hansard, Commons Debates, vol. 973, col. 37, 5 November 1979). Finally, the 1980 Education Act brought in the Assisted Places scheme, which gave poor but bright children access to private schools, something that West was to build on in his policy proposals.

In December 1979, FEVER presented a national petition supporting a voucher for all schools to the secretary of state for education. In December 1981, the new secretary of state, Sir Keith Joseph, invited FEVER to respond to a detailed summary of the problems that the Department of Education and Science saw with a voucher scheme. Importantly, in an accompanying letter, Sir Keith, writing from the Department, noted, 'I am intellectually attracted to the idea of education vouchers as a means of eventually extending parental choice and influence yet further and improving educational standards' (letter, Sir Keith Joseph to the chairman of FEVER, 16 December 1981, in Seldon, 1986, p. 36). FEVER invited 11 economists, lawyers and political scientists to respond in detail, including Professors E.G. West, Milton Friedman, Mark Blaug, Stanley Dennison, Alan Peacock, Jack Wiseman and Charles Rowley – all names we have already encountered in this book.

West's specific submission, as well as attending to some of the criticisms of vouchers in general, in particular also set out a scheme to extend the principles already embodied in the 1980 Education Act, including the Assisted Places scheme. The Assisted Places scheme (whereby the money went to the independent school, rather than to the parent, but having a similar effect to the voucher, as parents could also 'top up' the Assisted Place amount) could be provided to a greater number of children, and children of different abilities (not just the brighter ones, as was the case at the time); it could be offered to parents on different ranges of incomes and allow more schools to become part of the scheme. It would overcome the objection to the Assisted Places scheme that it was cream-skimming, and allowing only a tiny minority to benefit from private education (West, 1982b; see also Seldon, 1986, p. 51, and West 1986c for a response to some objections). Marjorie Seldon wrote to West saying that she had specifically highlighted West's submission 'because I thought Keith might be attracted by your idea of building onto the Assisted Places Scheme (which involves a tiny 2% of schoolchildren)'. She says her 'surmise was correct', and 'I have had two telephone calls from Keith and one from Rhodes' saying that they liked West's ideas. Furthermore, Marjorie Seldon had 'suggested to Keith that he might invite you over to mastermind an experiment ... Keith did say he would like a talk with you' (Marjorie Seldon to E.G. West, 11 March 1982, E.G. West Archives).

The academics' responses were submitted by FEVER in early 1982, and 'It was understood that the officials would be asked to respond to the academics' refutations' (Seldon, 1986, p. 15). But no reply was made during 1982 or 1983. The end result? In October 1983, the secretary of state, Sir Keith Joseph, announced (at the Conservative Party conference) that the voucher was 'dead' (ibid.).

Why? What caused the collapse of the scheme? In the 1981 memorandum setting out the Department of Education's discussion of vouchers, there were listed four perceived advantages that a voucher system would bring:

- There would be parity of choice between state and private schools.
- There would be parental choice between state and private schools.
- Schools would become accountable to parents.
- School standards would be raised.

But these advantages were outweighed for the Department by the ten objections raised. And in these objections, and in a May 1984 television interview and June 1984 statement to the House of Commons by the secretary of state, Sir Keith Joseph, we can see the huge bureaucratic impediments to the introduction of the kind of reforms that West and the IEA favored.

Many of the objections simply point to the undesirability of change, from the point of view of the Department, within the existing structures. One important sentence from the Department's memorandum neatly summarizes the whole position:

> If the voucher were the sole source of finance for a school which would have complete freedom of the way in which it disposed of its own resources, a voucher system *could lead to a situation in which parental choices and decisions undermined the character of the maintained school system.*
>
> (para. 10; quoted in Seldon, 1986, p. 40)

And if parents are in control, then what of the control currently vested in the teachers and unions, the LEAs, and the government department itself? For instance, it was argued that voucher-financed schools would be able to recruit and dismiss teachers, which would conflict with national salary scales; it would incur 'frictional costs', risk 'employee resistance' and undermine 'professional morale' (para. 11; quoted ibid., pp. 40–1). The teacher unions, in other words, would object to any changes that threatened hard-won positions. The Department, it was clear, was not going to countenance radical changes that would upset these vested interests, whatever their perceived advantages. And what about schools that, becoming unpopular, had lower incomes, because of per-capita pupil funding? Under 'sections 7 and 8 of the 1944 Act', the Department opined, the local education authority 'would be obliged . . . to prop up very badly resourced schools' (ibid., p. 41). Moreover, the Department asked, 'Would a voucher system be compatible with an individual LEA's management of the education service in its area?' (ibid., p. 42). Again, vested interests would object to these changes, and the Department was not overly inclined to challenge these vested interests.

Other of the objections raised questions about how a 'market' in education would operate. For instance, it was claimed that 'The ebb-and-flow of pupils at will could create difficult management and organisational problems for schools, at least in the short term' (memorandum, para. 8.iii, quoted in Seldon, 1986, p. 39). And again, there was a concern about whether private schools would expand or new ones open in response to demand: 'The scope and often the desire for existing schools to expand is limited. Starting a new independent school is a slow, expensive and risky business' (para. 6, quoted ibid., p. 38). The academic responses suggested that these concerns were not based on any evidence. On the 'ebb and flow' argument, this was, says Seldon, 'the characteristically corporatist view – that consumers should be subservient to producers' (ibid., p. 24). The 2,500 private schools in England and Wales were able to adapt to this feature of a competitive market with ease, and there would seem to be no reason, the academics argued, why new voucher schools should also not be able to adapt. Milton Friedman observed that the 'ebb and flow' difficulty is experienced only by government-operated monopolies and not by private institutions such as shops, hotels and restaurants (ibid., p. 29).

In other words, the responding academics, including West, offered their own views on how an education market could respond to price incentives. However, the only real *evidence* they could offer as a counter to the Department's position on inelasticity of educational supply was that of the Youth Training Scheme, where grants provided to young people had led to a huge expansion of suppliers willing to offer courses. But, of course, the Department could counter that schools were different. Importantly, Milton Friedman observed that if the voucher scheme 'were widely expected to be permanent, independent schools would be created to meet the demand' (ibid.), but this conceded that the problem of inelastic supply might be apparent if the voucher system were *trialed* as a short-term experiment.

The problem for the academics here was clear: They were in a catch-22 situation. They could offer no real evidence of how an educational market might operate, because there was a near-state education monopoly, both in the United Kingdom and overseas, so no obvious evidence could be forthcoming. Seldon suggests that 'the rejection of the voucher was based not on knowledge but on surmise' (ibid., p. 67) – which may have been true, but was just as true of the academics' defense of vouchers, too.

But the objections that seemed, in effect, able to carry the day against vouchers – this was one of the four main objections to the voucher scheme that the secretary of state offered in his television interview in May 1984 – concerned the additional costs of the system and the important issue of 'free' education. For there would be, said the Department, extra costs that would be incurred by a voucher system, because students currently in private schools would also have to be given the vouchers. 'These costs', the memorandum indicated, 'could be reduced by setting a lower value on a voucher used in the independent sector', but, crucially for the Department, 'the voucher would still need to entitle parents to a free education for their children at the maintained school of their choice, as long as section 61 of the Education Act 1944, which precludes charging, remains in force' (para. 5; quoted in Seldon, 1986, p. 38). But if top-ups were required from parents to send their children to private schools, then 'the value of the voucher as an agent of choice would diminish', with the result that 'at a certain point the vouchers would become little more than a straight subsidy for parents currently using the independent system' (para. 5; quoted ibid., p. 38). And the Department was not interested in that.

There was really no adequate response to these objections. On the costs issue, it was pointed out, among others by Milton Friedman, that if the voucher were set at 75 percent of school costs, total costs would actually fall. But then the issue of free education would be raised – for it would no longer be free to parents (who would have to pay at least 25 percent of the cost in state schools). It is all very well for commentators like Arthur Seldon to claim that the 1944 Act could be changed; he notes that not even the main architect of the 1944 Act, R.A. Butler, 'claimed that it set the optimum educational scene for all time, in the unforeseeable future of unceasing industrial, technical and social change' (ibid., p. 22). But it is very hard to see how the Department could have countenanced such a change, in view of the parallel requirements in the United Nations Charter of Human Rights. So, West's contribution that the 'tax system cannot raise enough funds for improved schooling, yet the egalitarian ethos of tax-financed education obstinately discourages or prevents parents from adding voluntary payments' to schools (ibid., p. 20) was in the end beside the point. The voucher, West argued, would encourage 'additional voluntary payments by parents'. Indeed, 'In time, voluntary payment, aided by reduced taxation, could replace the voucher' (ibid.). But the Department would not be interested in such bold claims; the law stated that education should be free, and the voucher proposals, challenging this, could henceforth be dismissed.

Moreover, the academics, including West, claimed that education markets would have benefits related to the costs of education. The idea that costs would rise would at most be limited to the short run:

> In the developing private sector the voucher would add a new inducement to cost reduction by offering an incentive to parents to shop around for schools that were run economically as well as efficiently in producing good results. Costs in an expanding market would be lower than in a monopoly because schools competing for voucher-pupils would offer required standards of teaching at the lowest possible costs, especially when parents could retain the difference between voucher values and school fees and put it to educational or other purposes.
>
> (ibid., p. 21)

Such incentives were not there in the state system. But again, this could be dismissed by the Department as mere speculation – where was the evidence of the market behaving in this way? The academics could offer none, stuck again in the same catch-22 situation as before: given state near-monopoly educational provision in the United Kingdom and competitor countries, from where could they find evidence showing the supposed virtues of educational markets?

In other words, *given the current system* that was pertaining in the 1980s, it might be hard to see how a change as radical as a voucher system could be brought in, such were the bureaucratic impediments. At most, an experiment in vouchers might be countenanced; but a short-term experiment, it was conceded by the academics, would not necessarily bring the advantages of a market in education, so might actually be counterproductive.

Seldon puts all of the Department's objections into the framework of the economics of bureaucracy: the teacher unions would object to it, because it would threaten their security and terms and conditions of service. And 'Self-interested politicians must be expected to oppose the voucher because it would undermine their control of education' (ibid., p. 101). The statement quoted above from the Department's memorandum about the effect of a voucher system putting control, undesirably, in the hands of parents succinctly summarizes this explicit objection. In summary, Seldon notes, 'the voucher was a challenge to the formidable fortress of paternalism, professional corporatism, monopoly and political authority that had long ruled British education. That the ramparts did not fall to the first intellectual assault was almost predictable' (ibid., p. 69).

This initial foray into political action inspired, in large part, by West's intellectual work was not successful. Indeed, the failure 'was almost predictable'. But what the Conservative government was to achieve later in education points even more to the difficulties of introducing the kinds of reform that West was advocating. Several of these reforms set out to strengthen parental choice vis-à-vis the suppliers of education. Crucially, as one observer put it, these reforms sought to address in a politically less dangerous manner the aspirations of those within the Conservative Party who were still seeking vouchers 'as a means to creating a free market for schooling and greater choice' (Harris, 1993, p. 160). For instance, the Education (No. 2) Act of 1986 gave parents 'a much greater involvement in the running of schools through their direct participation in new governing bodies with substantial powers', while the 1988 Education Reform Act brought in 'open enrollment', whereby schools were required 'to admit pupils up to their limits of their physical capacity' (West, 1994a, p. 235). One of the problems with parental choice introduced in the 1980 Education Act was that LEAs were allowed to fix an 'admissions limit', which effectively allowed a school not even operating at full capacity, given the way the limits were fixed, to turn pupils away. The provisions in the 1988 Act sought to challenge this.

'Open enrollment' meant much more effective parental choice, but, importantly, within state schools only. West saw some advantages in this system, but pointed out its inadequacies as compared with a proper voucher system. Obviously, there was a lack of price system operating in the schools, there was little likelihood of unpopular schools closing, there were few incentives for teachers and headteachers to welcome additional pupils (their salaries, for instance, were in no way related to enrollments), and, crucially, 'the full conditions of competition are not present . . . Choice that is constrained to exclude private schools cannot properly be called free choice' (West, 1989a, pp. 256–7). So, although '[a]t first sight the reforms . . . look impressive' (West, 1994a, p. 236), once examined they fail to meet the requirements for anything like true markets in education.

Crucially, the Department's apparent concessions allowing what was dubbed the 'internal market' in schools, namely open enrollment coupled with local management of schools (where state schools were given some control over their budgets), were 'balanced' by the need for tighter regulation of state schools (Department of Education and Science, 1989; Department of Education and Science and Welsh Office, 1987). The motivation for this was given as partly to ensure that parental choice was 'the same everywhere' (Bash and Coulby, 1989, pp. 19–20), and partly in order to give parents the required information to allow them to choose: the National Curriculum acts 'as justification for a massive programme of national testing at 7, 11, 14 and 16 which will, in turn, provide evidence to parents for the desirability or otherwise of individual schools' (Chitty, 1989, p. 218).

But the arrival of the National Curriculum, and the concomitant national testing and league tables, seemed to some to epitomize everything that was wrong with government intervention in general and in education in particular. Keith Joseph, now elevated to the Lords, put it like this: the government's philosophy, he said,

> is that we have been over-governed, and that in many fields the Government should provide a framework and leave people in their infinite variety to pursue their own purposes within that framework. Yet here, in the national curriculum, we have over-government and, in my view, straightjacket government.*

It is clear that West agreed with this kind of sentiment (see West, 1996e, p. 7). Indeed, he noted of the 1988 Act that 'despite its claim to be a movement largely for parental choice, the initial four clauses

---

* Official Report Fifth Series in Parliamentary Debates: Lords, Vol. 498, 1987–88, London HMSO, p. 607.

of this Act place extraordinary, and in some cases unprecedented, powers with the Secretary of State', pointing to the powers over curriculum and assessment in particular (West, 1994a, p. 237).

But again, we are drawn back to the 'almost predictable' aspect of it all. If one takes the economics of bureaucracy, or public choice, approach seriously, as does West, or even if one simply takes it as an empirical given about the growth of government departments, then perhaps it should not be a surprise that these extensions of bureaucratic powers emerged. With the reforms culminating in the 1988 Act – inspired, it has to be repeated, in part by the influence of West's intellectual work in favor of parental choice and markets – a huge extension of the 'mechanisms of central administration' emerged: 'The recent legislative thrust in Britain has amounted to a struggle for power between two types of bureaucracy, local and central, with the latter emerging triumphant.' Crucially, West went on to argue, 'The new powers the bureaucracy enjoys *are not likely to be reduced dramatically* in the near future. Indeed the economics literature predicts a strong *growth* of a bureaucracy's budget once it has removed or reduced the power of competing bureaus' (ibid., p. 239; first emphasis added).

Here emerges again the central paradox of West's writings. If it is 'almost predictable' that government bureaucracies will not simply bow down and accept the inevitable when confronted with intellectual arguments for reform, why continue arguing for such reform? For it is clear that West's experience, albeit at one step removed, with the policy reform process in the United Kingdom did not stop him writing in advocacy of vouchers and other school choice reforms (see, for instance, West, 1981c, 1983d, 1986c). So why bother? We come back again to the conclusion at the end of the previous chapter. The survival of the current system depends upon information asymmetries: 'teachers and officials' are able to mobilize information, and hence public opinion, more easily than can parents and children (West, 1994b, p. 13). Perhaps ultimately West saw his role, when writing in advocacy of vouchers and other similar reforms, as not specifically to influence policy but rather to influence *opinion*. If there were enough information around to show the inadequacies of the current system, the lack of substance in its supposed intellectual and historical foundations, and the coherence of an alternative, the information asymmetry could be redressed, and hence the political equilibrium in favor of current state education shifted. In the final chapter, I shall outline how the political equilibrium may indeed be changing, both as a direct result of the influence of people like Milton Friedman (hence directly through West's influence) and in places that neither West nor Friedman could have foreseen.

Part 4

The Relevance of West's Ideas Today

Chapter 7

An Enduring Legacy

The dissatisfaction with standards in state education that motivated West's enquiry in the 1960s into the role of government in education has not gone away. Around the world, governments of differing political complexions are exploring 'school choice' reforms that attempt to bring some aspects of 'markets' into the education system – whether it be through universal or targeted vouchers, tax credits or state subsidies to private schools (including specially created 'charter' schools in the United States and Canada, and city technology colleges and academies in the United Kingdom). What they have in common is an emphasis on parental choice as a mechanism for helping to make schools accountable to those using them, with the aim that this will, among other things, help to improve standards in education. With a few notable exceptions such as Denmark and the Netherlands, which instituted programs that could come under the rubric of 'school choice' in 1855 and 1917 respectively, the vast majority of the programs have been initiated since 1982, and most much later. Why the global movement since then? John Merrifield points to the influence of Milton Friedman's 1955 paper, but observes that the market-oriented reforms occurred 'especially after the election[s] of Margaret Thatcher and Ronald Reagan' (Merrifield, 2005, p. 175). If these governments influenced this global movement in school choice reforms – and it is not far-fetched to observe that they directly and indirectly influenced the privatization movements across the world in all other areas of the economy (see Yergin and Stanislaw, 1998) – then we can see in these global developments the enduring influence of E.G. West. For, as we saw in the previous chapter, West was one of the key intellectual figures behind the Thatcher government's early forays into education, which set the scene for the later reforms in the United Kingdom. And West, as we saw in that chapter, was also a key influence in the development of Milton Friedman's understanding of the role of government in education, and thus an important, although indirect, influence on developments in the United States.

In this chapter, I first outline some of the school choice developments that have taken place across the world, inspired in part by this influence. But this prompts us to ask the questions: To what extent would E.G. West have approved of these developments? Would he see them as moving us towards the goal of purely private education provision? Or would he be skeptical about their likely impact?

School choice reforms have been characterized as two 'ideal types' of privatization (Patrinos and Ariasingam, 1997), the first involving demand-side financing (e.g. vouchers and tax credits), the second involving reforms to the educational supply side (e.g. charter schools). Both of these bear the mark of West's direct or indirect influence. However, there is a further kind of privatization that, I argue here, may actually be much more closely relevant to West's ideas on education and the role of government, and a source of encouragement to those moved by West's ideals. There is no way, however, in which one could say that West influenced the early development of this area, although the lessons to be learned from it are directly relevant to much of West's discussion and critique – and his influence is obvious in recent research and development. This is what has been dubbed '*de facto*' privatization, where people, especially the poor, are opting for private education because of the perceived inadequacies of state intervention (see Tooley and Dixon, 2006c). Hence, responsibilities for education have been transferred *de facto* to the private sector, through the rapid growth of private schools, rather than *de jure*, through reform or legislation. We turn to the evidence of this, of the burgeoning of low-cost private schools, also a global movement, in the final section, to explore its significance and relevance for West's critique of the role of government in education.

Relevance: School Choice Reforms

Demand-Side Reforms: Vouchers – Universal and Targeted

We have already come across West's broad definition of an education voucher: 'A tax-funded education voucher in the broadest sense is a payment made by the government to a school chosen by the parent of the child being educated; the voucher finances all or most of the tuition charged' (West, 1997a, p. 83). This broad definition allows us to include in our discussion the two existing examples of *universal* voucher schemes – those in Sweden and Chile – and examples of *targeted* vouchers. However, as this book was being finalized, the bill for a third universal voucher scheme was passed, in the state of Utah in the United States, which may be the most important school choice reform to date – although of course it is too early to assess its impact, or even whether it will actually be implemented. I give brief details here, and spell out some possible implications in later sections.

The Swedish reforms occurred in 1991 and 1992, under the Government Bill on Freedom of Choice and Independent Schools, and the Government Bill on School Choice respectively. These established 'the right of any nongovernment school that fulfils certain basic requirements to receive public funding on terms equal to those of public schools' (Sandström and Bergström, 2002, p. 23). The 'equal' funding is calculated at 85 percent of the calculated average cost per student in the municipal schools, with the other 15 percent accounting for overhead and administration of the municipalities. The figure was reduced to 75 percent in 1995. Enrollment rules were also opened within the public sector, with money following pupils to public schools in other municipalities. As long as schools satisfy the National Agency for Education (NAE) that they are meeting certain quality requirements, including a general curriculum framework, and that they are non-discriminatory, *any* kind of school is eligible, from religious schools to schools run by for-profit corporations. However, no schools are allowed to charge tuition fees. Municipalities are allowed to say whether they consider that the establishment of a new independent school would be harmful to existing schools, and their views must be taken into account by the NAE. Importantly, however, they have no veto on a school's establishment, and must, by law, finance any independent school that has been approved by the NAE, which has on occasion approved schools against the municipality's will.

A rapid growth of independent schools has been experienced since reforms were introduced, although this differs between municipalities (in Sweden, schooling is primarily the responsibility of the municipalities, the lowest tier of government). Overall, only about 6 percent of children of compulsory school age are in private schools, though the proportion ranges from zero to nearly 20 percent in some municipalities, with about 10 percent in Stockholm.

Significantly, more than half of private schools are owned by limited liability companies, with several companies now running 'chains' of for-profit schools (Sandström and Bergström, 2002, p. 28). One of these is Kunskapsskolan (which translates as 'The Knowledge School'). This company currently operates more than 20 schools, with about 6,000 pupils. Other examples include the 'International English School', first opened in Stockholm in 1993 and with now six schools across the country; Pysslingen (with 12 schools); and Vittra (with 25 schools).

The second *universal* voucher program is in Chile, where students can choose to enroll in schools in either the government or the private sector. The scheme was started in 1982 when the government provided a per-student subsidy equal to the average per-student expenditure by the Ministry of Education on local municipalities, multiplied by the number of students in government schools. Private schools were also provided with the same subsidy on the condition that they did not charge fees. Private schools, from pre-primary to secondary, could therefore choose whether to accept the subsidy – that is, to participate in the scheme, along with all of its regulatory requirements – or to remain outside it and not accept the subsidy. These schools initially needed to comply with certain conditions laid down by the Ministry of Education and their services had to be provided free to those students who chose their institution as a learning environment. The government pays money directly to the voucher school either on a per-pupil basis or, in some cases (namely, vocational schools run by non-profit organizations), via a lump sum amount.

In 1990 and 1993, additional laws were passed that altered the existing system – most notably in 1993 with 'shared financing'. A law was passed that allowed private subsidized schools and public secondary schools to charge tuition fees. The value of the voucher subsidy provided to the school decreases on a sliding scale dependent upon the tuition charged.

Finally, the state of Utah, in February 2007, passed a bill to sign into law the first universal voucher scheme in the United States. The Parent Choice in Education Act will provide almost all Utah parents with school-aged children with a means-tested voucher ranging between $500 and $3,000, depending on income. The 'almost all' is because the vouchers will not be given to parents of children who are currently in private schools whose family incomes are above 185 percent of federal poverty guidelines: However, everyone else will be entitled to them – that is, the 95 percent of parents whose children currently attend public schools can use the vouchers, plus those poorer parents who are currently sending their children to private school. Importantly, the voucher can be used at either public or private schools. In the future, it is planned that the reach will be more or less universal: all students starting kindergarten in autumn 2007 will be entitled to scholarships, and thereafter will be allowed access to the state vouchers – so that by 2020 every child in the state will be able to participate in the program.

Private schools taking part in the Utah program will be required to satisfy a number of regulations, including the administration of a nationally norm-referenced test; providing reports to parents and a school report to the state; complying with health, safety and antidiscrimination laws; and employing teachers with college degrees or equivalent specialized training. Also, they must have at least 40 students. To soften the blow to government schools, if a student uses his or her voucher to transfer from a public to private school, the school district will continue to fund the school for a period of five years as if the student had not transferred, or until the student would have graduated (Legislative General Counsel, 2007).

Will the Utah scheme be implemented? As this book is being finalized, a group called the Utahns for Public Schools, formed by, among others, the Utah Education Association, the state teachers' union, is trying to stop the scheme. The group has applied for a referendum petition. There is a further complexity, however, in that a second bill amending the first was also passed by the Legislative Counsel, and the referendum petition apparently challenges only the first bill, not the second. 'Short of a court-ordered injunction,' the Senate majority leader Curtis Bramble is reported as saying, 'vouchers are going forward' (*Salt Lake Tribune*, 13 March 2007, www.sltrib. com/news/ci_5392186). Given what has happened to other voucher proposals in the USA, however, for what it is worth, I am sceptical that this will happen.

Prior to the Utah scheme, the voucher programs in America, operating in 11 states and Washington, DC, were all *targeted* voucher schemes aimed at specific groups of children, such as those in low-income families, those with special needs or those in failing (public) schools. For instance, the Milwaukee publicly funded voucher scheme – the Milwaukee Parent Choice Program (MPCP) – was introduced in 1990, specifically targeting low-income families to allow them to attend registered private schools. The voucher's value is set at the per-student subsidy rate provided to the government schools by the state. Parents qualify for a voucher only if their family income is no more than 1.75 times the official poverty level. In 1995, the program was expanded, allowing around 15,000 students to participate. In 1998, the growth of the program burgeoned when the Wisconsin Supreme Court ruled that religious schools could participate in the program, a decision endorsed by the US Supreme Court in 2002.

The Cleveland voucher program is similar, enacted in 1995 with legislation modeled on the Milwaukee system. Religious schools could participate in the program right from the start, and children who were currently attending private schools could apply for the vouchers. Families with incomes below the poverty line received 90 percent of tuition fees and those above the cut-off point 75 percent of the tuition fees. In its first year, 1996, the program was limited to 2,000 students and to children who were enrolled in kindergarten to grade 3. By the end of 1996, this target had been met – with around 2,000 children receiving vouchers, enrolled in the 55 private schools operating in the Cleveland voucher scheme.

An alternative 'targeted voucher' approach has been tried in Florida, the Florida A+ Plan for Education, which targets *failure* of state schools, rather than poverty. The program provides vouchers when a government school is rated a grade F twice in a period of four years. The grade is determined by students taking the Florida Comprehensive Assessment Tests (FCAT) in mathematics, reading and writing. The A+ Education Plan was introduced in Florida in June 1999 and became the first state-wide voucher program to be implemented in the United States. The idea is that schools will improve their performance owing to the fear of being shamed into closing or loosing students and revenue. The value of the voucher received by parents in Florida has a maximum limit of $4,000, and this may be spent in any independent secular, religious or government school.

Other targeted voucher schemes occur in developing countries. In Colombia, a targeted voucher system was introduced in 1992, aimed at providing wider access to private education for poor students, inspired by the realization that there was a shortage of places offered by state secondary schools. The proposal allowed poor children to benefit from private school provision, moving out of the overcrowded public sector. Central government shares the cost of the vouchers with the local governments participating in the scheme, although the financial burden is not equally distributed between them: 80 percent of the cost is financed by central government, with the remaining 20 percent being taken up by the municipalities. Importantly, the private schools taking part offer an educational service that had been estimated to be of comparable quality to that found in government schools, but the typical cost of sending a pupil to private school, via the voucher scheme, is around *two-thirds* of the per-pupil cost of sending him or her to a government school. After two years, the program was serving 90,807 low-income students in a total of 1,789 schools. By 1997, more than 100,000 students from very low-income families had received subsidies through the program.

Similarly, in 1982 in Bangladesh, the Female Secondary Education Scholarship Project piloted a targeted voucher scheme. This program was aimed at girls from low-income families who otherwise would not have been able to obtain a secondary school education; this program is therefore gender specific. Girls who receive the scholarships are able to attend secondary school at half the tuition cost for the first three grades of the school. Before the scheme was introduced, in areas participating in the project female enrollment in secondary education hovered at around 27 percent; by 1987, this figure had risen to almost 44 percent.

Demand-Side Reforms: Educational Tax Credits

A second kind of Demand-side reform is the educational tax credit, which can take one of three main forms:

- Non-refundable tax credits mean that a family pays for its child's education in private school, and then has this cost subtracted from its annual tax payment.
- Refundable tax credits mean that a sum more than one's tax burden can be claimed, so those who pay little or no tax receive additional funds.
- Tax credits may also be used to allow businesses or philanthropically minded individuals to fund a disadvantaged child's private education, and for the business or individual to count this contribution against their tax liability.

The first US states to introduce tax credits were Minnesota and Arizona in 1997, followed by Iowa in 1998, Illinois in 1999 and Pennsylvania in 2001. In Illinois and Iowa, the state matches 25 percent of the parental contribution in tax credit, but only up to a maximum of $500 in Illinois and $250 in Iowa. In Pennsylvania, corporations can receive tax credits to the amount of 75 percent of their contributions. In Minnesota, the scheme allows a $1,000 tax credit per student for families with incomes up to $37,500. Tax credits can be used for private tutoring, textbooks, school transport, computers and instructional materials, but not for school fees. Families with incomes above this level receive a tax deduction of up to $2,500 for private school fees, as well as the other expenses that are covered under the tax credit.

In all of the states apart from Minnesota and Arizona, tax credits can be set against tuition costs. All states allow the claim to be made against materials and other forms of schooling, apart from Arizona. The majority of the tax credit schemes are not means tested, although the maximum value of the tax credit is stated in each state.

In Arizona, taxpayers receive a dollar-for-dollar tax credit when they donate to scholarship organizations providing support for students who attend or wish to attend private school. Taxpayers can make an individual donation of up to $500 per year, and a married couple

$625 per year. This has led, between 1998 and 2000, to donations of approximately $32 million generated by these educational tax credits, funding 19,000 scholarships.

The Canadian province of Ontario has also introduced a tax credit scheme. The scheme allows a qualifying taxpayer to claim a tax credit of a certain percentage of eligible tuition fees paid to an eligible independent school. Starting in 2002, taxpayers could claim 10 percent of fees, rising by 10 percent each year until by 2006 50 percent could be claimed.

Supply-Side Reforms

The second approach to school choice reforms is through public funding of private schools. This is a model in common currency across the world, in Europe, the United States, New Zealand, Australia and Hong Kong. The oldest models are found in the Netherlands and Denmark. In the Netherlands, a scheme ensuring freedom of parental choice in education has been in operation for almost 100 years, enshrined in the Constitution of 1917. Altogether, about 70 percent of children attend private schools – of which the majority are church schools, with a total of 7 percent at non-religious private schools. Schools include Montessori and Steiner schools, together with Jewish, Islamic, Hindu and humanist schools.

Any group of parents or other interested parties can make application to the Ministry of Education, Culture and Science to establish a new school. The number of parents required to open a school varies with the size of the municipality, from 50 parents in small municipalities (those with fewer than 25,000 people) to 125 in municipalities with more than 100,000 people. If successful in their application, these groups are *guaranteed* to receive state funding to set up and maintain their private school. Capital and recurrent costs for the school are supplied by the state.

All government and private grant-aided schools are guaranteed the same financial support. Interestingly, although private schools are not allowed to charge top-up fees, they are allowed to receive contributions from parents to fund the purchase of teaching materials, fund extracurricular activities, employ additional staff or pay teachers a supplement to their regular salaries. These 'fees' range from $100 to $200 per year at most primary schools and are higher at secondary schools.

Denmark shares with the Netherlands the key feature that there is a constitutional right for parents to set up their own schools and receive state funding. Currently, about 12 percent of primary and lower-secondary students are in the private sector, and 5 percent of upper-secondary students. Twenty-one percent of schools at the primary and lower-secondary level are in the private sector.

Since the Free School Act of 1855, parents and organizations have been able to set up their own schools. Any private organization or group of adults or parents can set up a private school for children between 6 and 18 years of age. To receive government funding, the minimum size of primary or lower secondary private school is only 28 pupils after three years. At least 12 pupils have to be enrolled in the first year, 20 in the second year, and from then on, 28 pupils.

All approved private schools are entitled to receive state subsidies covering approximately about 80 percent of their operational expenditure on the basis of the number of pupils enrolled at the individual school in a given year, plus a capital allowance and other special grants. On top of these grants, parents pay a moderate fee. At primary and lower secondary level, parents pay DKK 8,100 a year per pupil on average, or about 19 percent of the total expenditure. At upper secondary level, parents pay on average DKK 10,400 a year per pupil.

In the United States and Canada, the model of public subsidy for private schools that has emerged is the 'charter school'. Charter schools are free from direct administrative government control and are under fewer regulatory constraints than state schools. They must, however, meet the performance standards set by their charter. This freedom allows charter schools to have more control over their curriculum, their hours of operation, the staff they employ, budget and internal organization, and schedule. The funding they receive is based upon the number of pupils in attendance – so fewer pupils mean less funding. The concept was first introduced in 1991 in Minnesota, and by January 2000 there was charter legislation in 36 states, plus Washington, DC, with over 500,000 students enrolled in charter schools.

Charter schools can be converted state schools, converted private schools, or new schools. In fact, about 70 percent of charter schools are brand-new schools. Charter schools are not allowed to charge tuition fees in any state, although it is possible to invite voluntary contributions from parents for building projects. In general, too, charter schools can – and do – go bankrupt; they are not protected by the state from bankruptcy, and will go bankrupt if they have not been able to attract sufficient students, or have managed their budgets poorly. In all states too, if there is excess demand for places – as there is in some 70 percent of charter schools – places are allocated by 'equitable means' such as a lottery. In 21 of the 36 states – including Arizona, Massachussetts and Michigan – for-profit companies are allowed to manage charter schools.

The 'Cheers' and the 'Jeers'

It is safe to say that all of these reforms have generated a huge amount of academic and policy-oriented controversy. For every 'cheer' that can be found from those in favor of choice in education, there is an equal and opposite 'jeer' from those opposed. The controversies have focused on the extent to which bringing in aspects of choice can, or cannot, raise standards in education, enhance equality of opportunity and extend access, and promote social cohesion. This is not the place to explore these controversies (although some evidence has been adduced in Chapter 2); interested readers are referred to some of the contrasting sources contained in the bibliography. The key question I want to explore here is, instead, the extent to which any of these school choice reforms can be seen as moving forward West's agenda, in particular towards his preferred model of a genuine market in education.

A key source here is the economist John Merrifield (2005). Merrifield is a keen admirer of the work of E.G. West and in his recent work has spelled out strong principles of market reform that clearly owe much to the influence of West – and with which, I suggest, West would largely concur. Merrifield outlines what he argues should be five basic tenets of any 'choice-based, market accountability approaches to reform' (Merrifield, 2005, p. 183), if the reforms are to reveal anything like the virtues of educational markets that their proponents claim, and likewise if they are to reveal anything like the vices that opponents of markets claim too. (Merrifield refers to 'schools' in the passages that are quoted below. It may be preferable to think of these more broadly as 'educational opportunities', as market-based reform in education is likely to involve innovation and exploration of opportunities wider than schooling.) These are:

- 'Opportunity to specialize/innovate' – for 'Parental choice legislation has little relevance to parents unless there are noteworthy differences between educational opportunities. The opportunity to specialize underpins the exploitation of producer comparative advantage and the ability to experiment, innovate, and adjust to changing costs' (ibid.).
- Non-discrimination: per-child funding for all schools on the same basis – for there should be a 'level playing field' between all types of school, public or private. A scheme involving targeted vouchers that limit school choices to only, for instance, the poor, 'stifles innovation' in the market, and is in any case an implicit 'endorsement' of the current system, indicating that it is adequate for the majority (ibid., p. 187).
- 'Unbiased, low formal entry barriers' – for otherwise the benefits of full market competition will not be felt. This must include allowing for-profit providers.
- 'Avoidance of price control' – because 'Freedom to determine price and freedom to start a school on formally equal terms are essential partners because customers willingness to buy depends on the availability of reasonable alternatives. Without the actual and potential rivalry that results from freedom to start a private school, schools could exploit the absence of alternatives by selling minimally effective schooling at a very high price' (ibid., p. 190).
- 'Minimal regulation of private schools' – so as to avoid 'regulatory strangulation of the parental choice reform catalyst' (ibid., p. 194).

The key question then is: to what extent do any of the programs outlined earlier in the chapter meet these requirements? Merrifield was clearly writing prior to the passing of the Utah Bill, so his comments do not take into account events in Utah. Concerning the other US cases, Milwaukee, Florida and Cleveland, the picture is rather mixed but generally not hopeful, says Merrifield. While they may feature at least low levels of regulation of private schools, the per-child funding is not the same in public and private schools, they are in any case targeted at a very small proportion of the population, while price control, in the form of 'caps' to what can be added on to the vouchers by parents, is prevalent. In short, 'none of the publicly funded US programs approaches the key conditions' that a genuine voucher system would require (ibid., p. 202).

It would seem that Milton Friedman might have concurred with Merrifield's analysis – again, writing before the Utah bill, which was passed three months after his death. One clear issue for him was the tiny scale of the US experimental reforms. Taking all of the school choice reform programs in the United States together, 'they cover only a small fraction of all children in the country' (Friedman, 2006a, p. ix). And interestingly – statements that lend themselves to analysis in the light of West's discussion of public choice theory – Friedman expresses how he has been 'repeatedly frustrated', over the past 50 years of advocating vouchers, by the 'adamant and effective opposition of trade union leaders and educational administrators to any change that would in any way reduce their control of the educational system' (ibid.). For instance, he gives the example of his (and Rose's) involvement in trying to bring about not a small-scale experiment but a statewide universal voucher system in California in 1993 and 2000. In both cases, he writes, 'the initiatives were carefully drawn up and the voucher sums moderate'. The costings had been carefully worked out to show the advantages. Public opinion polls only nine months or so before the elections showed 'a sizable majority in favor of the initiative', plus 'a sizable group of fervent supporters' active. But then, on each occasion, about six months before the election, 'opponents of vouchers launched a well-financed and thoroughly unscrupulous campaign against the initiative. Television ads blared that vouchers would break the budget', even though the carefully worked out sums clearly showed a reduction in government spending, given that the vouchers for private schools were 'only a fraction of what government was spending per student'. Most sinisterly, for Friedman, 'Teachers were induced to send home with their students misleading propaganda against the initiative. Dirty tricks of every variety were financed from a very deep purse.' In each case, these tactics won the day: 'The result was to convert the initial majority into a landslide defeat' (ibid.). The same thing occurred, Friedman says, in Washington State, Colorado and Michigan. 'Opposition like this explains why progress has been so slow in such a good cause' (ibid., p. x).

But nonetheless, Friedman was still optimistic, despite these 'setbacks', an optimism perhaps vindicated by the Utah Bill – and, as the Milton & Rose D. Friedman Foundation had been active for seven years in, among other things, providing educational funding for the proposers of the Utah Bill, he may have known that the Bill would be passed there (author's interview with Robert Enlow, Milton & Rose D. Friedman Foundation, 13 March 2007). Friedman points to the growing 'public interest in and support for vouchers and tax credits'. And, he says,

> Sooner or later there will be a breakthrough; we shall get a universal voucher plan in one or more states. When we do, a competitive private educational market serving parents who are free to choose the school they believe best for each child will demonstrate how it can revolutionize schooling.
>
> (Friedman, 2006a, p. x).

Friedman pointed out why such a 'universal' voucher experiment is required, rather than the limited experiments that have taken place, if we are really to see the virtues and benefits of markets in education. He outlines what those benefits are and what the 'prescription' required to transform education is:

> Change the organization of elementary schooling and secondary schooling from top-down to bottom-up. Convert to a system in which parents choose the schools their children attend – or, more broadly, the educational services their children receive, whether in a

brick-and-mortar school or on DVDs or over the Internet or whatever alternative the ingenuity of man can conceive. Parents would pay for educational services with whatever subsidy they received from the government plus whatever sum they want to add out of their own resources. Producers would be free to enter or leave the industry and would compete to attract students. As in other industries, such a competitive free market would lead to improvements in quality and reductions in cost.

(ibid., p. 156)

But, says Friedman, the problem is 'how to get from here to there' (ibid.). For the kinds of vouchers that have been tried in the United States are not the solution at all, 'limited, directly or indirectly, to low-income families', and not allowing parental add-ons. Crucially for Friedman, everyone involved in the education system, particularly the rich and middle classes, needs to be involved in a voucher system, to stimulate the kind of innovation in education that he envisages:

One function of the rich is to finance innovation. They bought the initial cars and TVs at high prices and thereby supported production while the cost was being brought down, until what started out as a luxury good for the rich became a necessity for the poor.

(ibid., p. 157)

The crucial point, however, Friedman noted, was that progress towards that kind of educational voucher had been almost non-existent. And the reason he gives is that

centralization, bureaucratization, and unionization have enabled teachers' union leaders and educational administrators to gain effective control of government elementary and secondary schools. The union leaders and educational administrators rightly regard extended parental choice through vouchers and tax-funded scholarships as the major threat to their monopolistic control. So far, they have been extremely successful in blocking any significant change.

(ibid.)

Would the Utah scheme, if implemented, change any of this discussion? In terms of Merrifield's framework, it clearly would be much more advanced than any of the other US voucher schemes, if it were to survive any referendum challenge. Crucially, while the Bill does not explicitly mention this, it appears that *any* type of private school will be allowed to receive vouchers, including for-profit ones (Legislative General Counsel, 2007). While there are certainly regulatory hurdles that the private schools have to meet, these are not as onerous as Merrifield might have feared, and would seem to allow schools the '[o]pportunity to specialize/innovate', and to ensure '[u]nbiased, low formal entry barriers'. One main problem for Merrifield's criteria is that public schools that lose students will not feel any pain as a result of this, or at least not for five years: the legislation allows them to carry on receiving their funding however many students exit to private schools. This will seriously undermine the 'level playing field' required for genuine competition between public and private schools. And, of course, something that is unknown as this book goes to press, the teacher unions may yet succeed in blocking the proposals in any case.

If we now move away from the United States and back to Merrifield's framework for analysis of global reform, there are similar grounds for skepticism about the potential of school choice to bring in genuine market reforms. In the Chilean voucher system, there is not equal funding of public and private schools – with preferential funding of public schools commonplace. Importantly,

> Public schools work under a system of 'soft' budget constraints and are not influenced by the competition from private voucher schools. Municipal schools with important competition from private voucher schools may actually want their students to leave, since they can preserve their jobs (no municipal schools have closed) while teaching smaller classes.
>
> (Merrifield, 2005, p. 197)

While the education ministry does allow 'add-ons', these are capped and progressively taxed, so that if a school charges more than the approved level, the ministry gets to keep a proportion. Regulations are very tight on private schools, with inspections to check that all schools follow the national curriculum, organize themselves in the standard way, operate in a traditional school building and have similarly trained teachers. The barriers to entry for new schools 'are formidable', including that 'Regional offices of the Ministry of Education have to certify that there is no an excess of educational services before a private school can be formed' (ibid., p. 198). In other words, far from being, as some economists, including those sympathetic to market-oriented reforms, have claimed, 'a textbook voucher scheme' (ibid., p. 199), Chile's voucher system falls short at almost every level – or at least in terms of the criteria put forward by Merrifield, which I have argued would probably have been endorsed by West.

Sweden perhaps satisfies more of the requirements than any other, but even here, very heavy regulation, including the following of the national curriculum, means that there is very little room for specialization, and the barriers to entry for new schools are high. Price control 'is nearly ubiquitous', as add-ons are banned. Here, then, 'there is still little basis for substantial optimism. Key reform catalyst elements are absent or hobbled' (ibid., p. 208). Merrifield would level similar objections against any of the other school choice reforms noted above, and others around the world, in terms of his criteria.

In other words, for Merrifield – and, by inference, for West – there would be little room for optimism that any of the global 'school choice' reforms actually bring in genuine market elements. 'The parental choice programs have generally amounted to slightly increased mobility within a system of little-changed, largely uniform schooling alternatives' (ibid., p. 212). On the basis of this analysis – and bearing in mind that the Utah program may or may not affect this assessment – Merrifield suggests that the current, limited school choice experiments could actually have precisely the opposite impact to that which Friedman and West might have hoped for. Rather than moving the political equilibrium away from the kinds of state intervention to which we are used, and towards market reform, they could have the effect of actually alienating support for genuine school choice reform. The important point is that the proponents of school choice point to the evidence from these small-scale changes around the world as being of significance. But, says Merrifield, the evidence is extraordinarily limited, and usually 'unspectacular' (ibid., p. 213). The 'excessively exuberant or inappropriately alarmist' responses to these – the cheers and the jeers noted above – are thus entirely unfounded. But if the perception grows that for all the political effort put into these programs, only unspectacular changes result, and 'core problems remain' (ibid., fn. 113, p. 219), then '[t]hat would be catastrophic' – for genuine market reform, with programs 'that could actually harness and test market forces, would probably become increasingly politically infeasible' (ibid., p. 213). Reform, says Merrifield,

> is inadequate, perhaps even counterproductive, if it leaves the beneficiaries of the status quo in positions of power from which they can at least try to stifle competition and specialization or use regulatory micromanagement to extend government control to private schools.
>
> (ibid., p. 214)

In other words, tinkering at the margins with state intervention, and then claiming that important market reform is the result, could have the impact of reinforcing or even extending the government status quo, rather than undermining it.

To return to the question raised at the beginning of this section: to what extent would West have approved of these 'top-down' school choice developments? The suggestion was that the framework used by Merrifield would have been compatible with West's own understanding. Hence, it is likely that West would have concurred with Merrifield in his conclusions and, unless the Utah program is implemented successfully and changes this analysis, would *not* see much grounds for optimism that the kind of reforms espoused around the world under the rubrics of 'school choice' and 'markets' would be successful in moving towards the goal of his favored genuine markets in education.

Relevance: Private Schools for the Poor

The opposite conclusion, however, might be reached about the final strand that illustrates the relevance of West's ideas for today: the *de facto* privatization of education that is taking place around the world. For a remarkable phenomenon, now widely reported in the development literature, would have greatly interested and inspired E.G. West: the existence of a low-cost private education sector serving low-income families. The *Oxfam Education Report*, for instance, notes, 'the notion that private schools are servicing the needs of a small minority of wealthy parents is misplaced ... a lower cost private sector has emerged to meet the demands of poor households' (Watkins, 2000, pp. 229–30). Reporting on evidence from three states of India – Haryana, Uttar Pradesh and Rajasthan – De et al. note that 'private schools have been expanding rapidly in recent years' and that these 'now include a large number of primary schools which charge low fees', in urban as well as rural areas (2002, p. 148). For the poor in Calcutta (Kolkata), there has been a 'mushrooming of privately managed unregulated ... primary schools' (Nambissan, 2003, p. 52). Research in Haryana, India, found that unrecognized private schools 'are operating practically in every locality of the urban centres as well as in rural areas', often located adjacent to a government school (Aggarwal, 2000, p. 20). In Lahore, Pakistan, research suggests that 51 percent of children from families earning less than \$1 a day attend private schools, even when there are government alternatives (Alderman et al., 2003). From sub-Saharan Africa, in Uganda and Malawi private schools have 'mushroomed due to the poor quality government primary schools' (Rose, 2002, p. 6; 2003, p. 80). In Nigeria, 'unapproved [private] schools are providing schooling opportunities to a significant number of children, particularly in urban and peri-urban areas' (Adelabu and Rose, 2004, p. 64). And such private schools for the poor have been reported in many countries across the developing world.

Significantly, the low quality of government schools for the poor is often reported as a major reason for the 'mushrooming' of private schools: Venkatanarayana notes that the 'failure of public school in terms of meeting parents' expectations/aspirations' has led to a 'growing demand' for private schools in rural Andhra Pradesh, India (ibid., p. 40). The Human Development Report 2003 notes that in India and Pakistan, 'poor households cited teacher absenteeism in public schools as their main reason for choosing private ones' (UNDP,

2003, p. 112). The Probe Team reports that 'even among poor families and disadvantaged communities, one finds parents who make great sacrifices to send some or all of their children to private schools, so disillusioned are they with government schools' (1999, p. 103). In Kenya, 'the deteriorating quality of public education ... created demand for private alternatives' (Baurer et al., 2002).

My own recent research, funded by the John Templeton Foundation, has investigated the phenomenon in selected officially designated 'poor' areas of Nigeria, Ghana, Kenya, India and China. My research teams found that in most urban and peri-urban areas surveyed, the *vast majority* of school children were found to be in 'budget' private schools. For instance, in the poor urban and peri-urban areas of Lagos State, Nigeria, 75 percent of schoolchildren were in private schools. In the peri-urban district of Ga, Ghana, the figure was 64 percent, while in the slums of Hyderabad, India, 65 percent of schoolchildren were in private unaided schools. Private schools for the poor were found not just to be an urban or peri-urban phenomenon, either. In the deprived district of Mahbubnagar, rural Andhra Pradesh, India, roughly half of all schoolchildren were in private unaided schools. In the remote villages of rural Gansu, China, official figures showed no private schools at all; but we found 586, serving 59,958 children (see Tooley, 2005, 2006; Tooley and Dixon, 2006a, b, c).

The existence of this private sector serving the poor opens up a whole new horizon of relevance – as well as research opportunities – for those interested in the kinds of questions raised by E.G. West about the role of government in education. For recall one of the major problems that West had in moving the agenda forward, particularly in convincing those antagonistic to his views: the problem was his evidence base. West's major contribution *qua* economist can in fact be seen as his pointing to the need for evidence to challenge the accepted wisdom of the economic justifications for state intervention. And although in his later work, he was able to point to some of the growing evidence about the mostly small-scale voucher schemes that were being trialed in the United States and elsewhere, for West and others like him, this evidence was clearly not totally satisfactory: as John Merrifield (2005) has pointed out most clearly, as discussed earlier, nowhere in any of these so-called market experiments do we have anything like a genuine market in education. They are only heavily constrained quasi- or even *bogus* markets, which do not reveal the true potential (or, of course, some might argue, dangers) of real markets in education.

Instead, the evidence base that West was to rely on for all his conclusions was historical, particularly the history of education in the nineteenth century. But historical evidence, as he was quite aware, is open to different, even conflicting, interpretations. On the quantity of schooling and other educational opportunities, West was on firmest ground. To scholars who are willing to go back to the original sources, rather than rely on secondhand historical summaries, there appears to be little real dispute about the ways in which private sources – the churches and philanthropists, and small-scale proprietors – largely independent of any government assistance, were able to bring about literacy and provide schooling for the vast majority, including the poor. This was true in England and Wales, Scotland, and New York, and, to a smaller extent, in New South Wales. In other words, wherever West looked in detail at the data, he was able to show the prevalence of private educational opportunities. Yes, there are some details that can be disputed, but, by and large, his figures on quantity appear no longer controversial.

Where he had greatest difficulty in persuading others of his case concerned the quality of educational provision without the state. For, again as he was quite aware, there were plenty of *first-hand* accounts of educational *inadequacy* in the private schools, and very little if any contemporaneous evidence to counter those impressions. One of West's major contributions was to suggest that such damning evidence of low-quality private education was largely written by administrators, politicians, intellectuals and social reformers who had a vested interest in showing how bad things were, and hence showing how much their reforms and interventions were desperately required. We can, as West did, deconstruct what these sources were saying and point to likely reasons why they came out with the interpretation they did, and that an alternative, more positive interpretation is available. But ultimately, we do not know what the quality of education without the state was like in the nineteenth century. And so in the end, we cannot convince those like Chelly Halsey, in his irascible review of *Education and the State*, or Mark Blaug in his more tempered criticisms in *Education: A Framework for Choice*. They write that the actual words of the social reformers – where the social reformers write explicitly about the low quality of private provision – are the ones to examine, rather than any sophisticated deconstruction of them. And these words, as they correctly point out, contradict West's version of events. And if West is wrong about the quality of private educational provision in the nineteenth century, particularly vis-à-vis that obtainable in state education, then many (although of course not all) of his conclusions are ultimately weakened.

But this brings us to the relevance of the low-cost private schools that are burgeoning today in developing countries. These are genuine markets in education, where the majority of people go to private school. This is quite unlike in the developed world, where private education is always a small minority of total enrollment, around 7 percent in the United Kingdom, for instance, or only 6 percent in Sweden, which has a universal 'voucher' system. This is true even if one focuses instead on urban areas, which have a particularly high concentration of private education: in central London, for instance, private school enrollment is still only about 15 percent. In such circumstances, studying private education is not likely to lead to much understanding of how authentic educational markets might work: such private education 'markets' are unlikely to illustrate real competitive behavior and are likely to exhibit complacency among the providers, because the 'market' is very small, has a largely captive audience and is competing against a near-monopoly state provider.

The situation is completely different in the poor areas of developing countries, where private education forms the greater part of provision. In these areas, parents have genuine choices of a number of competing private schools within easy reach and are sensitive to the price mechanism; schools do close if demand is low, and new schools open to cater for expanded demand. In these genuine markets, educational entrepreneurs are apparently responding to parental needs and requirements.

Hence, these genuine markets are open to researchers who, like E.G. West was, are interested in questions of quality and the economic justifications for state intervention in education. Rather than relying on the impressions filtered through the lenses of the past, any interested researcher can in principle see for themselves what these low-cost private schools are like, can explore the dynamics of these markets and conduct research to see how they compare with the government alternative. Researchers can talk to parents and children, see at first hand what their relative perceptions of the public and private alternatives are, and explore why these might be the case, and whether they are valid. Importantly, the evidence can be fed back into the questions that West raised: Do the economic arguments for state intervention, based on the existence of externalities and the protection of minors principle, justify the kinds of state intervention we are used to? Do they in fact justify any state intervention at all? And predictions derived from public choice theory can be explored in real time, rather than retrospectively, without all the concomitant difficulties faced by West. Through the growing evidence about this low-cost private education sector, West's questions, and his answers, can be explored in ways that West would have welcomed but did not envisage.

For instance, some of the arguments that are used today against educational vouchers – and were used to challenge West when he was advocating them in England and Wales in the 1980s – can be informed by this evidence from developing countries. One of these objections the Friedmans characterize as '[d]oubt about new schools' (Friedman and Friedman, 1980, p. 204). Given that when they were writing, private schools were either 'parochial [religious] schools or elite academies', critics of the voucher proposal wanted to know what reason there was 'to suppose that alternatives will really arise'. The Friedmans were convinced that 'a market would develop where it does not exist today', attracting 'many entrants, both from public schools and from other occupations'. Their conviction came from talking to many people about vouchers:

> [W]e have been impressed by the number of persons who said something like, 'I have always wanted to teach (or run a school) but I couldn't stand the educational bureaucracy, red tape, and general ossification of the public schools. Under your plan, I'd like to try my hand at starting a school.'
>
> (ibid., pp. 204–5)

But just as we noted with the discussion of objections to vouchers in England and Wales in 1981, the Friedmans had no real evidence to support this claim. However, the evidence from developing countries today suggests that their confidence in the entrepreneurial spirit may be justified: it appears that educational entrepreneurs do emerge to provide educational opportunities, including among some of the poorest members of society. They emerge because parents and poor communities are concerned about education; it is a fundamental priority. When they have (well-founded) doubts about the efficiency and effectiveness of public schools, they will create alternatives of their own.

The evidence from developing countries could also help challenge another of the fundamental objections to vouchers in the United States, that prosperous families would 'top up', or supplement, the state provision with their own funds, which would penalize poor parents who *would not* spend their resources on education. The Friedmans replied that

> this view . . . seems to us another example of the tendency of intellectuals to denigrate parents who are poor. Even the very poorest can—and do—scrape up a few extra dollars to improve the quality of their children's schooling, although they cannot replace the whole of the present cost of public schooling.
>
> (ibid., pp. 203–4)

The evidence from developing countries supports this argument: some of the poorest parents on this planet do appear willing to 'scrimp and save' to pay for their children's education. This evidence is available to inform the parallel school choice debate within the United States.

Moreover, the perspectives of public choice theory can also be brought to bear on the evidence of what is happening in developing countries today – providing further evidence that can be used both to reflect back on West's analysis of nineteenth-century reforms and to add further insight into the questions of the role of government in education. West would have been particularly interested to see how international agencies and national governments are not sympathetic to the private schools for the poor, seeing them as a hindrance rather than a help in reaching their targets of 'education for all'. He would have noted that the objections raised against low-cost private schools – of their low quality, because they do not have trained teachers and are in poor-quality buildings – exactly parallel the criticisms of the private schools in Victorian England (see, for instance, Adelabu and Rose, 2004, p. 48; Save the Children UK, South and Central Asia, 2002, p. 8). And he would have been intrigued by the observation that the official agencies were deriving figures for the numbers of children out of school – and hence the numbers of children in dire need of international assistance – that simply excluded those in the unregistered private schools. This is so even though recent research suggests that very large minorities of children might be in these schools – perhaps 40 percent of all schoolchildren (Adelabu and Rose, 2004) – and that if such schoolchildren are taken into account, the numbers out of school and hence needing international assistance are dramatically reduced, perhaps in some cases almost to zero (Tooley and Dixon, 2006a, b, c). Here, for example, we might find firmer evidence of the kind of 'erroneous calculations' that West suggested were put forward by educational reforms in nineteenth-century England, America and Australia, and, crucially, be able to examine their origin and the motivations and intentions of those putting forward contemporary statistics in a way that was unavailable to West, focusing only on historical debates.

West would have noted with interest how particular vested interests are served by these calculations of educational need. He might also have observed that the research methods used by the Newcastle Commission in 1858 appear more sophisticated than those used by international agencies today: for the Newcastle Commission was very aware of the existence of the unregistered private schools – the commissioners termed them 'un-inspected' schools. Thus, they devised a method of sampling a number of areas to find out how many of these there were, and extrapolated from these figures to estimate how the educational needs of the population more generally were being met by them. Today's agencies in general simply look at the number of children officially in government and inspected private schools, and ignore those in unregistered schools altogether.

West's work also provides a framework to challenge reasons given by development agencies today as to why these private schools have no role to play in meeting the educational needs of the poor. In particular, two major objections would have deeply interested West:

First, it is argued by development agencies that governments should 'finance and provide' primary education because it 'benefits not only the individual who gains knowledge, it also benefits all members of society by improving health and hygiene behaviour and raising worker productivity' (UNDP, 2003, p. 111). Similarly, primary education is 'replete with market failures – with externalities as when . . . a farmer benefits from a neighbor's ability to read. So the private sector, left to its devices, will not achieve the level of . . . education that society desires' (World Bank, 2003, p. 3). In other words, this is precisely the externalities or neighborhood effects argument, applied to developing countries. But again, the existence of the private sector serving the poor provides a way in which researchers today can explore these arguments – with none of the disadvantages that West had in exploring the evidence from the nineteenth century. A first consideration would have to be that large numbers of the poor are using private provision, suggesting that state intervention might not be required to serve the majority. It would then be a matter for research to explore whether universal provision could better be provided through state intervention, and what level of state intervention might be required – for instance, targeted vouchers rather than universal subsidies. Furthermore, the existence of this sector allows us to explore empirically, rather than theoretically, whether or not private provision can produce some of the other externalities of education, such as education for democracy or social cohesion. The important point is that, in principle, it is possible to explore whether the private schools are delivering these, and whether or not this is better than the government alternative, by conducting research in these countries today. Where West had to rely on historical interpretation, empirical researchers today can get their boots muddy and go into the field.

The second major justification for state intervention in developing countries today is given as the argument from history: 'only when governments intervened [in education] did these services become universal in Canada, Western Europe and the United States' (UNDP,

2003, p. 111). Similarly, 'in practice no country has achieved significant improvement in ... primary education without government involvement' (World Bank, 2003, p. 11). Therefore, state intervention is also required in developing countries. For readers of West, this reason may not appear strong. Chapters 3 and 4 laid out in detail West's arguments that suggest this is a complete misreading of the historical evidence. It is certainly not the case that, in terms of quantity of provision, government intervention was required in order to provide universal or near-universal schooling for the poor. The discussion of quality is more controversial – but, crucially, we no longer have to rely on the historical evidence, but can look to the relative quality of private provision in developing countries today to help inform the debate about what the private sector for the poor can deliver.

When Edwin George West wrote *Education and the State* in 1965, he was plowing a lonely intellectual furrow. His was one of only a small number of voices raised questioning the role of government in education, and the position he took, after reflecting on historical evidence and economic arguments, was on the extremes of the debate, allowing for its ready dismissal by his many opponents. Today, those exploring West's agenda can be seen as moving towards the mainstream of educational policy ideas. Perhaps this might be because of the range of governments, of multifarious political complexions, that are exploring and espousing school choice reforms, of the kinds we have touched on briefly in this chapter. Perhaps a program like the Utah voucher scheme will be implemented and provide the type of educative experience that will shift the political equilibrium further towards support for educational markets. But even more strongly, it would be because of the ways in which people, especially the poor, are embracing the private education alternative in developing countries as a response to the inadequacies of state provision. Given West's interest throughout his life in the ways in which the poor were served by private education historically, he would be very comfortable that his life's work provided a framework through which to explore and evaluate – and even celebrate – this growing movement.

Bibliography

This section includes first a complete bibliography for E.G. West, followed by references in the text and other relevant texts for further reading.

West's publications: sole authorship

An asterisk (*) indicates sources that have been referred to in the text.

(*)West, E.G. (1963) The Treatment of Education in the Writings of the Classical Economists, unpublished PhD thesis, University of London, October (awarded 1964).

(*)West, E.G. (1964a) Adam Smith's Two Views on the Division of Labour, *Economica*, vol. 31, no. 121, pp. 23–32.

West, E.G. (1964b) The Role of Education in Nineteenth-Century Doctrines of Political Economy, *British Journal of Educational Studies*, vol. 12, no. 2, May, pp. 161–72.

West, E.G. (1964c) Private versus Public Education: A Classical Economic Dispute, *Journal of Political Economy*, vol. 72, no. 5, October, pp. 465–75.

(*)West, E.G. (1964d) Parents' Choice in Education, *The Rebirth of Britain: A Symposium of Challenging Essays on Britain in the Mid-1960's and the Splendid Opportunities before Her*, London: Pan Books (in association with the Institute of Economic Affairs).

West, E.G. (1965a) *Education and the State: A Study in Political Economy*, London: Institute of Economic Affairs.

West, E.G. (1965b) Liberty and Education: John Stuart Mill's Dilemma, *Philosophy*, vol. 27, no. 2, April, pp. 35–48.

West, E.G. (1966) Regional Planning: Fact and Fallacy, *Lloyds Bank Review*, April, pp. 35–48.

(*)West, E.G. (1967a) The Political Economy of Public School Legislation, *Journal of Law and Economics*, vol. 10, October, pp. 101–28.

West, E.G. (1967b) Tom Paine's Voucher Scheme for Public Education, *Southern Economic Journal*, vol. 33, no. 2, January, pp. 378–82.

(*)West, E.G. (1968a) *Economics, Education and the Politician*, Hobart Paper 42, London: Institute of Economic Affairs.

West, E.G. (1968b) The Propriety of Migration Controls, *Il Politico*, vol. 33, pp. 360–75.

West, E.G. (1968c) Social Legislation and the Demand for Children, *Economic Inquiry*, vol. 6, no. 5, December, pp. 419–24.

(*)West, E.G. (1969a) *Adam Smith: The Man and His Works*, New Rochelle, NY: Arlington House.

West, E.G. (1969b) The Political Economy of Alienation: Karl Marx and Adam Smith, *Oxford Economic Papers*, vol. 21, no. 1, March, pp. 1–23.

(*)West, E.G. (1969c) Adam Smith's Philosophy of Riches, *Philosophy*, vol. 44, no. 168, April, pp. 101–15.

West, E.G. (1969d) Private and Political Markets in Education, *Economic Age*, no. 1, April, pp. 12–15.

West, E.G. (1969e) Classical Economic Views of the Role of the State in Victorian Education: Comment, *Southern Economic Journal*, vol. 35, no. 4, April, pp. 185–7.

West, E.G. (1969f) Welfare Economics and Emigration Taxes, Southern Economic Journal, vol. 36, no. 1, July, pp. 52–9.

West, E.G. (1969g) The Evolution of Britain's Minimum Wage Policy: An Economic Assessment, *Moorgate and Wall Street*, pp. 52–66.

(*)West, E.G. (1970a) Resource Allocation and Growth in Early Nineteenth Century British Education, *Economic History Review*, vol. 23, no. 1, April, pp. 68–95.

West, E.G. (1970b) Forster and After: 100 Years of State Education, *Economic Age*, vol. 2, no. 5, August, pp. 14–18.

(*)West, E.G. (1970c) *Education and the State: A Study in Political Economy*, 2nd edn, London: Institute of Economic Affairs.

West, E.G. ([1967] 1970d) Dr. Blaug and State Education: A Reply, in Beales et al. ([1967]1970).

West, E.G. (1970e) Private versus Public Education, in A.W. Coats (ed.) *The Classical Economists and Economic Policy*, London: Methuen.

(*)West, E.G. (1971a) The Interpretation of Early Nineteenth Century Education Statistics, *Economic History Review*, vol. 24, no. 4, November, pp. 633–42.

West, E.G. (1971b) Subsidized but Compulsory Consumption Goods: Some Special Welfare Cases, *Kyklos*, vol. 24, pp. 534–45.

(*)West, E.G. (1971c) Adam Smith and Rousseau's Discourse on Inequality: inspiration or provocation? *Journal of Economic Issues*, vol. 5, Summer, pp. 56–70.

West, E.G. (1971d) Going Comprehensive in Two County Boroughs, *Journal of Educational Administration and History*, November, pp. 33–36.

West, E.G. (1973a) *'Pure' versus 'Operational' Economics in Regional Policy: Regional Policy Forever?* London: Institute of Economic Affairs.

West, E.G. (1973b) The Bilateral Monopoly Theory of Public Goods, *Journal of Political Economy*, vol. 81, no. 5, August–September, pp. 1226–35.

West, E.G. (1974a) The Economics of Compulsory Education, in W.F. Rickenbacker (ed.) *The Twelve Year Sentence,* La Salle, IL: Open Court.

West, E.G. (1974b) Vote Earning versus Vote Losing Properties of Minimum Wage Laws, *Public Choice*, 19, Fall, pp. 133–7.

(*)West, E.G. (1975a) *Education and the Industrial Revolution*, London: Batsford.

(*)West, E.G. (1975b) Education Slowdown and Public Intervention in 19th-Century England: A Study in the Economics of Bureaucracy, *Explorations in Economic History*, 12, pp. 61–87.

(*)West, E.G. (1975c) Adam Smith and Alienation: A Rejoinder, *Oxford Economic Papers*, vol. 27, no. 2, July, pp. 295–301.

West, E.G. (1975d) Public Debt Burden and Cost Theory, *Economic Inquiry*, vol. 13, June, pp. 179–90.

West, E.G. (1975e) Student Loan: A Reappraisal . . . with Special Reference to Canada's Changing Needs in Educational Finance, Ontario Economic Council, Toronto Working Paper Series 4/75.

West, E.G. (1975f) Adam Smith and Alienation, in A. Skinner and T. Wilson (eds) *Essays on Adam Smith*, Oxford: Clarendon Press; Ames: Iowa State University Press.

West, E.G. (1976a) An Economic Analysis of the Law and Politics of Non-Public School 'Aid', *Journal of Law and Economics*, vol. 19, no. 1, April, pp. 79–101.

West, E.G. (1976b) The Yale Tuition Postponement Plan in the Mid-Seventies, *Higher Education*, vol. 5, no. 2, pp. 169–75.

West, E.G. (1976c) The Radical Economics of Public School Breakdown: A Critique, *Review of Social Economy*, vol. 34, no. 2, pp. 125–46.

(*)West, E.G. (1976d) *Nonpublic School Aid: The Law, Economics, and Politics of American Education*, Lexington, MA: Lexington Books.

(*)West, E.G. (1976e) *Adam Smith: The Man and His Works*, new edition, Indianapolis: Liberty Fund.

(*)West, E.G. (1976f) Adam Smith's Economics of Politics, *History of Political Economy*, vol. 8, no. 4, November, pp. 515–39.

West, E.G. (1977a) The Perils of Public Education, *The Freeman*, vol. 27, no. 11, November, pp. 13–17.

(*)West, E.G. (1977b) Adam Smith's Public Economics: A Re-evaluation, *Canadian Journal of Economics*, vol. 10, no. 1, pp. 1–18.

West, E.G. (1977c) Introductory essay and index, in A. Smith, *The Theory of Moral Sentiments*, new edition of Adam Smith's 1759 classic, Indianapolis: Liberty Fund.

West, E.G. (1978a) J.S. Mill's Redistribution Policy: New Political Economy or Old?, *Economic Inquiry*, vol. 41, no. 4, pp. 570–86.

West, E.G. (1978b) Literacy and the Industrial Revolution, *Economic History Review*, new series, vol. 31, no. 3, pp. 369–83.

West, E.G. (1978c) American Public Schools on Trial, *New Society*, January.

West, E.G. (1978d) A Prince Replies to Machiavelli: Philip of England on the Erosion of Freedom, *The Freeman*, vol. 28, no. 2, February.

West, E.G. (1978e) Tuition Tax Credit Proposals: An Economic Analysis of the 1978 Packwood/Moynihan Bill, *Policy Review*, vol. 3, Winter, pp. 17–21.

West, E.G. (1978f) The Burdens of Monopoly: Classical versus Neoclassical, *Southern Economic Journal*, vol. 44, no. 4, pp. 829–45.

West, E.G. (1978g) Scotland's Resurgent Economist: A Survey of the New Literature on Adam Smith, *Southern Economic Journal*, vol. 45, no. 2, October, pp. 343–69.

West, E.G. (1979a) Free Education: A Re-examination, in R.E. Wagner (ed.) *Government Aid to Private Schools: Is It a Trojan Horse?*, Menlo Park, CA: Institute for Human Studies.

West, E.G. (1979b) Voters versus the Public Schools, *Policy Report*, CATO Institute, vol. 1, no. 2, February, pp. 9–11.

West, E.G. (1979c) Challenging the Public School Monopoly, *Reason*, vol. 11, no. 8, December, pp. 17–25.

West, E.G. (1980a) Education and Crime: A Political Economy of Interdependence, *Character*, vol. 8, no. 4, June.

West, E.G. (1980b) The 'Exploitation' of Bob Cratchit: In Defense of Scrooge, *Competition*, vol. 1, no. 2, April.

West, E.G. (1980c) *New U.S. Plans for Jobless Youth*, Policy Report, CATO Institute, vol. 11, no. 3, May.

West, E.G. (1980d) Policies to Reduce Criminal Activity: Do Schools Make a Difference?, *Character*, University of Illinois, vol. 3, April, pp. 7–9.

West, E.G. (1980e) Canada's Oil Price Dilemma, *Journal of Economic Affairs*, vol. 1, no. 1, October, pp. 63–4.

West, E.G. (1980f) The Public School System and the Deterioration of Free Exercise, *Review Journal of Philosophy and Social Science*, vol. 4, no. 2, pp. 10–15.

West, E.G. (1981a) The Role of the State in Financing Recurrent Education: Lessons from European Experience, Commentary, *Public Choice*, vol. 36, no. 3, pp. 579–82.

(*)West, E.G. (1981b) *The Economics of Education Tax Credits*, *Critical Issues*, Washington, DC: Heritage Foundation.

(*)West, E.G. (1981c) Education Vouchers: New Perspectives in the Eighties?, *Policy Review*, Washington, vol. 15, Winter, pp. 7–12.

West, E.G. (1981d) The Education Tax Credit Proposal, *CATO Institute Policy Report*, vol. 3, no. 9, September.

West, E.G. (1981e) An analysis of the District of Columbia: Education Tax Credit Initiative, *CATO Policy Analysis*, October 1981, pp. 27–33.

West, E.G. (1982a) The Prospects for Education Vouchers: An Economic Analysis, in R.B. Everhart (ed.) *The Public School Monopoly: A Critical Analysis of Education and the State in American Society*, San Francisco: Pacific Research Institute for Public Policy.

(*)West, E.G. (1982b) Education Vouchers – Evolution or Revolution?, *Journal of Economic Affairs*, vol. 3, no. 1, October, pp. 14–18.

West, E.G. (1982c) The Public Monopoly and the Seeds of Self-Destruction, in M.E. Manley-Casimir (ed.) *Family Choice in Schooling: Issues and Dilemmas*, Lexington, MA: Lexington Books.

West, E.G. (1982d) Ricardo in Historical Perspective: Review Article, *Canadian Journal of Economics*, vol. 15, no. 2, May, pp. 308–26.

West, E.G. (1982e) The Public Monopoly and the Seeds of Self-Destruction, in M.E. Manley-Casimir (ed.) *Family Choice in Schooling: Issues and Dilemmas*, Lexington, MA: Lexington Books.

West, E.G. (1982f) Commentaries: The Role of the State in Financing Recurrent Education: Lessons from European Experience, in M.J. Bowman (ed.) *Collective Choice in Education*, The Hague: Kluwer Nijhoff.

(*)West, E.G. (1983a) Nineteenth-Century Educational History: The Kiesling Critique, *Economic History Review*, vol. 36, no. 3, pp. 426–34.

West, E.G. (1983b) Marx's Hypotheses on the Length of the Working Day, *Journal of Political Economy*, vol. 91, no. 2, April, pp. 266–81.

West, E.G. (1983c) Parental versus State Goals in Education: Comments on Arthur E. Wise and Linda Darling-Hammond's 'Education by Voucher', *Educational Theory*, vol. 34, no. 1, Winter, pp. 51–3.

(*)West, E.G. (1983d) Tuition Tax Credits: Equity Issues, *American Education*, vol. 2, July.

West, E.G. (1983e) Quality Trends in U.S. Public Schools, CATO *Institute Policy Report*, Fall, pp. 21–30.

West, E.G. (1983f) Are American Schools Working? Disturbing Cost and Quality Trends, *CATO Policy Analysis*, no. 26. Washington, DC: CATO Institute.

West, E.G. (1984a) Failing School Systems in America and Elsewhere, *Journal of Social, Political and Economic Studies*, vol. 9, no. 1, Spring.

West, E.G. (1985a) The Real Cost of Tuition Tax Credits, *Public Choice*, vol. 46, no. 1, pp. 61–70.

West, E.G. (1985b) The Demise of 'Free' Education, *Challenge: The Magazine of Economic Affairs*, vol. 27, no. 6, January–February, pp. 13–20.

West, E.G. (1985c) The Economics of Performing Shakespeare: Comment, *American Economic Review*, vol. 75, no. 5, pp. 1206–9.

West, E.G. (1985d) Public Aid to Ontario's Independent Schools, *Canadian Public Policy*, vol. 11, no. 4, pp. 701–10.

West, E.G. (1985e) Richard Cantillon and Adam Smith: A Reappraisal, *Research in the History of Economic Thought and Methodology*, vol. 3, pp. 27–51.

West, E.G. (1985f) The Shapiro Report on Ontario's Private Schools, *Fraser Forum*, Vancouver: Fraser Institute, November.

West, E.G. (1985g) Literacy and the Industrial Revolution, in J. Mokyr (ed.) *The Economics of the Industrial Revolution*, Totowa, NJ: Rowman & Allenheld.

West, E.G. (1985h) The Universal Student Grant Option in the Federal Financing of Post-secondary Education. In A. Noordeh (ed.) *Reforming the Financing Arrangement for Post-secondary Education in Canada*, Ontario Economic Council Conference Proceedings.

(*)West, E.G. (1986a) An Economic Rationale for Public Schools: The Search Continues, *Teachers College Record*, vol. 88, no. 2, Winter, pp. 152–62.

West, E.G. (1986b) Arts Vouchers to Replace Grants, *Journal of Economics Affairs*, vol. 6, no. 3, pp. 9–11.

(*)West, E.G. (1986c) Education Reform: Administrative Objections Over-ruled, *Journal of Economic Affairs*, vol. 6, no. 4, May, pp. 24–5.

West, E.G. (1987a) Constitutional Decisions on Non-public School Aid, *Emory Law Journal*, vol. 16, no. 1, April, pp. 795–851.

West, E.G. (1987b) Monopoly, published in *The New Palgrave: A Dictionary of Economic Thought and Doctrine*, J. Eatwell, M. Milgate and P. Newman (eds), New York: Stockton Press.

West, E.G. (1988) *Higher Education in Canada: An Analysis*, Vancouver: Fraser Institute.

(*)West, E.G. (1989a) Open Enrollment: A Vehicle for Market Competition in Schooling?, *CATO Journal*, vol. 9, no. 1, Spring/Summer, pp. 253–62.

West, E.G. (1989b) The Economics of Charities: Revised Theory and New Evidence, *Economic Affairs*, vol. 9, no. 3, March, pp. 22–4.

West, E.G. (1989c) Non-profit Organizations: Revised Theory and New Evidence, *Public Choice*, vol. 63, no. 2, November, pp. 165–74.

West, E.G. (1989d) *The Education Monopoly Problem*, CIS Occasional Papers 26, Sydney: Centre for Independent Studies.

(*)West, E.G. (1990a) Public Education via Exclusive Territories, *Public Finance Quarterly*, vol. 18, no. 4, October, pp. 371–94.

West, E.G. (1990b) *Education and Choice*, CIS Occasional Paper, Sydney: Centre for Independent Studies.

West, E.G. (1990c) Restoring Family Autonomy in Education, *Chronicles*, vol. 13, October, pp. 11–15.

West, E.G. (1990d) Adam Smith's Revolution: Past and Present, in *Adam Smith's Legacy: His Thought in Our Time* (other contributors: N. Barry, W. Letwin, N. Ridley and J. Shearmur), London: Adam Smith Institute.

West, E.G. (1990e) *Adam Smith and Modern Economics: From Market Behaviour to Public Choice*, Aldershot, UK: Edward Elgar.

West, E.G. (1990f) Educación y Libertad, *Revista Acta Académica*, no. 6, May, Universidad Autónoma de Centroamérica.

(*)West, E.G. (1991a) Public Schools and Excess Burdens, *Economics of Education Review*, vol. 10, no. 2, pp. 159–69.

(*) West, E.G. (1991b) Rejoinder, *Economics of Education Review*, vol. 10, no. 2, pp. 177–8.

West, E.G. (1991c) Secular Cost Changes and the Size of Government: Towards a Generalized Theory, *Journal of Public Economics*, vol. 45, no. 3, pp. 363–81.

West, E.G. (1991d) Comments: The Welfare Implications of International Intergovernmental Cooperation, in S. Gordon and T.K. Rymes (eds) *Welfare, Property Rights, and Economic Policy: Essays and Tributes in Honor of H. Scott Gordon*, Ottawa: Carleton University Press.

West, E.G. (1991e) Comment: Merit Wants and Public Goods Theory, in L. Eden (ed.) *Retrospectives on Public Finance*, Durham, NC: Duke University Press.

(*)West, E.G. (1992a) The Benthamites as Educational Engineers: The Reputation and the Record, *History of Political Economy*, vol. 24, no. 3, Fall, pp. 595–621.

West, E.G. (1992b) Autonomy in School Provision: Meanings and Implications – Review Essay, *Economics of Education Review*, vol. 11, no. 4, pp. 417–25.

(*)West, E.G. (1993a) The 'Opting Out' Revolution in British Education: Real versus Fictitious Opportunities, *Economic Affairs*, vol. 13, no. 3, pp. 18–21.

West, E.G. (1993b) Simplicity versus Complexity in Adam Smith: The Intellectuals' Dilemma, *Quadrant: Australian Review of Ideas*, vol. 38, no. 3.

West, E.G. (1993c) *Education and Competitiveness*, Discussion Paper 93–02, Government and Competitiveness School of Policy Studies, Queen's University, Kingston, Ontario, Canada.

(*)West, E.G. (1993d) *Higher Education and Competitiveness*, Discussion Paper 93–26, Government and Competitiveness School for Policy Studies, Queen's University, Kingston, Ontario, Canada.

(*)West, E.G. (1993e) Why Adam Smith Burned His Clothes, *The Freeman*, vol. 43, no. 10, October.

(*)West, E.G. (1994a) *Education and the State: A Study in Political Economy*, 3rd edn (revised and expanded), Indianapolis: Liberty Fund.

(*)West, E.G. (1994b) Education without the State, *Economic Affairs*, vol. 14, no. 5, pp. 12–15, p. 17.

(*)West, E.G. (1994c) Interview with Adam Smith, *The Region*, vol. 8, no. 2, June, Federal Reserve Bank of Minneapolis.

West, E.G. (1994d) Joint Supply Theory before Mill, *History of Political Economy*, vol. 26, no. 2, Summer, pp. 267–78.

West, E.G. (1994e) *Britain's New Student Loan System in World Perspective: A Critique*, London: Institute of Economic Affairs.

West, E.G. (1995a) *Education with and without the State*, World Bank, HCO Working Paper 61, September.

West, E.G. (1995b) *Mr. Axworthy's Proposals for Reforming Canadian University Finance: A World Perspective*, Vancouver: Fraser Forum.

West, E.G. (1995c) The Economics of Fundamental Research, in J.W. Sommer (ed.) *Academy in Crisis: The Political Economy of High Education*, New Brunswick, NJ: Transaction Publishers.

(*)West, E.G. (1996a) *Education Vouchers in Practice and Principle: A World Survey*, HCO Working Paper 64, World Bank.

West, E.G. (1996b) The Spread of Education before Compulsion: Britain and America in the 19th Century, *The Freeman*, vol. 46, no. 6, July.

(*)West, E.G. (1996c) Adam Smith on the Cultural Effects of Specialization: Splenetics versus Economics, *History of Political Economy*, vol. 28, no. 2, Spring, pp. 83–105.

(*)West, E.G. (1996d) *Adam Smith into the Twenty-first Century*, Fairfax, VA: The Locke Institute.

(*)West, E.G. (1996e) Foreword to J. Tooley, *Education without the State*, London: Institute of Economic Affairs.

(*)West, E.G. (1997a) Educational Vouchers in Principle and Practice: A Survey, *World Bank Research Observer*, vol. 12, no. 1, pp. 83–103.

(*)West, E.G. (1997b) Adam Smith's Support for Money and Banking Regulation: A Case of Inconsistency?, *Journal of Money, Credit and Banking*, vol. 29, February, pp. 127–34.

West, E.G. (1997c) C.D. Howe's Report on Canadian Student Loans, *Fraser Forum*, Fraser Institute, pp. 25–6.

West, E.G. (1997d) *Student Loans under New Scrutiny*, Public Policy Sources 1, Fraser Institute.

(*)West, E.G. (1998a) The Role of Income Tax in Student Loan Repayments, *Economic Affairs*, vol. 18, no. 3, pp. 24–30.

(*)West, E.G. (1998b) Supplying and Financing Education: Options and Trends under Growing Fiscal Restraints, in H. Giersch (ed.) *On the Merit and Limits of Markets*, Berlin: Springer-Verlag.

(*) West, E.G. (1999a) *First acquaintances with James Buchanan's Scholarship: A Personal Reminiscence on the Occasion of His 80th Birthday*, Fairfax, VA: Public Choice Center.

(*)West, E.G. (1999b) Adam Smith and *The Wealth of Nations*, in R.M. Ebeling (executive ed.) *The Age of Economists: From Adam Smith to Milton Friedman*, Champions of Freedom, vol. 26, Hillsdale, MI: Hillsdale College Press.

West, E.G. (2000a) Unilateral Free Trade versus Reciprocity in *The Wealth of Nations*, *Journal of the History of Economic Thought*, vol. 22, no. 1, pp. 29–42.

West, E.G. (2000b) Public Education and Imperfect Democracy, in T.R. Machan (ed.) *Education in a Free Society*, Stanford, CA: Hoover Institution Press.

(*)West, E.G. (2001a) *Education and the Industrial Revolution*, 2nd edn, Indianapolis: Liberty Fund.

West, E.G. (2001b) Charles L. Griswold: *Adam Smith and the Virtues of Enlightenment*, *Public Choice*, vol. 104, pp. 183–91.

West's publications: joint authorship

Beales, A.C.F., Blaug, M., Veale, D., and West, E.G. ([1967] 1970) *Education: A Framework for Choice. Papers on Historical, Economic and Administrative Aspects of Choice in Education and its Finance*, Readings in Political Economy 1, London: Institute of Economic Affairs.

Chen, Z., and West, E.G. (1997) *Education as a Positional Good: The Role of Vouchers*, Working Paper Series, Carleton University, Ottawa.

Chen, Z., and West, E.G. (2000) Selective versus Universal Vouchers: Modelling Median Voter Preferences in Education, *American Economic Review*, vol. 90, no. 5, December, pp. 1520–34.

Constantatos, C., and West, E.G. (1991) Measuring Social Returns from Education: Some Neglected Factors, *Canadian Public Policy*, vol. 7, no. 2, June, pp. 127–38.

Diman, R.W., and West, E.G. (1989) Destutt de Tracy: A French Precursor of the Virginia School of Public Finance, *History of Economics Society Bulletin*, vol. 11, no. 2, Fall, pp. 210–15.

Ferris, J.S., and West, E.G. (1996a) Changes in the Real Size of Government: U.S. Experience 1948–1989, *Southern Economic Journal*, vol. 62, no. 1, pp. 537–53.

Ferris, J.S., and West, E.G. (1996b) The Cost Disease and Government Growth: Qualifications to Baumol, *Public Choice*, vol. 89, no. 1–2, pp. 35–52.

Ferris, J.S., and West, E.G. (1999) Cost Disease versus Leviathan Explanations of Government Growth, *Public Choice*, vol. 98, no. 3–4, March, pp. 307–16.

Ferris, J.S., and West, E.G. (2002) Education Vouchers, the Peer Group Problem and the Question of Dropouts, *Southern Economic Journal*, vol. 68, no. 4, pp. 774–93.

Grossman, P., and West, E.G. (1994) Federalism and the Growth of Government, *Public Choice*, vol. 79, no. 1–2, pp. 19–32.

Martinello, F., and West, E.G. (1988) The Optimal Size of the Tuition Tax Credit, *Public Finance Quarterly*, vol. 16, no. 4, November, pp. 425–38.

Martinello, F., and West, E.G. (1991) Education Budget Reductions via Tax Credits: Some Further Considerations, *Public Finance Quarterly*, vol. 19, no. 3, July, pp. 355–68.

Staaf, R.J., and West, E.G. (1980) Limits on Public Provision of Private Goods, *American Economic Review*, vol. 70, no. 3, June, pp. 461–5.

Tooley, J., and West, E.G. (1998) Student Loans in Developing Countries: Government versus Company Loans, *Economic Affairs*, vol. 18, no. 3, September, pp. 31–5.

West, E.G., and Hafer, R.W. (1978) J.S. Mill, Unions, and the Wages Fund Recantation: A Reinterpretation, *Quarterly Journal of Economics*, vol. 92, no. 4, November, pp. 603–19.

West, E.G., and Hafer, R.W. (1981) J.S. Mill, Unions, and the Wages Fund Recantation: A Reinterpretation – Reply, *Quarterly Journal of Economics*, vol. 96, no. 3, August, pp. 543–9.

West, E.G., and McKee, M. (1983) De Gustibus Non Est Disputandum: The Phenomenon of 'Merit Wants', *American Economic Review*, vol. 73, no. 5, December, pp. 1110–21.

West, E.G., and Palsson, H. (1988) Parental Choice of School Characteristics: Estimation using State-Wide Characteristics, *Economic Inquiry*, vol. 26, no. 4, pp. 725–40.

West, E.G., and Staaf, R.J. (1979) The Distributional Implications of Public Goods Revisited, *Econometrica*, vol. 47, no. 4, May, pp. 1031–7.

West, E.G., and Staaf, R.J. (1981) Extra Governmental Powers in Public Schools: The Unions and the Courts, *Public Choice*, vol. 36, no. 3, pp. 619–37.

(*)West, E.G., Blaug, M., Beales, H., and Veale, D, (1967) *Readings in Political Economy*, London: Institute of Economic Affairs.

References and Further Reading

Adelabu, M., and Rose, P. (2004) Non-state Provision of Basic Education in Nigeria, in G. Larbi, M. Adelabu, P. Rose, D. Jawara,

O. Nwaorgu and S. Vyas, *Nigeria: Study of Non-state Providers of Basic Services*, commissioned by Policy Division, Department for International Development (DFID), UK, and Country Studies, International Development Department, Birmingham: University of Birmingham and DFID.

Aggarwal, Y. (2000) *Public and Private Partnership in Primary Education in India: A Study of Unrecognised Schools in Haryana, New Delhi*, New Delhi, National Institute of Educational Planning and Administration.

Alderman, H., Kim, J., and Orazem, P.F. (2003) Design, Evaluation, and Sustainability of Private Schools for the Poor: The Pakistan Urban and Rural Fellowship School Experiments, *Economics of Education Review*, vol. 22, pp. 265–74.

Angrist, J.D., Bettinger, E., Bloom, E., King, E., and Kremer, M. (2001) Vouchers for Private Schooling in Colombia: Evidence from a Randomized Natural Experiment, *NBER Working Paper Series*, no. 8343, Cambridge, MA: National Bureau of Economic Research.

Bash, L. and Coulby, D (1989) *The Education Reform Act: Competition and Control*, London: Cassell Education.

Baurer, A., Brust, F., and Hybbert, J. (2002) Entrepreneurship: A case study in African Enterprise Growth, Expanding Private Education in Kenya: Mary Okelo and Makini Schools, *Chazen Web Journal of International Business*, Fall.

Belfield, C.R., and Levin, H.M. (2002) *What Does the Supreme Court Ruling on Vouchers Mean for School Superintendents?*, Columbia University and American Association of School Administrators.

Blaug, M. ([1967] 1970), Economic Aspects of Vouchers for Education, in Beales et al. ([1967]1970).

Borg, W.R., and Gall, M.D. (1989) *Educational Research: An Introduction*, 5th edn, New York and London: Longman.

Bosetti, L. (2000) Alberta Charter Schools: Paradox and Promises, *Alberta Journal of Educational Research*, vol. 46, no. 2, pp. 179–90.

Boyson, R. (1970) Appraisal, in Beales et al. ([1967]1970).

Bray, M. (1996) *Counting the Full Cost: Parental and Community Financing of Education in East Asia*, Washington, DC: World Bank.

Bray, M., and Mukundan, M.V. (2003) Management and Governance for EFA: Is Decentralisation Really the Answer? Global

Monitoring Report Background Paper, UNESCO, available from portal.unesco.org/education/en/ev.php-URL_ID = 25755& URL_DO = DO_TOPIC&URL_SECTION = 201.html (accessed June 2006).

Brennan, G., and Buchanan, J.M. (1988) Is Public Choice Immoral? The Case of the 'Nobel' Lie, *Virginia Law Review*, vol. 74, March, pp. 179–89.

Brighouse, H. (1998) Why Should States Fund Schools?, *British Journal of Educational Studies*, vol. 46, no. 2, pp. 138–52.

Brighouse, H. (2004) What's Wrong with Privatising Schools?, *Journal of Philosophy of Education*, vol. 38, no. 4, pp. 617–31.

Bryant, A. (1940) *English Saga, 1840–1940*, London: Collins.

Buchanan, J.M. (1978) From Private Preferences to Public Philosophy: The Development of Public Choice, in *The Economics of Politics*, London: IEA.

Buchanan, J.M. (1999a) Politics without Romance: A Sketch of Positive Public Choice Theory and Its Normative Implications, in *The Collected Works of James M. Buchanan*, vol. 1, *The Logical Foundations of Constitutional Liberty*, Indianapolis: Liberty Fund.

Buchanan, J.M. ([1968] 1999b) *The Collected Works of James M. Buchanan*, vol. 5, *The Demand and Supply of Public Goods*, Indianapolis: Liberty Fund.

Buchanan, J.M., and Tullock, G. (1962) *The Calculus of Consent: Logical Foundations of Constitutional Democracy*, Ann Arbor: University of Michigan Press.

Buchanan, J.M., Tollison, R.D., and Tullock, G. (eds) (1980) *Toward a Theory of the Rent-Seeking Society*, College Station: Texas A & M University Press.

Castañeda, T. (1992) *Combating Poverty: Innovative Social Reforms in Chile during the 1980s*, San Francisco: International Center for Economic Growth.

Chitty, C. (1989) *Towards a New Education System: The Victory of the New Right?*, Lewes, UK: Falmer Press.

Cockett, R. (1994, 1995) *Thinking the Unthinkable: Think-Tanks and the Economic Counter-revolution, 1931–1983*, London: HarperCollins.

Curtis, S.J. (1965) *History of Education in Great Britain*, London: University Tutorial Press.

Dalrymple, W. (2005a) Inside Islam's 'Terror Schools', *New Statesman and Society*, 28 March.

Dalrymple, W. (2005b) Inside the Madrasas, *New York Review of Books*, vol. 52, no. 19, 1 December, pp. 16–20.

De, A., Majumdar, M., Samson, M., and Noronha, C. (2002) Private Schools and Universal Elementary Education, in R. Govinda (ed.) *India Education Report: A Profile of Basic Education*, Oxford and New Delhi: Oxford University Press.

Department of Education and Science (1989) *National Curriculum: From Policy to Practice*, London: HMSO.

Department of Education and Science and Welsh Office (1987) *The National Curriculum 5–16: A Consultation Document*, London: HMSO.

Devine, N. (2004) *Education and Public Choice: A Critical Account of the Invisible Hand in Education*, Westport, CT: Praeger.

Dore, R. (1976) *The Diploma Disease*, Berkeley: University of California Press.

Downs, A. (1957) *An Economic Theory of Democracy*, New York: Harper.

Easterly, W. (2001) *The Elusive Quest for Growth*, Cambridge, MA: MIT Press.

Enlow, R.C., and Ealy, L.T. (eds) (2006) *Liberty and Learning: Milton Friedman's Voucher Idea at Fifty*, Washington, DC: Cato Institute.

Evans, A. (2006) Understanding Madrasahs, *Foreign Affairs*, vol. 85, no. 1, January–February, pp. 9–16.

Fay, C.R. (1956) *Adam Smith and the Scotland of His Day*, Cambridge: Cambridge University Press.

Fisher, A. (1947) *The Case for Freedom*, London: Runnymede Press.

Fisher, A. (1974) *Must History Repeat Itself?*, London: Churchill Press.

Forster, G. (2006) *Segregation Levels in Cleveland Public Schools and the Cleveland Voucher Program*, Milton & Rose D. Friedman Foundation and The Buckeye Institute.

Friedman, M. (1955) The Role of Government in Education, in R.A. Solo (ed.) *Economics and the Public Interest*, New Brunswick, NJ: Rutgers University Press.

Friedman, M. (1956) *Studies in the Quantity Theory of Money*, Chicago: University of Chicago Press.

Friedman, M. (1962) *Capitalism and Freedom*, Chicago: University of Chicago Press.

Friedman, M. (1968) The Role of Monetary Policy, *American Economic Review*, vol. 58, no. 1, pp. 1–17.

Friedman, M. (1976) Are Externalities Relevant?, in E.G. West (ed.) *Nonpublic School Aid: The Law, Economics and Politics of American Education*, Lexington, MA: Lexington Books, D.C. Heath & Co.

Friedman, M. (2006a) Prologue: A Personal Retrospective, in R.C. Enlow and L.T. Ealy (eds) *Liberty and Learning: Milton Friedman's Voucher Idea at Fifty*, Washington, DC: Cato Institute.

Friedman, M. (2006b) Epilogue: School Choice Turns 50, but the Fun Is Just Beginning, in R.C. Enlow and L.T. Ealy (eds) *Liberty and Learning: Milton Friedman's Voucher Idea at Fifty*, Washington, DC: Cato Institute.

Friedman, M., and Friedman, R. (1980) *Free to Choose*, Harmondsworth, UK: Pelican Books.

Friedman, M., and Schwartz, A.J. (1963) *Monetary History of the United States, 1867–1960*, Princeton, NJ: Princeton University Press.

Fuller, H.L., and Greiveldinger, D. (2002) The Impact of School Choice on Racial Integration in Milwaukee Private Schools, American Education Reform Council manuscript, August.

Fuller, H.L., and Mitchell, G.A. (1999) *The Impact of School Choice on Racial and Ethnic Enrollment in Milwaukee Private Schools*, Institute for the Transformation of Learning, December.

Fuller, H.L., and Mitchell, G.A. (2000) *The Impact of School Choice on Integration in Milwaukee Private Schools*, Institute for the Transformation of Learning, June.

Gallagher, T. (2005) Faith Schools and Northern Ireland: A Review of Research, in R. Gardner, J. Cairns and D. Lawton (eds) *Faith Schools, Consensus or Conflict?*, London: RoutledgeFalmer.

Garforth, F.W. (1980) *Educative Democracy: John Stuart Mill on Education in Society*, Oxford: Oxford University Press.

Glass, D. (1962) Education and Social Change in Modern England, in A.H. Halsey (ed.) *Education, Economy and Society*, Glencoe, IL: Free Press.

Green, A. (1990) *Education and State Formation*, Basingstoke, UK: Macmillan.

Greene, J.P. (1998) Civic Values in Public and Private Schools, in P. Peterson and B. Hassel (eds) *Learning from School Choice*, Washington, DC: Brookings Institution.

Greene, J.P. (1999) The Racial, Economic and Religious Context of Parental Choice in Cleveland, paper presented at the Association for Public Policy Analysis and Management meeting, November.

Greene, J.P. (2005) Choosing Integration, in J.T. Scott (ed.) *School Choice and Diversity: What the Evidence Says*, New York: Teachers College Press.

Greene, J.P., and Mellow, N. (2000) Integration Where It Counts, *Texas Education Review*, vol. 1, no. 1, Spring, pp. 15–26.

Greene, J.P., and Winters, M.A. (2005) *An Evaluation of the Effects of D.C.'s Voucher Program on Public School Achievement and Racial Integration after One Year*, New York: Manhattan Institute.

Griffiths, D.C. (1957) *Documents on the Establishment of Education in New South Wales, 1789–1880*, Melbourne: Australian Council for Educational Research.

Halstead, M., and McLaughlin, T. (2005) Are Faith Schools Divisive? In R. Gardner, J. Cairns and D. Lawton (eds) *Faith Schools, Consensus or Conflict?*, London: RoutledgeFalmer.

Harris, N. (1993) *Law and Education: Regulation, Consumerism and the Education System*, London: Sweet & Maxwell.

Harris, R. and Seldon, A. (1979) *Over-ruled on Welfare*, Hobart Paperback 1, London: Institute of Economic Affairs.

Hartwell, R.M. (1995) *A History of the Mont Pelerin Society*, Indianapolis: Liberty Fund.

Hayek, F.A. ([1944] 1999) *The Road to Serfdom*, London: Institute of Economic Affairs.

Hayek, F.A. ([1954] 1963) History and Politics, in F.A. Hayek (ed.) *Capitalism and the Historians*, Chicago: University of Chicago Press.

Hayek, F.A. (1960) *The Constitution of Liberty*, London: Routledge & Kegan Paul.

Hayek, F.A. (1967) *Studies in Philosophy, Politics and Economics*, London: Routledge & Kegan Paul.

Hayek, F.A. (1973) *Law, Legislation and Liberty: A Statement of the Liberal Principles of Justice and Political Economy*, London: Routledge & Kegan Paul.

Hirschman, A.O. (1970) *Exit, Voice, and Loyalty: Responses to Decline in Firms, Organizations, and States*, Cambridge, MA: Harvard University Press.

Hurt, J.S. (1971) Professor West on Early Nineteenth-Century Education, *Economic History Review*, vol. 23, pp. 624–32.

Jakobsen, J.R., and Alpert, R.T. (2002) Faith Based on What? A Roundtable Discussion, *Journal of the American Academy of Religion*, vol. 70, no. 4, December, pp. 821–32.

Kelman, S. (1987) 'Public Choice and Public Spirit', *Public Interest*, vol. 87, pp. 93–4.

Kiesling, H.J. (1983) Nineteenth-Century Education according to West: A Comment, *Economic History Review*, 2nd series, vol. 36, pp. 416–25.

King, E.M., and Bellew, R. (1993) Educating Women: Lessons from Experience, in E.M. King and M.A. Hill (eds) *Women's Education in Developing Countries: Barriers, Benefits and Policy*, Baltimore, MD: Johns Hopkins University Press.

King, E., Rawlings, L., Gutierrez, M., Pardo, C., and Torres, C. (1997) Columbia's Targeted Education Voucher Program: Features, Coverage, and Participation, *Development Economics Research Group*, Working Paper Series on Impact Evaluation of Education Reforms, Paper 3, World Bank.

Krashinsky, M. (1986a) Why Educational Vouchers May Be Bad Economics, *Teachers College Record*, vol. 88, no. 2, Winter, pp. 139–51.

Krashinsky, M. (1986b) Educational Vouchers and Economics: A Rejoinder, *Teachers College Record*, vol. 88, no. 2, Winter, pp. 163–7.

Krueger, A.B., and Malečková, J. (2003) Education, Poverty and Terrorism: Is There a Causal Connection?, *Journal of Economic Perspectives*, vol. 17, no. 4, pp. 119–44.

Lee, D.R. (1988) Politics, Ideology, and the Power of Public Choice, *Virginia Law Review*, vol. 74, no. 2, pp. 191–8.

Lees, D.S. (1962) The Role of Government in Relation to Health Services, in papers of the Mont Pelerin Society Thirteenth Annual Meeting, 9–15 September, Knokke, Belgium, Section III, The Role of Government in Relation to Education, Health Sciences and Support of Science, pp. III.35–45.

Legislative General Counsel (2007) Education Vouchers, 2007 General Session, State of Utah, Chief Sponsor: Stephen H. Urquhart. HB 148.

Levin, H.M. (1991a) The Economics of Educational Choice, *Economics of Education Review*, vol. 10, no. 2, pp. 137–58.

Levin, H.M. (1991b) Views on the Economics of Educational Choice: A Reply to West, *Economics of Education Review*, vol. 10, no. 2, pp. 171–5.

Lippmann, W. (1937) *The Good Society*, London: George Allen.

Lott, J.R. Jr (1987) Juvenile Delinquency and Education: A Comparison of Public and Private Provision, *International Review of Law and Economics*, vol. 7, pp. 163–75.

Lott, J.R. Jr, and Fremling, G.M. (1980) *Juvenile Delinquency and Education: An Econometric Study*, International Institute for Economic Research.

McKinney, S.J. (2006) Review Article – The Faith-Based Schools Debate: Challenging Assumptions and Stereotypes, *Journal of Moral Education*, vol. 35, no. 1, pp. 105–15.

Makdisi, G. (1981) *The Rise of Colleges: Institutions of Learning in Islam and the West*, Edinburgh: Edinburgh University Press.

Merrifield, J. (2005) Choice as an Education Reform Catalyst: Lessons from Chile, Milwaukee, Florida. Cleveland, Edgewood, New Zealand and Sweden, in D. Salisbury and J. Tooley (eds) *What America Can Learn from School Choice in Other Countries*, Washington, DC: Cato Institute.

Mill, J.S. (1873) *Autobiography*, London: Longmans.

Mill, J.S. (1909) *Principles of Political Economy*, Ashley edition, London: Longmans.

Mueller, D.C. (2003) *Public Choice III*, 3rd edn, Cambridge: Cambridge University Press.

Nambissan, G.B. (2003) Educational Deprivation and Primary School Provision: A Study of Providers in the City of Calcutta, IDS Working Paper 187 (Institute of Development Studies).

Niskanen, W.A. (1971) *Bureaucracy and Representative Government*, Chicago: Aldine.

Noah, H.J. (2000) Book Review: *Education as a Commodity*, *Comparative Education Review*, vol. 44, no. 2, pp. 220–1.

Nsiah-Peprah, Y. (2004) Assessment of the Role of Private Schools in the Development of Education in Ghana: A Study of the Kumasi Metropolis, *Journal of Science and Technology*, vol. 24, no. 2, pp. 54–75.

Orchard, L., and Stretton, H. (1997) Critical Survey, *Cambridge Journal of Economics*, vol. 21, pp. 409–30.

O'Reilly, R., and Bosetti, L. (2000) Charter Schools: The Search for Community, *Peabody Journal of Education*, vol. 75, no. 4, pp. 19–36.

Parker-Jenkins, M., Hartas, D., and Irving, B.A. (2005) *In Good Faith: Schools, Religion and Public Funding*, Aldershot, UK: Ashgate.

Patrinos, H.A., and Ariasingam, D.L. (1997) *Decentralization of Education: Demand-Side Financing*, Washington, DC: World Bank.

Peacock, A.T., and Wiseman, J. (1964) *Education for Democrats: A Study of the Financing of Education in a Free Society*, London: Institute of Economic Affairs.

Perelman, L.J. (1992) *School's Out: A Radical New Formula for the Revitalization of America's Educational System*, New York: Avon Books.

Pride, R.A., and Woodard, J.D. (1985) *The Burden of Busing: The Politics of Desegregation in Nashville, Tennessee*, Knoxville: University of Tennessee Press.

Pring, R. (2005) Faith Schools: Are They Justified?, in R. Gardner, J. Cairns and D. Lawton (eds) *Faith Schools, Consensus or Conflict?*, London: RoutledgeFalmer.

Probe Team, The (1999) *Public Report on Basic Education in India*, Oxford and New Delhi: Oxford University Press.

Randall, M. (1871) *History of the Common School System of New York*, Ivison, Blakeman, Taylor, & Co.

Ravitch, D. (1985) *The Troubled Crusade: American Education, 1945–1980*, New York: Basic Books.

Reid, T.W. ([1888] 1970) *Life of the Rt Hon.W.E. Forster*, New York: Augustus M Kelly.

Ritter, G., Rush, A., and Rush, J. (2002) How Might School Choice Affect Racial Integration in Schools? New Evidence from the ECLS-K, *Georgetown Public Policy Review*, Spring.

Rose, P. (2002) Is the Non-State Education Sector Serving the needs of the Poor? Evidence from East and Southern Africa, paper prepared for Department for International Development Seminar in preparation for 2004 World Development Report.

Rose, P. (2003) From the Washington to the Post-Washington Consensus: The Influence of International Agendas on Education Policy and Practice in Malawi, *Globalisation, Societies and Education*, vol. 1, no. 1, pp. 67–86.

Rothbard, M.N. (1976) Total Reform: Nothing Less, in E.G. West (ed.) *Nonpublic School Aid: The Law, Economics and Politics of American Education*, Lexington, MA: Lexington Books, D.C. Heath & Co.

Rowley, C.K. (1969) The Political Economy of British Education, *Scottish Journal of Political Economy*, vol. 16, pp. 152–76.

Rowley, C.K. (2002) E.G. West: Champion of the Market for Education, *Ideas on Liberty*, vol. 52, no. 4, April, pp. 33–7.

Salmi, J. (2000) Equity and Quality in Private Education: The Haitian Paradox, *Compare*, vol. 30, no. 2, pp. 163–78.

Sandström, F.M. and Bergström, F. (2002) *School Vouchers in Practice*, The Research Institute of Industrial Economics, Working Paper 578, Stockholm, 30 April.

Save the Children, UK, South and Central Asia (2002) Private Sector Involvement in Education: A Perspective from Nepal and Pakistan, submission to 'The Private Sector as Service Provider and Its Role in Implementing Child Rights', Office of the High Commissioner for Human Rights, Geneva, 20 September.

Seldon, A. (1965) Preface, in E.G. West, *Education and the State: A Study in Political Economy*, London: Institute of Economic Affairs.

Seldon, A. (1986) *The Riddle of the Voucher: An Inquiry into the Obstacles of Introducing Choice and Competition in State Schools*, London: Institute of Economic Affairs.

Seldon, A. (2005) *The Collected Works of Arthur Seldon*, vol. 7, *The LEA, the LSE, and the Influence of Ideas*, Indianapolis: Liberty Fund.

Smith, A. ([1759] 1976) *The Theory of Moral Sentiments*, Oxford: Clarendon Press.

Smith, A. ([1776] 1976) *An Inquiry into the Nature and Causes of the Wealth of Nations*, 2 vols, ed. R.G. Campbell, A.S. Skinner and W.B. Todd, Oxford: Oxford University Press.

Smith, F. (1931) *A History of English Elementary Education, 1760–1902*, London: London University Press.

Stephens, W.B. (1987) *Education, Literacy and Society, 1830–70: The Geography of Diversity in Provincial England*, Manchester: Manchester University Press.

Swift, A. (2003) *How Not to Be a Hypocrite: School Choice for the Morally Perplexed Parent*, London and New York: Routledge.

Thomson, J. (1832) *The Life, Lectures and Writings of William Cullen, M.C.*, vol. 1, Edinburgh: Blackwood.

Thornton, W.T. (1846) *Over Population and Its Remedy*, London: Longman, Brown, Green & Longmans.

Tooley, J. (1995) *Disestablishing the School*, Aldershot, UK: Avebury Press.

Tooley, J. (1996) *Education without the State*, London: Institute of Economic Affairs.

Tooley, J. (2000) *Reclaiming Education*, London: Cassell.

Tooley, J. (2005) Private Schools for the Poor, *Education Next: A Journal of Opinion and Research*, vol. 5, no. 4, Fall, pp. 22–32.

Tooley, J. (2006) From Universal to Targeted Vouchers: The Relevance of the Friedmans' Proposals for Developing Countries, in R. Enlow and L. Ealy (eds) *Liberty and Learning: Milton Friedman's Voucher Idea at Fifty*, Chicago: Cato Press.

Tooley, J., and Dixon, P. (2006a) Private Education for Low Income Families: Research from a Global Research Project, in P. Srivastava and G. Walford (eds) *Private Schooling in Developing Countries*, Didcot, UK: Symposium Books.

Tooley, J., and Dixon, P. (2006b) The Failures of State Schooling in Developing Countries and the People's Response, in M. Miles, K.R. Homes and M.A. O'Grady (eds) *2006 Index of Economic Freedom*, Washington, DC: Heritage Foundation and Wall Street Journal.

Tooley, J. and Dixon, P. (2006c) '*De Facto*' Privatisation of Education and the Poor: Implications of a Study from Sub-Saharan Africa and India, *Compare*, vol. 36, no. 4, December, pp. 443–62.

Tooley, J., and Stanfield, J. (eds) (2003) *Government Failure: E.G. West on Education*, London: Profile Books.

Tooley, J., Dixon, P., and Stanfield, J. (2003) *Delivering Better Education: Market Solutions to Education*, London: Adam Smith Institute.

Trevelyan, G.M. (1922) *British History in the Nineteenth Century*, London: Longmans.

UNDP (2003) *Human Development Report 2003*, New York: United Nations Development Programme.

UNESCO (2004) *Education for All: The Quality Imperative*, EFA Global Monitoring Report 2005, Paris: UNESCO.

Venkatanarayana, M. (2004) *Educational Deprivation of Children in Andhra Pradesh: Levels and Trends, Disparities and Associate Factors*, Working Paper 362, Centre for Development Studies, Trivandrum, Kerala, India, available online at www.cds.edu (accessed August 2005).

Watkins, K. (2000) *The Oxfam Education Report*, Oxford: Oxfam in Great Britain.

Watkins, K. (2004) Private Education and 'Education for All' – or How Not to Construct an Evidence-Based Argument, *Economic Affairs*, vol. 24, no. 4, pp. 8–11.

Webb, R.K. (1950) Working Class Readers in Early Victorian England, *English Historical Review*, vol. 65, no. 256, pp. 333–51.

Webb, R.K. (1963) The Victorian Reading Public, in *From Dickens to Hardy*, Harmondsworth, UK: Pelican.

Weisbrod, B.A. (1962a) *External Benefits of Public Education*, Princeton, NJ: Princeton University Press.

Weisbrod, B.A. (1962b) Education and Investment in Human Capital, *Journal of Political Economy*, vol. 70, no. 5, October, pp. 106–23.

Winder, G. (1955) *The Free Convertibility of Sterling*, London: Institute of Economic Affairs.

Witte, J.F. (1996) Who Benefits from the Milwaukee Choice Program?, in B. Fuller and R. Elmore with G. Orfield (eds) *Who Chooses? Who Loses? Culture, Institutions and the Unequal Effects of School Choice*, New York: Teachers College Press.

Wolf, A. (2002) *Does Education Matter? Myths about Education and Economic Growth*, London: Penguin.

World Bank (2003) *Making Services Work for Poor People: World Development Report 2004*, Washington, DC: World Bank; Oxford: Oxford University Press.

Yergin, D., and Stanislaw, J. (1998) *The Commanding Heights: The Battle for the World Economy*, New York: Simon & Schuster.

Yun, J.T. and Reardon, S.F. (2005) Private School Racial Enrollments and Segregation, in J.T. Scott (ed.) *School Choice and Diversity: What the Evidence Says*, New York: Teachers College Press.

Index